99 Episodes
That Defined the '90s

ALSO BY CHRIS MORGAN
AND FROM MCFARLAND

*The Nickelodeon '90s: Cartoons, Game Shows
and a Whole Bunch of Slime* (2021)

The Comic Galaxy of Mystery Science Theater 3000:
Twelve Classic Episodes and the Movies They Lampoon (2015)

99 Episodes That Defined the '90s

Television Milestones from Arsenio to Homer to Yada Yada Yada

CHRIS MORGAN

McFarland & Company, Inc., Publishers
Jefferson, North Carolina

LIBRARY OF CONGRESS CATALOGING-IN-PUBLICATION DATA

Names: Morgan, Chris, 1986– author.
Title: 99 episodes that defined the '90s : television milestones from Arsenio to Homer to yada yada yada / Chris Morgan.
Other titles: Ninety-nine episodes that defined the '90s
Description: Jefferson, North Carolina : McFarland & Company, Inc., Publishers, 2024. | Includes index.
Identifiers: LCCN 2024026100 | ISBN 9781476694191 (paperback : acid free paper) ∞
    ISBN 9781476653334 (ebook)
Subjects: LCSH: Television programs—United States—History—20th century. | Nineteen nineties. | LCGFT: Television criticism and reviews.
Classification: LCC PN1992.3.U5 M627 2024 | DDC 791.45/750973—dc23/eng/20240614
LC record available at https://lccn.loc.gov/2024026100

BRITISH LIBRARY CATALOGUING DATA ARE AVAILABLE

ISBN (print) 978-1-4766-9419-1
ISBN (ebook) 978-1-4766-5333-4

© 2024 Chris Morgan. All rights reserved

No part of this book may be reproduced or transmitted in any form or by any means, electronic or mechanical, including photocopying or recording, or by any information storage and retrieval system, without permission in writing from the publisher.

Front cover image © Shutterstock

Printed in the United States of America

McFarland & Company, Inc., Publishers
  Box 611, Jefferson, North Carolina 28640
    www.mcfarlandpub.com

Table of Contents

Must-See TV: An Introduction 1
Twin Peaks: "Pilot" 5
Tales from the Crypt: "The Switch" 7
Family Matters: "Rachel's Place" 10
Newhart: "The Last Newhart" 13
Saved by the Bell: "Jessie's Song" 15
Cop Rock: "Cop-a-Feeliac" 18
Married ... with Children: "I'll See You in Court" 20
In Living Color: "February 10, 1991" 23
Full House: "Joey Goes Hollywood" 26
Shop 'til You Drop: "July 10, 1991" 28
Darkwing Duck: "Comic Book Capers" 30
Blossom: "Rockumentary" 32
Columbo: "No Time to Die" 34
The Ren & Stimpy Show: "Stimpy's Invention" 37
Barney & Friends: "When I Grow Up..." 39
The Arsenio Hall Show: "June 3, 1992" 42
Clarissa Explains It All: "Total TV" 44
Murphy Brown: "You Say Potatoe, I Say Potato" 46
Quantum Leap: "Lee Harvey Oswald" 49
Martin: "Forever Sheneneh" 52
Saturday Night Live: "Tim Robbins/Sinead O'Connor" 54
Baywatch: "Rookie of the Year" 57
Where in the World Is Carmen Sandiego?: "Bad Day on Broadway" 59
The Fresh Prince of Bel-Air: "A Night at the Oprah" 62

The Ben Stiller Show: "With Rob Morrow"	64
Seinfeld: "The Contest"	67
Law & Order: "Point of View"	72
X-Men: The Animated Series: "Days of Future Past"	74
The Young Indiana Jones Chronicles: "Young Indiana Jones and the Mystery of the Blues"	76
Beverly Hills, 90210: "Something in the Air"	78
Beavis and Butt-Head: "Scientific Stuff"	81
Cheers: "One for the Road"	83
Late Show with David Letterman: "August 30, 1993"	86
Melrose Place: "Much Ado About Everything"	89
Animaniacs: "Episode 15"	91
Saved by the Bell: The College Years: "The Poker Game"	94
Diagnosis: Murder: "Murder at the Telethon"	97
Lois & Clark: The New Adventures of Superman: "Pheromone, My Lovely"	100
Home Improvement: "The Eve of Construction"	102
Space Ghost Coast to Coast: "Spanish Translation"	104
Frasier: "My Coffee with Niles"	107
Dinosaurs: "Changing Nature"	110
The Real World: "Getting Dropped"	112
My So-Called Life: "Why Jordan Can't Read"	114
Silk Stalkings: "The Mud-Queen Murders"	116
Picket Fences: "Rebels with Causes"	118
Sister, Sister: "Get a Job"	120
Living Single: "There's No Ship Like Kinship"	122
The Parent 'Hood: "Ring Around the Nosey"	125
All That: "Da Brat"	128
All-American Girl: "Pulp Sitcom"	132
The Critic: "Siskel & Ebert & Jay & Alice"	135
The X-Files: "Humbug"	137
The Tonight Show with Jay Leno: "April 11, 1995"	140
ER: "Motherhood"	143
The Wayans Bros.: "Blood Is Thicker Than Watercolor"	146
Goosebumps: "The Haunted Mask"	150

Table of Contents

Xena: Warrior Princess: "Prometheus"	153
Ace Ventura: Pet Detective: "The Reindeer Hunter"	156
Muppets Tonight: "Michelle Pfeiffer"	158
Mad About You: "The Finale: Part 1"	160
Dexter's Laboratory: "Dexter's Rival / Dial M for Monkey: Simion"	164
Clueless: "As If a Girl's Reach Should Exceed Her Grasp"	167
7th Heaven: "No Funerals and a Wedding"	170
Judge Judy: "Episode 30"	173
Mystery Science Theater 3000: "Revenge of the Creature"	176
The Simpsons: "The Itchy & Scratchy & Poochie Show"	179
Friends: "The One with the Morning After"	183
Buffy the Vampire Slayer: "Angel"	188
King of the Hill: "Keeping Up with Our Joneses"	190
Ellen: "The Puppy Episode"	193
Todd McFarlane's Spawn: "Burning Visions"	196
Roseanne: "Into That Good Night"	198
Emeril Live: "Dueling Woks"	201
Walker, Texas Ranger: "Lucas"	203
Jerry Springer: "I Refuse to Wear Clothes"	205
Ally McBeal: "Cro-Magnon"	208
3rd Rock from the Sun: "36! 24! 36! Dick"	211
Veronica's Closet: "Veronica's $600,000 Pop"	214
South Park: "Mecha-Streisand"	216
Boy Meets World: "If You Can't Be with the One You Love…"	219
The Larry Sanders Show: "Another List"	222
The Drew Carey Show: "What's Wrong with This Episode?"	225
Monday Night RAW: "April 27, 1998"	228
Cousin Skeeter: "Mo' Skeeter Blues"	232
Will & Grace: "A New Lease on Life"	235
Hang Time: "High Hoops"	238
Sports Night: "Intellectual Property"	241
Celebrity Deathmatch: "Masters of Martial Arts"	244
That '70s Show: "That Disco Episode"	246
Total Request Live: "November 9, 1998"	249
NYPD Blue: "Hearts and Souls"	251

The PJs: "Rich Man, Porn Man"	254
The Sopranos: "College"	256
Futurama: "Space Pilot 3000"	259
Star Trek: Deep Space Nine: "What You Leave Behind"	262
The West Wing: "Pilot"	264
Felicity: "The List"	267
Who Wants to Be a Millionaire? "November 19, 1999"	269
Warm Glow: A Conclusion	272
Index	277

Must-See TV:
An Introduction

When *Lilyhammer* dropped on Netflix in February of 2012, the argument that the 1990s was the most transformative decade for television as a medium went out the window. As always, Steven Van Zandt proved prescient. The concept of original streaming programming truly changed the landscape, and the reverberations of that paradigm shift have proven irrevocable in a variety of ways. In a sense, "TV" became a non-literal description, a term of art we use to categorize both what is watched on actual television channels and also the programs you find on services like Netflix, Hulu, and the rest of that ilk.

Of course, innovation is notable, but it is not inherently interesting. The history of Netflix dropping a show with that one guy from Bruce Springsteen's band (but not the guy who was Conan O'Brien's bandleader, the one most of us cared about) is significant and, if you care about television, worth cataloging away in your brain. What's truly interesting is what happens within these shows. I like to think about, talk about, and write about the content that makes up television's contribution to popular culture, not technological evolution. In that sense, are the '90s the most interesting decade for television? Are they the best decade for television? I've dedicated much of my professional writing career to the TV of the 1990s, so my argument would be to answer in the affirmative to both of those leading questions I asked myself.

Due to the proliferation of cable channels and "not TV" HBO's foray into original programming, in the 1990s people were given more choices of what to watch. Even so, network channels ruled the roost. Maybe teenagers were watching MTV and younger kids were tuned into Nickelodeon, but adults were watching networks in prime time. Many kids were too. There were the family shows, designed for parents and children to watch together, but of course kids also enjoyed peering into the world of adulthood by catching some *Seinfeld* or *Friends*. That was certainly my experience as a child of the '90s. As a kid, one of my favorite shows was *Dragnet*, which I watched on Nick at Nite. The 1960s version of the show was mostly star and creator Jack Webb railing against hippies, but it fascinated me for whatever reason. It was adult. Also, it was on TV. As George Costanza said to Russell Dalrymple when asked why anybody would watch a show about nothing, the answer is "because it's on television."

In the era of binge watching, it is worth remembering that television used to exist as a somewhat passive medium, at least to many. TV was something to "have on" while you did other things. You watched *The Price Is Right* when you were home sick. In the era before the proliferation of the internet and mobile phones, sometimes you found yourself watching TV because you were home and you needed something to do. I have heard an anecdote—and I pass it along anecdotally, so grab a few grains of salt if you are so inclined—that back in the day you were considered a "regular" watcher of a TV show if you caught one out of every three episodes. Back then, if you missed an episode, you were waiting for reruns or for syndication. I missed *The Simpsons* episode "I'm with Cupid" when it aired in 1999. It was a couple years before I finally saw it. I don't know what I was doing on Valentine's Day that year. I would have been 12. It was definitely not romantic, whatever it was.

Television is also interesting to me because it both creates cultural content and best reflects the culture surrounding it. After all, TV can move faster than other mediums. There were, and still are, television shows that literally will create five new episodes of television the day of for a given week. *Saturday Night Live* can do sketches about stuff that just happened. Even scripted shows—non-animated category—can turn things around fairly fast. If something is in the zeitgeist, television can reflect upon it. Additionally, those who work in TV don't have to sweat the zeitgeist changing. They are going to keep producing more episodes. I love television, but it can be "disposable" in a way that other mediums cannot. Who cares if an episode from two years ago is about something that nobody thinks about anymore? There have been dozens of episodes since. People are also ready to accept the ephemeral nature of TV episodes, having been doing so for years.

Movies can't do that. It takes months, and often years, to get a movie from conception to release. The films that reflected America after 9/11 couldn't hit theaters until a lot of processing of the events of that day had already occurred. Oliver Stone's *World Trade Center* came out in 2006, as did Paul Greengrass's *United 93*. Music needs to be written, recorded, and released, and that is a medium that has been less concerned with the cultural movements of the time than with, say, love, heartbreak, and where in the city the factory is where the man puts peaches in a can (it's downtown, for the record). Books? Unless you are actively looking to churn out something for a quick turnaround—which is often felt by the reader—books are less interested in immediacy than any other medium. Hell, some jerks are writing books about what happened in TV decades ago. These days, podcasts have surpassed TV as the swiftest turnaround in terms of reflecting the current landscape, but in the 1990s, that was TV's job.

Given this, by delving into the TV offerings of the '90s, we can define the decade with a good amount of accuracy. Also, talk about a lot of great, bad, and weird shows that are worthy topics in and of themselves. There are episodes of 1990s television that are defining moments of culture in the decade and also episodes that successfully captured something about the culture of the time. So while this book is a discussion of TV in the '90s, it also goes well beyond simply talking TV. Popular culture, and culture in general, is trapped within the proverbial four walls of these episodes of television. Can I cover every single moment of import from the 1990s in this assortment of television episodes? Probably not, but I can get close, and I didn't even include the series finale of *ALF*, which was not supposed to be the series finale and thus ends on a grim cliffhanger where the US government captures the titular alien from Melmac.

This book covers 99 episodes of television that define the 1990s as a decade. Yes, that number was chosen because this is a book about the '90s, but it also helps me really run the gamut in terms of programs. Each episode comes from a different show as well. I could, in theory, have easily chosen multiple episodes from certain shows. Honestly, I could have probably done, like, 50 episodes of *The Simpsons* and really tackled the zeitgeist of the decade. The episode I chose isn't even the "Treehouse of Horror" with Bob Dole and Bill Clinton! There are shows I love in the mix, shows I don't like, and shows I didn't really watch then. Some of them, frankly, I was exploring with intent for the first time in writing this book. That's part of the fun of writing a book like this. Oh, and these are all American shows, I should note. I did not feel up to the task of delving into British or Canadian or French shows with any accuracy. I grew up with American pop culture, and it is what I know best. Although, growing up in Michigan, I did get CBC, so I have a working knowledge of Don Cherry that many Americans lack.

As the 1990s went on, the world changed. Of course it did. The '90s weren't static. Neither was television in the '90s. Shows got canceled, shows debuted, casts changed—you name it. Television was more than an avenue for episodic entertainment. It was more than a way to kill time after school on a Tuesday. TV is a time capsule. So what were the 1990s? How do you define the decade? Well, in this case, with these 99 episodes of television from the '90s. Hopefully you will learn a few things, recall a few fond memories, and take a trip back to the world of 1990s television. Don't change the channel. It's time to get started.

While 99 Episodes That Defined the '90s *does cover everything from Arsenio to Homer to Yada Yada Yada (and beyond, though former NHL defenseman Zarley Zalapski does not make any appearances aside from this reference), telling the story of the '90s through television in an alphabetical sense is not the most conducive. Thus, I have placed these episodes, and the chapters on each episode, chronologically. We will travel through time, based on episodes airing, not through the alphabet. This way, you can watch the '90s unfold. Or, of course, you are free to pop in and out of chapters as you desire. It's my book, but it's your copy of my book. You can even burn it if you want, you weirdo!*

Twin Peaks: "Pilot"

This book is organized by original airdate for all of these episodes, or at least to the best of my abilities based on the information I could find. Of course, thanks to *TV Guide*, it is usually easy to be reliable in terms of airdates for TV episodes. Fittingly, we unwrap the plastic on this list of episodes with the pilot episode of the cultish TV show *Twin Peaks*.

I say "cultish," because the pilot of *Twin Peaks* hit the cultural landscape too hard for this to be a "cult classic." *Twin Peaks* permeated the firmament of pop culture. It remains a reference point. David Lynch knew his way around imagery. Did he prove too weird for mainstream audiences? Did he (and Mark Frost) run out of ideas for *Twin Peaks* by, say, the second season? I would say so, and the fact the show was canceled indicates that a lot of folks agreed with me.

The idea of Lynch finding success on network television always felt unlikely, dare I say improbable. This is the dude who debuted with *Eraserhead*, a tedious art film built around weird, gross imagery. He tried to adapt *Dune* and failed. Denis Villeneuve proved that Frank Herbert's books are, indeed, adaptable. *Blue Velvet* is probably still his defining film, but Roger Ebert and I both hated it (although for different reasons). I'm not here to talk about movies, though.

Lynch and Frost pitched *Twin Peaks* (originally called *Northwest Passage*) on concept in 1988, and the pilot debuted on April 8, 1990. Co-written by Frost and Lynch and directed by Lynch, "Pilot" is effectively a TV movie setting up a show, as it runs 94 minutes. Laura Palmer, a high school student from the small town of Twin Peaks, Washington, washes up on shore wrapped in plastic. In time, Kyle MacLachlan's Agent Dale Cooper comes to town to figure out what is going on. Thus begins a murder mystery, but not your typical murder mystery.

The Lynchian touches of *Twin Peaks* were probably alluring at first.

In 1990, there were only so many television channels. A lot of people still just had network TV. People were watching *Twin Peaks* because it was on, not because they were big fans of Lynch's movies. In fact, a lot of them had likely never heard of Lynch. They wanted to watch the murder mystery show.

The pilot of *Twin Peaks* was watched by more than 30 million people. As the first season rolled on, the ratings dropped. That first season was also only eight episodes. The second season was 22, traditional for network TV at the time. This ... did not work. Even fans of *Twin Peaks*, and it has its ardent supporters, recognize the faults of the second season. There is a reason the show got canceled, even if the second season ended on a cliffhanger. People, it would seem, got tired of Lynch's eccentricities, or maybe they just noticed a show spinning its wheels, and they stopped caring about who killed Laura Palmer.

That is how things played out, though. The pilot brimmed with potential. It had that iconic image of Palmer being unwrapped. It had MacLachlan's idiosyncratic performance. Even if you haven't seen *Twin Peaks*, you have picked up some of the cultural references over time. Dale Cooper had an understandable love of coffee and an unusual love for cherry pie. There was the "red room" and the backwards talk. Lynch threw a lot of weird images at the wall, and some of them stuck.

Twin Peaks is probably the defining cult show of the 1990s, and it was also one of the opening salvos the decade delivered in terms of television. Certainly, television fans remember *Twin Peaks*. We remember Laura Palmer. Maybe Lynch proved too weird for TV, and when he got a delayed third season it was on Showtime, which was basically just letting him do his thing, and, man, did he get self-indulgent. I give him credit, though. With the *Twin Peaks* pilot, he showed that he knew how to hook people ... for a little while, anyway.

Tales from the Crypt: "The Switch"

In truth, the biggest impact that EC Comics made on culture was in the 1950s, not the 1990s. This was when *Tales from the Crypt* arrived on shelves. Comics were already under fire. Psychologists were wringing their hands about violent comics warping the youth. Were comics causing juvenile delinquents? In a sense, comics were to the 1950s what video games were to the 1990s. That is to say, a convenient scapegoat.

EC Comics was an easy target, as the company's bailiwick was horror and gore. *Tales from the Crypt* was an anthology series of comics that would tell macabre stories with lush graphics, but that just made them scarier to the pearl clutchers and (one assumes) more enticing to kids. I can imagine Marion Cunningham saying, "Howard, I am worried about the comics that Richie has been reading." Howard, in turn, sighs and says, "Marion, why won't you admit that Chuck has disappeared? Why won't you acknowledge our other son is gone?" Anyway, the anguish piled up at EC's doorstep, and eventually they started to focus on their humor publication, something called *Mad* magazine.

In the 1990s, though, pushing the boundaries was a feature, not a bug, for HBO. As a premium cable channel, they could do what they pleased. They could be as violent, vulgar, and sexual as they wanted. *Tales from the Crypt* may have been a bygone title by the 1990s, but with a title that evocative, and with plenty of stories from EC comics available to adapt, HBO turned the comics series into an anthology show that ran 93 episodes from 1989 until 1996.

As an anthology show, each episode featured a different cast. There is only one recurring character, the iconic figure of *Tales from the Crypt*, the Cryptkeeper. Akin to horror hosts like Vampira and Ghoulardi, the Cryptkeeper was a puppet of a living corpse, though he was kind of a palatable version of grotesquery. The Cryptkeeper was almost kind of charming, even if he was a rotting human, which is probably how he ended up with his own kids' show and game show. Voiced by John Kassir, the Cryptkeeper would introduce every episode from his coffin, replete with an abundance of puns.

Tales from the Crypt was for the horror hounds, and it did not shy away from gore. Since it was on HBO, though, it could also bring the profanity and the nudity. Sex and violence: In the 1990s, they were still among the pillars of American television (though when it came to sex, we were still light years behind European television). The appeal to the show was that it was lurid and tawdry, but not overly sordid. It wasn't like *Faces of Death* or something truly depraved. It was just TV. You could hear somebody swear and maybe see a naked woman, and it was on your television screen. Before the internet was really a thing, *Tales from the Crypt* could be a fix for certain interests. Having the Cryptkeeper there, a puppet loaded

The Cryptkeeper (voiced by John Kassir) flips through one of his tale-filled tomes (HBO).

with puns speaking with an eerie, funny falsetto voice, made it all feel safe too. *Tales from the Crypt* was palatable prurience.

"The Switch" is a fairly typical episode of the show. William Hickey plays an old man who wants to marry a young woman played by Kelly Preston. She rebuffs him, so Hickey and an unethical doctor help him take over the body of a young man named Hans. It doesn't work out as Hickey hopes. Twist ending! Be careful what you wish for! It's facile, but it is also the end note for, like, 80 percent of *Tales from the Crypt* episodes.

Here's what makes "The Switch" the episode of this show that defines the '90s: It was directed by Arnold Schwarzenegger. Yes, *that* Arnold Schwarzenegger. He even appears alongside the Cryptkeeper in the opening. By 1990, when this episode aired, Schwarzenegger was already a huge star. He would also be one of the defining stars of the ensuing decade. In 1990 he was in *Total Recall* and *Kindergarten Cop*, and then the next year he was in *Terminator 2: Judgment Day*.

A lot of actors like to flex their muscles once they have some cachet, and not just actors who are former bodybuilders like Arnold. That can mean producing, but it can also mean directing. *Tales from the Crypt* gave Schwarzenegger a chance to try out directing. Michael J. Fox would direct an episode in season 3. Tom Hanks directed the first episode of season 4. This was a show that wasn't afraid to let actors try directing. It took for Hanks. Schwarzenegger never directed a feature film. In fact, his only other directing credit is 1992's made-for-TV movie version of *Christmas in Connecticut* starring Dyan Cannon, Kris Kristofferson, and Tony Curtis.

Two of the iconic figures of the 1990s came together in this episode of TV: Arnold Schwarzenegger and the Cryptkeeper. The most interesting thing about "The Switch" is who directed it. *Tales from the Crypt* comics scared adults in the 1950s. In the 1990s, *Tales from the Crypt* allowed people to see gore, nudity, and what the Terminator could do as a director.

Family Matters: "Rachel's Place"

Family Matters ran for 215 episodes. It was the last live-action show that debuted in the 1980s that was still running, as it ran from 1989 until 1998. *Family Matters* covered much of the '90s and was a staple of ABC's TGIF lineup. It was, ostensibly, a family sitcom. It's right there in the name. It is fitting, however, that the episode I decided to include in this book, "Rachel's Place," name drops a character who is not a member of the Winslow family, the ostensible center of this family sitcom. That's because *Family Matters* quickly became a show where the titular family was arguably an afterthought.

Jo Marie Payton played Harriette Winslow on *Perfect Strangers*, an elevator operator who interacted with the mismatched main characters from that show. Her husband, Carl, played by Reginald VelJohnson, was introduced as a police officer. The two had a winning chemistry, and VelJohnson was riding high on the wave of being in *Die Hard*. He is great in that movie, to be clear. This led to the spinoff *Family Matters*. Carl and Harriette had three kids. Harriette's sister Rachel Crawford and her infant son Richie were already living with the Winslows after her husband died. In the pilot, Carl's mom moves in as well. Can this extended family, all under one roof, get along?

Who cares? Well, that seemed to be the consensus of viewers. Oh, *Family Matters* became a success. It just had little to nothing to do with the Winslows. In the 12th episode of the first season, Laura wants a date for the dance. Carl, trying to help out, turns to the Winslow's odd neighbor. He had an odd style of dress and an unusual demeanor. His name is Steve Urkel. He changed the show—and '90s pop culture.

That was supposed to be the only appearance of Urkel. He was a one-off joke character. Something about Jaleel White's character clicked with audiences, though. "Rachel's Place" is the first episode of the second

Family Matters: "Rachel's Place"

Steve Urkel (Jaleel White, left) ended up overtaking *Family Matters* from Carl Winslow (Reginald VelJohnson) and his family (ABC).

season. It's about Rachel wanting to open her own diner to replace Leroy's, the local teen hangout. What happened to Leroy's? Urkel burnt it down. This episode is the first in which Steve Urkel is a main character. He would swiftly come to dominate *Family Matters*. It became a show not about the Winslows, but about Urkel and his interaction with the Winslows. A show where Carl, a devoted father and police officer, spends his time, say, traveling through time with Urkel.

How much did Urkel take over *Family Matters*? The Winslows' youngest daughter, Judy, was written off the show and retconned as having never existed. It all began with "Rachel's Place." This is the episode where the producers on the show decided this Steve Urkel was going places. His obsessive crush on Laura, his love of cheese, his clumsiness, his suspenders, his catchphrases, it all would come to overwhelm *Family Matters*. Truly, Steve Urkel came to be a defining character of the 1990s. He is the quintessential annoying neighbor. Usually, that character is relegated to a supporting role. When has the annoying neighbor archetype ever taken over a show? It has only ever happened with *Family Matters* and with Steve Urkel.

Sure, I've barely talked about the titular Rachel, and there are members of the Winslow family I have not mentioned. That is in keeping with the cultural legacy of *Family Matters*, though. "Rachel's Place" is when *Family Matters* started to become Steve Urkel's show. It became "Urkel: Featuring the Winslows." He showed up on *Full House* and *Step by Step*. He had his own novelty dance. Could *Family Matters* have survived as a sitcom about the Winslow family? Would it have ever lasted 215 episodes? I doubt it. Urkel may have taken over *Family Matters*, but he also kept it going and going and going. Rachel's Place gets opened, by the way. Urkel would start working there. Of course he did. The thing is, somehow, the family didn't matter. Urkel mattered.

Newhart:
"The Last Newhart"

It makes sense that a defining moment early in the 1990s would be the end of a 1980s TV show. *Newhart* was very much a "1980s TV show," and not just because it began in 1982 and barely squeaked into the 1990s, airing its final episode on May 21, 1990. While I consider *Newhart* perhaps the best sitcom of the '80s, were it to have aired in the '90s it would have felt a little out of place. Stephanie and Michael, played with gusto by Julia Duffy and Peter Scolari in performances that should have won them both an Emmy, are '80s yuppies through and through. A new decade cannot begin until the last one ends, and that means seeing the vestiges of the preceding decade come to a conclusion.

Now, *Newhart* is not the last sitcom that is synonymous with the 1980s to be airing into the next decade. There is another indelible sitcom of that decade that does not come to a conclusion for a couple more years, and it will be featured in this book as well. I have another reason to be writing about the aptly titled "The Last Newhart," though. It is a defining series finale, one that still gets talked about to this day. Not so much because of quality, but because it took a big swing that made sure it was splashy and memorable. Weirdly, it seems to have worked entirely, as opposed to a certain snow globe–centric finale that is more lampooned than lauded.

Newhart starred Bob Newhart as Dick Loudon. This was a time when a TV show would be named after its star, even if the character did not share that name. He lives in a small Vermont town where he and his wife, Joanna, run an inn. Dick is also a writer of how-to books and hosts a local TV show. *Newhart* is often pointed to as a show that took some time to find its footing. The cast changed after the first *and* second seasons. Eventually, Stephanie and Michael came into their own as foils to Dick and Joanna, and *Newhart* started to excel as a show about Newhart as the straight man in a town teeming with eccentrics.

If not for the tail end of "The Last Newhart," this would not be a memorable finale. It gently pokes fun at the fear and anger that was fomenting in America in the 1980s about Japan as a rising economic power. It is not the final word on this phenomenon, as the film *Rising Sun* would still be on the horizon, landing in theaters in 1993. That movie is built around a then-ebbing anxiety about Japan. "The Last Newhart" is sillier, and more infused with the energy of Gedde Watanabe, than other examples of this.

After Dick is hit in a head with a golf ball, the screen cuts to black. Then, we find ourselves in a TV bedroom, but not Dick's. Instead, we are in the bedroom of Bob and Emily Hartley from *The Bob Newhart Show*. Newhart is once again playing Hartley, and then suddenly there is Suzanne Pleshette reprising her role as Emily. The studio audience is stunned by the turn of events. Yes, "The Last Newhart" is from the school of "It was all a dream!" For whatever reason, however, this was the dream ending people viewed joyously, and not as a cheap ploy or cop-out.

Maybe it was fondness for *The Bob Newhart Show* and seeing Bob and Emily back together, even if Pleshette's voice carried with it another decade or so of cigarette detritus (the actress would spend the end of her life dealing with lung cancer that led to her death). Maybe it was easier to accept such a turn from what was an absurdist sitcom to begin with. Although, I will say as I was watching the series for the first time, I did so knowing how it ended. At some point in the middle of its run, it struck me that, even within the world of this show, technically all these characters were fake. I was, in theory, watching a dream Bob Hartley was having. That kind of makes it hard to invest in anybody. How can I care about Larry, Darryl, or Darryl if they ceased to exist the moment Bob Hartley opened his eyes?

"The Last Newhart" brought an end to a staple '80s sitcom, helping to continue the process of turning the culture over to the new decade. It also served as a "water cooler moment," something that still existed in the 1990s. "Did you see *Newhart* last night?" one might ask a coworker, though when spoken I imagine the show's title was not italicized. Style guides have yet to dictate human speech. Now, the closest you get to that is, "Have you watched all of *Stranger Things* yet?" This is not a lament, just a statement of observation.

Honestly, "The Last Newhart" is an unremarkable series finale save for that twist. The twist did still work on me, though. It's not one of the, like, 30 best episodes of *Newhart*, but it is the one that the show is remembered for, and it is the one that helped put a demarcation point at the end of the 1980s. Dick Loudon was gone. He never existed. Some TV character from the 1970s dreamt him up. It's over. Time for the 1990s to take over in earnest.

Saved by the Bell: "Jessie's Song"

The Pointer Sisters released the song "I'm So Excited" in 1982; it peaked at 30 on the *Billboard* Hot 100. In 1984, the sister act (not to be confused with the Whoopi Goldberg vehicle *Sister Act*, which also involved a fair amount of singing) released a remixed take on their song. This time, it was paired with a music video. It was a shrewd move, as the remix of "I'm So Excited" hit number nine on the charts. And yet, the most indelible version of "I'm So Excited" was belted out, in unfinished fashion, by Elizabeth Berkley.

Good Morning, Miss Bliss debuted on the Disney Channel in 1988, and was positioned as a vehicle for Hayley Mills, once a Disney star herself. It took place at a junior high school in Indiana. Kids would get into scrapes and thorny situations, with the sensible teacher there to impart a lesson to them. *Good Morning, Miss Bliss* lasted for 13 episodes, and nobody cared.

NBC took *Good Morning, Miss Bliss*, kicked Mills to the curb, moved the show to California, and decided to focus on the kids. They called this show *Saved by the Bell*. It debuted in prime time, but it would become a staple of NBC's Saturday-morning lineup aimed at teenagers. This time around, NBC crafted an indelible piece of '90s pop culture.

Is *Saved by the Bell* a good show? No, it is not. It's cheesy and ridiculous and filled with jokes penned by writers who were probably in their fifties and were just using gags and references from their childhoods. Have I also seen every episode of *Saved by the Bell* multiple times? Absolutely. I grew up watching it in reruns every morning before school. I watched it in college and somehow always seemed to see only the first part of the two-parter about Jessie's half brother.

Jessie Spano is at the center of this story, though she was by no means at the center of *Saved by the Bell* by and large. Zack Morris was the star attraction, a carryover from the *Good Morning, Miss Bliss* days.

Samuel "Screech" Powers was Bayside's answer to Steve Urkel. Kelly Kapowski was the distaff equivalent of Zack, and the two were often paired together romantically (and ended up getting married in Las Vegas in the made-for-TV movie that served as the note of finality for these characters until the meta reboot on Peacock). A.C. Slater was the "jock," and he got plenty of shine. In truth, Lisa Turtle was also the most underserved of the six main characters from the bulk of the show's run (no time to talk about Tori, a character who only engenders apathy on my part).

Then, there is Jessie Spano. She was smart, but not an archetypal "nerd" like Screech. No, Jessie was an ambitious striver. Also, the writer's conception of a "feminist," an ethos that seemed to only encompass calling Slater a "pig" for his casual sexism. It was her intense ambition that proved to be her downfall in "Jessie's Song," a second-season episode that aired on November 3, 1990.

Young Ms. Spano finds herself burning the candle at both ends, studying extremely hard for her midterms while simultaneously attempting to serve as a member of the burgeoning all-girl pop trio Hot Sundae. OK, so the second half of this conundrum likely needs more elaboration. Jessie, Lisa, and Kelly are singing together for fun, but Zack sees a moneymaking scheme in becoming their manager and turning them professional. Naturally, this plan involves Screech dressing in drag and as a janitor to sneak into the girls' locker room to surreptitiously record the girls singing, a turn of events that does not even scratch the top 10 most egregious things done in an episode of *Saved by the Bell*.

I will skip some key details along the way—and avoid an in-depth discussion of the high-budget music video Hot Sundae somehow manages to make heavily indebted to Olivia Newton-John's "Physical"—to get to the core of the matter at hand. Jessie turns to over-the-counter caffeine pills in order to stay awake and have the energy to both study for her midterms and be a member of Hot Sundae. Purportedly, the original plan was for Jessie to take amphetamines, but NBC balked at illicit drug use, so they just swapped in caffeine pills and kept everything else the same.

Jessie doesn't listen to warnings from Slater, and Zack doesn't at first either. However, Jessie's behavior and health deteriorates more and more until she goes MIA and Zack shows up to her place and finds she has crashed and is delirious. Finally, Zack confronts Jessie, who breaks down, is comforted by Zack, and realizes she has a problem. Lesson learned. Ah, but about that breakdown. You see, Hot Sundae had made a habit of singing "I'm So Excited" as one of their signature songs, and Jessie tries to sing it to prove to Zack that she is fine. Jessie is able to yell-sing "I'm so excited!" a couple times before collapsing into a tearful breakdown, proclaiming, "I'm so scared!"

"I'm so excited.... I'm so scared." Say this to a child of the '90s, or rather sing it at first and then fake sob through the second part, and they will likely remember it. "Jessie's Song" is the iconic *Saved by the Bell* episode, and Jessie's singing breakdown is the indelible moment from said episode. Berkley even recreated it when on *Dancing with the Stars*. It's not the dumbest moment in the show's history. It probably isn't even the most unintentionally funny moment from *Saved by the Bell*. Everybody was able to glom onto "I'm so scared" though.

For decades, "Jessie's Song" has been a calling card of '90s pop culture. In fact, it's overly worn at this point. Comedian April Richardson, host of the departed *Go Bayside!* podcast, did not personally consider it the best, or most sublimely ridiculous, episode, and it feels like a true connoisseur of this slice of '90s teen trash would be reticent to go all-in on "Jessie's Song" as a fave, as it feels like too facile a choice in some ways. It's like saying your favorite Beatles song is "Yesterday" or something. On the other hand, "Jessie's Song" has become the shorthand encapsulation for a defining, if lousy, '90s show. It is also a sterling example of the heavy-handed, clumsy "very special episode" trend of the decade, which *Saved by the Bell* would tackle in even sweatier fashion in episodes such as "No Hope with Dope." You could likely never intentionally create a moment as sublimely absurd as Jessie Spano's "I'm So Excited" breakdown, which in a way makes it feel special, even more so for those of us who found it organically and not in meme form. If you were putting together a montage of '90s pop culture, it would be a miscarriage not to include it.

Cop Rock: "Cop-a-Feeliac"

A decade is defined not just by its greatest successes, but also by its greatest failures. If I were writing a book about films of the 1990s, *Titanic* would be there, but so would *Waterworld*. Also, some middling film that hinged on water as well. Maybe *The Mighty Ducks*? Ice is water, after all. Like literally every decade of television, the '90s were littered with cop shows. Some were quite good. *Cop Rock*, on the other hand, is a defining fiasco of the decade. Were there worse shows in the '90s? Sure, but few, if any, were as misguided as *Cop Rock*.

Steven Bochco has a tremendous television resume, even going back to writing "Murder by the Book," the first proper episode of *Columbo*. The one directed by Steven Spielberg. He was a creative force on *Hill Street Blues*, *L.A. Law*, *NYPD Blue*, and *Doogie Howser*. Yes, Bochco, who passed away in 2018, had a great career. Great, but not unimpeachable, because he also co-created *Cop Rock*.

I could probably just give you the simple gist of *Cop Rock* and that would likely be enough. *Cop Rock* is a musical police procedural. If you, like me, have an affinity for pop cultural ephemera and esoterica, you probably already know about *Cop Rock*. It's one of those shows you mention when talking about the sublimely baffling shows from TV's past. *Cop Rock* is mentioned in the same breath as *Shasta McNasty* and *Small Wonder*. It was a flop critically and commercially, and any forays into watching clips from it show why.

The program served no audience well. It was unsuccessful as a police procedural, which is hard to do with one of the most plug-and-play genres out there. Doing integrated musicals—which is to say musicals where characters break out into song and dance within the characters' universe—is trickier. Some people just won't accept musicals where characters will just start singing and dancing. Personally, I have always had a problem with integrated musicals, other than when done archly and with a wink. I can accept, say, the hurricane episode of *Daria*, but I'm not sitting through *West Side Story*. Many people will, but they wouldn't sit through *Cop Rock*, because it also failed as a musical. It was the inverse of a "you got your chocolate in my peanut butter" situation.

It is hard to see *Cop Rock*'s musical moments out of context and not assume the show was a gag. The vibe is reminiscent of the ironic *Reefer Madness* musical, but it was all too real. Even as somebody who generally doesn't like this style of storytelling, even I can tell that the songs, and choreography, of *Cop Rock* are subpar. These are the elements that make it a fiasco. Nobody would remember the show it if were just a bad police procedural. No, it had to be the cop show where people since and dance.

The show lasted for 11 episodes in 1990. I chose "Cop-a-Feeliac" as an example of the overarching terrible nature of *Cop Rock*. For starters, the title sucks, a lame joke that is also staggeringly ribald for the era. The episode also features a song called "Burning Crosses," which is about, yes, burning crosses. Even the KKK was worth a toe-tapping ditty in the world of *Cop Rock*. This is, after all, a show where a guy who traffics children on the black market gets his own song. Now, "Baby Merchant" is from a different episode, but you can't tell the story of the disaster that was *Cop Rock* without mentioning "Baby Merchant." There is no way outside of the most deranged of minds that song is fully sincere, but it is still way too sincere in execution.

"Cop-a-Feeliac" is laden with tedium and absurdity. It's not as amusingly bad as I would hope. The fun reaches diminishing returns quickly. Now, Bochco did rebound with *NYPD Blue*, which was a definitive success. Even so, *Cop Rock* sits there like an albatross around his neck. I don't know if there was a bigger swing and miss in the 1990s than *Cop Rock*. It is a show where somebody could say, "How about a song about the KKK burning crosses?" and it was met with, "Sure, let's do that!" I may not be the audience for a musical, but I am the audience for "so-bad-it's-good" pop culture. Even I can't muster much enthusiasm for *Cop Rock*. It amuses me that it exists, and the story of '90s TV definitely needs to mention the show. Maybe it is better to just imagine the idea of a musical police procedural in your head. When you open the door to *Cop Rock* to satisfy your morbid curiosity, you might just end up being bummed out. Keep the beautiful, absurd dream alive in your mind.

Married ... with Children: "I'll See You in Court"

In the '90s, there became an increasing drive to push the envelope in television. Whether it was network TV or cable, there were shows trying to entice viewers by offering up an increased level of sexuality, violence, profanity, and all that good stuff. If the content proved controversial, even better. That was marketing. The very idea that something could be "too hot for TV" was a siren song to many. Before the '90s even began, though, *Married ... with Children* was out there scandalizing television viewers and stirring up controversy. In fact, the FOX sitcom proved so provocative that a 1990 episode ... didn't air in 1990 in the United States.

Much like the 2 Live Crew, "I'll See You in Court" was banned in the United States. It all began with a popular occurrence of the 1990s: a boycott campaign. Before I get to the fuss around "I'll See You in Court," though, which was really the end point of a snowballing controversy, a brief history of *Married ... with Children*, one of the burgeoning FOX network's first successes, even predating *The Simpsons*.

The family sitcom has been around forever, and *Married ... with Children* was a funhouse mirror version of those shows. George H.W. Bush once said that families needed to be more like the Waltons and less like the Simpsons, but my guess is that he said that because he didn't even know about the Bundys. What's tricky about *Married* is trying to thread the needle of intent. I don't think it is a *Seinfeld* type show where you are supposed to despise the main characters. Yes, the joke is often on the Bundys, and to a degree their behavior is supposed to be viewed with a wink and a raised eyebrow. The humor is partially born from people acting inappropriately, but I also can't help but feel sometimes you are supposed to laugh at that because the show thinks it is funny. It's the "every joke has a kernel of truth" corollary. Some of Al Bundy's misogyny feels like the show's misogyny, or at least tolerance of misogyny for the sake of a joke.

Personally, I have a bit of a disdain for both "my husband is such an idiot" sitcoms and "my wife is such a shrew" sitcoms, and *Married ... with Children* is both. Al Bundy is an idiot still pining for his high school football stardom as he toils away in a shoe store where he deals with a series of women he finds repugnant. All he wants to do is flip through his porno magazines and watch his trash TV. Peg Bundy (whose maiden name is Wanker, if the vibe of this show wasn't clear enough as is) is lazy and constantly complaining about Al. She watches Oprah's show, which makes her vapid by the show's logic. Hey, I am one of the rare people who is happy to trash Oprah Winfrey's show, but even I will call that facile. Al and Peg despise each other. They both are horny, but rarely for one another.

Al and Peg have two kids. Kelly is dumb and promiscuous. That is effectively her entire character. Her sex-positive nature, though, made Kelly Bundy a real key figure of '80s and '90s TV for ... well, since Christina Applegate was 16 when the show started, let's naively pretend it was for teenagers and teenagers alone. There's Bud Bundy, who is also very interested in sexual matters. Marcy D'Arcy is the neighbor who is Peg's best friend and Al's nemesis, what with her being—get this—a feminist. Of course, in the world of *Married ... with Children* she is the broadest feminist killjoy possible.

To me, this is a sitcom that is hit or miss. The raunchiness was considered novel during the early days of its run, a big swing from the new FOX network. I don't mind that as much as I mind the facile jokes and one-dimensional characters. Ed O'Neill, Katey Sagal, and Applegate are all talented actors (David Faustino isn't bad either), but the writing on *Married ... with Children* wasn't always great, or even good. What it was, though, is controversial.

Enter Terry Rakolta. Rakolta is a woman who lived, and apparently still lives, in Bloomfield Hills, Michigan. As a native of Metro Detroit, this actually means something to me, as I know Bloomfield Hills intimately. It's a place for super-rich conservatives to live. They are the one percent. Rakolta, née Stern, married John Rakolta, a former construction company CEO who was the ambassador to the United Arab Emirates for Donald Trump. Terry's sister Ronna was previously married to Scott Romney, Mitt Romney's brother and son of George Romney, former governor of Michigan. Ronna is a conservative talk show host. In short, Terry sucks. Her husband sucks. Her sister sucks. Terry also decided she wanted to make it her business what aired on TV.

Rakolta happened to see the *Married ... with Children* episode "Her Cups Runneth Over," which is centered on Al and Marcy's first husband, Steve, buying a bra for Peg. It had a woman covering her naked breasts with her arm (a classic '90s move), a mannequin in S&M gear, and a couple things I am sure Rakolta really didn't like: a man in women's stockings and a gay dude. Rakolta started a letter-writing campaign to sponsors, trying to get them to boycott the show. Eventually, all the fervor would lead to increased ratings for *Married ... with Children*, and the sponsors all came back. Before that, though, the show was moved to 9 p.m. (8 p.m. central) and toned down. In fact, FOX declined to air an episode they thought might prove too controversial, at least in the United States. While "I'll See You in Court" aired in Europe, it did not air in America until 2002, when it was shown on FX.

"I'll See You in Court" sees Steve and Marcy suggest that Al and Peg go to a sleazy motel in order to actually get them interested in having sex with each other. At said motel, Al and Peg find that the proprietors had secretly taped Marcy and Steve having sex, and then Al and Peg have sex and the same thing happens. The two couples take the Hop-On-Inn to court, Al and Peg don't get a settlement because the jury didn't believe they actually had sex, and then they have sex in the courtroom.

This was the episode FOX decided to pull to appease Rakolta and her weird conservative compatriots. I am sure they would have indeed all had a beef with an episode of TV this overtly sexual, though there aren't any gay guys for Rakolta to bristle at (though I will add that the "joke" of the gay guy in "Her Cups Runneth Over" is pretty cringey in its stereotyping). Having an episode that was "too hot for TV" probably helped pull eyes to *Married ... with Children*. You tell people that "this show had an episode that was banned from airing!" and they are going to want to check it out. What's funny is that "I'll See You in Court" isn't good. It's lame and cheesy and inane. It wasn't worth waiting 12 years for, that's for sure.

Parsing *Married ... with Children* in modern times is a little difficult. What is for sure, though, is that Rakolta utterly failed in her quest, and whatever my thoughts on this particular show, I am glad that happened. FOX won in multiple ways. They got a ton of attention and also avoided airing an episode of TV that wasn't worth the controversy, or even really watching.

In Living Color: "February 10, 1991"

Saturday Night Live has long been the hegemonic force in sketch comedy. That hasn't stopped others from giving it a shot and trying to carve out a slice of sketch comedy television for themselves. In the 1990s, a few shows threw their hats into the ring. Personally, my favorite '90s sketch show is *The State*, MTV's Gen X comedy extravaganza that spawned many people who would come to define popular comedy, cult comedy, and those VH1 talking head shows for years to come. From *The State* we got Michael Ian Black, Thomas Lennon, Kerri Kenney-Silver, and one of our worst studio movie directors, Michael Showalter. That being said, my affinity for *The State* will not lead me to eschew the truth. Among '90s sketch shows, none had the popularity or impact of *In Living Color*. In fact, I would say it was as popular as *Saturday Night Live* for a moment.

Much like *Married ... with Children*, *In Living Color* was an attempt by the burgeoning FOX network to make a splash in network television. By the time the sketch show debuted, FOX had found its footing, as the first season of *The Simpsons* had begun airing in December of 1989. *In Living Color* would debut in April 1990, and it quickly made a splash, helping turn the Wayans family into some of the foremost faces of comedy in the United States.

Keenen Ivory Wayans had already made a splash in comedy. He was in Robert Townsend's satire *Hollywood Shuffle*, which he also co-wrote. The next year he wrote, directed, and starred in the blaxploitation parody *I'm Gonna Get You Sucka*, the cachet of which likely helped him create and develop a show for FOX, and also to hire a few of his family members as well. When *In Living Color* began, Keenen, Damon, and Kim were all starring on the show, with Shawn a featured player.

This was not merely a family affair, though. Beyond the assorted Wayans, Rosie Perez was one of the show's dancing "Fly Girls," and also served as their choreographer. Jennifer Lopez was famously a Fly Girl, though she joined during season 3, and the episode in this chapter is from season 2. In terms of cast members, there was stalwart TV staple David Alan Grier, as well as Tommy Davidson, a recognizable face who has had a spottier career since the end of *In Living Color*. Then, there is the breakout star of the show, a young, expressive Canadian lad by the name of Jim Carrey.

Look, *In Living Color* was historically significant as a sketch show created by a Black American, with a cast that was largely Black as well. As such, I don't want to just be like, "Now, let's talk about the white guy." But this is Jim Carrey we are talking about here. You could argue that he is the most important, most popular person in American comedy in the 1990s. Maybe the legacy of *In Living Color* should go beyond, "It's the show where Jim Carrey and Jennifer Lopez" got their starts, but, well, we love celebrities and movie stars in this country. Although, I will note that Carrey had been in a few movies by the time he joined the cast of *In Living Color*, including *Earth Girls Are Easy*. None of them were big films, though, not to throw shade at the vampire comedy *Once Bitten*.

The episode from the week prior to the February 10, 1991, episode featured two staple sketches: Homey D. Clown and Fire Marshall Bill, though apparently this episode was not shown in syndication, so I am left to wonder what might have occurred for that to be the case. *In Living Color* was not unfamiliar with controversy and questionable content. This episode, though, speaks to the cultural power of *In Living Color* at the time. Yes, Carrey is the focus, but it is what it is.

Late in August 1990, Vanilla Ice released his single "Ice Ice Baby." It would become the first rap song to top the *Billboard* Hot 100. The fact that Vanilla Ice was a white rapper—or, to translate sociological perception into grammatical choices, a *White Rapper*—certainly played a role in that. Obviously, Vanilla Ice was quite popular for a minute there. The Teenage Mutant Ninja Turtles loved him, and vice versa. Not everybody liked him, though, and that crossed racial lines. *In Living Color* was not the first time Vanilla Ice was lampooned in pop culture, but it was so effective it may have really helped turn the tide on the overarching opinion of the rapper.

Carrey, who is dressed ridiculously but not any more ridiculously than how Vanilla Ice really dressed, comes out to perform as the rapper. Instead of "Ice Ice Baby," though, Carrey's Ice is performing a parody of that song called "White White Baby." The song is about how Vanilla Ice is, yes, white, and were it simply about that the parody would be extremely facile. Instead it's ... just kind of facile. Look, "White White Baby" is sub-"Weird Al" parody. The show made a point of noting that Vanilla Ice's real name is Robert Van Winkle, as if every rapper before him used their real name. I hate to pop any balloons, but Dr. Dre's name isn't really Dr. Dre, and he's not even a doctor.

What "White White Baby" also did, though, is assert that Vanilla Ice was not a "real" rapper, that he just saw hip-hop on the rise and decided to capitalize on that. This is an assertion that is easier to make stick. Even if you didn't have a beef with Vanilla Ice being a white rapper, you could have a beef with him being a poseur rapper. Now, the dude was likely to always just be a gimmick, and *In Living Color* didn't necessarily bring down Van Winkle entirely. That being said, "White White Baby" is certainly the defining bit of anti–Vanilla Ice culture.

In Living Color would run until 1994, but by the last season every Wayans member had left the show, including Keenen. Carrey was still there, though in 1994 he would star in *Ace Ventura*, *The Mask*, and *Dumb and Dumber*, turning him into the biggest movie star in the world in one year's time. There is one other defining moment in the history of *In Living Color* that I have to mention. They decided to air a live episode during the halftime of Super Bowl XXVI. Their halftime show was a salute to winter. *In Living Color*'s gambit worked. They got huge ratings, and hurt the ratings of the second half of the Super Bowl. The NFL decided this could never happen again. They got Michael Jackson for the next Super Bowl, and this began the idea of a massive musical act doing the Super Bowl halftime show. The show changed the racial makeup of sketch comedy in the United States, but *In Living Color* also changed the defining sporting event of the country.

Full House: "Joey Goes Hollywood"

Full House may have begun in 1987, but to a child of the '90s that just meant it got momentum going to deliver reruns to watch in syndication as soon as we found the show. I don't know if I ever saw a *Saved by the Bell* episode in its original run, but I know I saw it every morning before school for a couple of years. *Full House* reruns were definitely part of my television diet as a child as well, though there is a chance I caught some of it as it aired, given that it ended in 1995. Nowadays, *Full House* is also significant as one of the first signifiers of the coming "what is dead will never truly die" ethos of modern pop culture. The show was rebooted, many years later, on Netflix with *Fuller House*. I watched a few episodes. It was terrible! For some, though, I am sure it scratched a nostalgic itch. That's fitting, as this is a key element of the fourth-season episode "Joey Goes Hollywood."

Uncle Joey, as played by non–Canadian Dave Coulier, was the "funny one" of the main trio of adult men. His storylines, when he had them, tended to be less substantive. Just look at season 4 for a clear example of that. "Joey Goes Hollywood" aired during a chunk of episodes between Jesse and Becky's wedding and the season finale built around Becky getting pregnant with Nicky and Alex. As an aside, one of the only good things about *Fuller House* was that they actually got the actors who played Nicky and Alex back for the show. That was totally unnecessary. I appreciated it.

Because *Full House* was a family sitcom with a family audience in mind, this Joey-centric episode did find two subplots for the kids. Michelle gets in trouble for calling Tokyo, and Stephanie tries to change her name because the kids at school are calling her…. Step on Me? I get that the show wanted to do a storyline about one of the kids being teased for their name, a classic thing that happens to children. Also, obviously the show had to keep things family friendly, so they didn't go with, off the top of my head, "Sniffin' Pee" or, hell, even "Stupid-nie" was right there. The intent of the kids was negative, but if all they landed on was "Step on Me" and you were a kid in the '90s, you kind of got off easily. In real life, I assume she would just have been called fat and constantly had it brought up that her mom is dead and also had it intimated that her mom was in Christian hell and was being exceedingly promiscuous while there.

"Joey Goes Hollywood," though, is focused on Joey getting the opportunity to co-star in a new TV show starring.... Frankie Avalon and Annette Funicello. Frankie and Annette were the stars of AIP's *Beach Party* movies. These movie musicals typically took place at the beach; involved a lot of surfing, dancing, and bathing suits; and were pretty fun, all things considered. I have seen most of them now as an adult. In the '90s, though, only a select few children were likely aware of a series of films that were released in the 1960s.

No, Frankie and Annette were there for nostalgia. They were there for the parents who were teens in the 1960s, or perhaps early 1970s, and remembered Frankie and Annette. I mean, it was a nostalgia play when Avalon showed up in *Grease* to sing "Beauty School Dropout," and that movie came out in 1978. At least the writers on the show were aware enough to have it explained to the kids who Frankie and Annette are, and why the adults are so enthused to meet them. Their show that Joey gets a part on is called *Surf's Up*, so they kept the beach motif going, but that was presumably because *Full House* had gotten Frankie and Annette to be on the show. I doubt the beach came first.

Ultimately *Surf's Up* is turned into a cartoon, which allows Joey to return to San Francisco and not have to move to Los Angeles. First, though, the family did get to take a trip to LA. That makes "Joey Goes Hollywood" an example of two classic staples of '90s television: cameos from people who were famous in the 1960s and the "we're going to Hollywood!" episode. I doubt anybody thought Joey was going to be written off of the show. Just a couple episodes earlier *Full House* had shoehorned in a way for Jesse and Becky, two recently married adults, to still live at the Tanner house. The family unit could only be allowed to grow stronger and larger. Not even the stars of *Muscle Beach Party* could change that.

Shop 'til You Drop: "July 10, 1991"

Time marches on. I know that. Certainly cultural touchstones fell by the wayside before I had any cognizance of them, and I do not miss them, because I never truly knew them. Does it make sense that the shopping mall is archaic at best, obsolete at worst? With the way consumerism has changed with technological advances, sure. Am I bummed that malls aren't really a thing anymore? Honestly, yeah. Now, I will admit I am part of the problem. I have maybe been to a shopping mall once in adulthood, but you know what? I enjoyed going into all the different stores and I ate a cookie from Mrs. Fields and it ruled. There is a place for the mall in my heart, even if there are few places left in the world for them.

Now, the mall did not arrive as a hub for shopping and hanging out in the 1990s. Just watch a movie like *Valley Girl* or that one season of *Stranger Things* for proof of that. In the 1990s, though, the concept of the shopping mall was turned into the bones of a game show. That show was *Shop 'til You Drop*. The show had three lives. First, it aired on Lifetime from 1991 until 1994. In 1996, it was rebooted on The Family Channel until 1998. Lastly, it ended up on PAX from 2000 until 2005. This episode here is the first episode, the premiere of *Shop 'til You Drop*, because, honestly, the show basically all bleeds together.

The game show was largely hosted by Pat Finn. Previously, he had briefly hosted a reboot of *The Joker's Wild*, and then he hosted some California Lottery show, and then at some point I am guessing he updated his own Wikipedia page, based on the way it is written. If I had to summarize *Shop 'til You Drop*, I would call it *Supermarket Sweep*, but in a fake mall instead of a fake grocery store. *Shop 'til You Drop* took place in a facsimile of a shopping mall with 14 stores, though the stores would change from episode to episode. Most of the show was built around answering questions about pop culture and consumer goods. Then, the winning duo would make it to the "Shop 'til You Drop" bonus round. This was sort of a Yankee swap type deal that involved running around the fake mall. The couple would keep everything on the "prize table," and if their prizes totaled at least $2,500, they would also win a trip.

I watched *Shop 'til You Drop* as a kid, and I remember it as being fine. It wasn't my favorite game show, but it was watchable. Sure, it wasn't as good as *Supermarket Sweep*, but if I was in a pinch, I could watch *Shop 'til You Drop* and kill half an hour. The fake mall was maybe a little too artificial, and the running around the mall wasn't as fun as watching the shoppers on *Supermarket Sweep* run around picking up hams and such. That being said, of course they decided to do a "shopping mall game show." It made total sense in the '90s, when people were going to the mall all the time, to either shop or just hang out. Malls were central to the lives of many. You might go to a mall every week. Truly, you might go to the mall as often as you go to the grocery store in the 1990s. If you were a teenager, you were probably going to the mall more.

There are still some malls these days, though the number has diminished. A lot of malls are now "outdoor malls," which doesn't quite feel like a mall to me. Dead malls abound, as certain Instagram accounts have chronicled. The mall of my childhood has seen better days, or so I hear. *Supermarket Sweep* got rebooted during the surge in prime-time reboots for classic game shows like *Match Game* and *Password*. I highly doubt *Shop 'til You Drop* ever gets rebooted. The mall's time has come and gone. In the '90s, the shopping mall was a hub, especially in suburban life. It is where you would take your kids to meet Santa Claus and/or the Easter Bunny. It is where teenagers could go hang out at Hot Topic or Spencer's until mall security kicked them out for sitting on the escalator rail. The shopping mall is never coming back. The further we get into the future, the more striking it will be to remember that, in 1991, a game show debuted that was based around the idea of the mall. There was no Mrs. Fields, sure, but you could shop 'til you dropped nevertheless.

Darkwing Duck: "Comic Book Capers"

Superheroes are serious business these days. That has been the case since the double dose of *Iron Man* and *The Dark Knight* in 2008. Comic books, mostly of the Marvel and DC ilk, became adapted to the point of oversaturation. Not that you can blame Disney and Warner Bros. There was money to be had. *Avengers: Endgame* was, for a moment, the highest-grossing movie in history. There was also, on occasion, some prestige to be found. Multiple actors have won Oscars for playing Joker. These days, the seriousness of superhero stories could use a puncturing, but in the '90s, silly takes on superheroes were the ones on the forefront. Sometimes, they even involved a duck.

Following in the success of *DuckTales*—and a quasi spinoff of said show—*Darkwing Duck* was a superhero parody that carried over the energy of *DuckTales*. In a way, *Darkwing Duck* was to Batman what *DuckTales* was to Indiana Jones. We were immediately spammed heavily with *Darkwing Duck* by Disney, as the first season, which was syndicated as part of the Disney Afternoon block, ran from September 6, 1991, through May 20, 1992. Simultaneously, what is now called "season 2" aired 12 episodes on ABC on Saturdays. That is some aggressive scheduling, especially for animation. Also, it means that, even when you throw in the 12 episodes of the third season, *Darkwing Duck* was airing original episodes for barely over one calendar year, but squeezed out 91 episodes. I assume they then aired in reruns repeatedly, which is how they got burnt into the brains of '90s kids. It's much how I was stunned in adulthood when I found out there are only 26 total episodes of *Salute Your Shorts*. Nickelodeon just ran them in a constant churn.

Drake Mallard is a seemingly mild-mannered suburban dad living in St. Canard. Yes, that is already three duck puns. Secretly, though, he is also Darkwing Duck. When you're in trouble, you call "D.W." Dressed in a style more akin to a '30s serial masked crime-fighter (his name is a parody of Kent Allard, the alter ego of The Shadow, so that is fitting), Darkwing Duck dealt each episode with some villain while also balancing fatherhood. The humor, such as it is, often comes out of Mallard desperately wanting the kudos for being Darkwing Duck but needing to protect his daughter, Gosalyn, which is a goose pun, but avian enough to, ahem, fly.

There is already plenty of superhero parody to be found in just the premise, but the first-season episode "Comic Book Capers" took it to the next level—and even got somewhat meta. A Darkwing Duck comic book comes out in St. Canard, but the man himself hates how he is portrayed in it. He sets out to create his own Darkwing Duck comic, but it becomes an unwilling group project, with even the villainous Megavolt getting into the mix. Megavolt is the only villain I remembered off the top of my head before delving back into this show for the book. That's because I remember having the action figure of the electricity-based rat baddie. You could make his battery backpack spark, and I would always see if I could ignite a fire with said spark. This was being a child in the '90s.

If you ask somebody in modern times to articulate the status of superheroes in popular culture, they would say something like, "They become the dominant force in films. The Marvel Cinematic Universe defined the 2010s, before fatigue started to set in during the 2020s. Batman got super grim and serious, and then Zack Snyder made the whole world of DC super grim and serious. People got mad that comic book movies like *Black Panther* didn't get taken seriously by the Oscars. Superheroes kind of defined 15 years of film and television." Back in 1991, though, somebody might say, "I hear they are doing a sequel to that Batman movie with Jack Nicholson in it. Also, remember how bad those last couple of Superman movies sucked?" When *Darkwing Duck* aired, we had not yet gotten *Batman Returns*, much less Joel Schumacher's campy *Batman Forever* and *Batman & Robin*, films that were so non-serious they basically sparked the backlash that begat, well, the entire reframing of the movie landscape.

A Disney superhero parody about a duck that fought crime didn't really need to wrestle with anything. It was more a *DuckTales* extension than a response to superheroes overcrowding the landscape. Darkwing Duck writing his own comic was the kind of meta fun a lot of animation creatives like to have, but reading comics was practically an esoteric hobby in 1991. It made sense that such a joke would be in a show for kids, because, to many, comic books were "kids stuff." These days, Disney owns Marvel, and alongside the whole MCU on Disney+ you can find old episodes of *Darkwing Duck*. Weirdly, it serves as a reasonable palate cleanser to all that overwrought universe building. It just happened to arrive a full 25 years before it was needed. "Comic Book Capers" walked so *Teen Titans Go!* could run.

Blossom: "Rockumentary"

Admittedly, I had not seen any *Blossom* prior to writing this book. Cultural magpie that I am, I was aware of plenty of aspects of it. I knew it starred Mayim Bialik as a teenager, and that she had a distinctive way of dressing. Granted, that came entirely from one joke from *The Simpsons*, but if not for *The Simpsons*, I would be 27 percent less culturally aware. On top of that, I knew Jenna von Oÿ played her best friend Six, and that Joey Lawrence said "Whoa!" a bunch. Turns out he played Blossom's brother, fittingly named Joey Russo. It was successful enough to run for five seasons and 114 episodes. I just missed it at the time.

Due to my cultural awareness of the show, "Whoa!" alone secured *Blossom* a spot in this book. I just needed an episode, perhaps one that had an overarching tie to the firmament of the '90s. Then I found out there is a dream episode where Blossom is sick in bed and imagines herself to be a '90s pop star. Immediately I knew that "Rockumentary" was the episode for this book.

Had "Jessie's Song" not been the only choice for *Saved by the Bell*, the dream episode where the gang are rock stars behind their hit song "Friends Forever" would have been a great choice. Weirdly, that episode is also called "Rockumentary." However, the Zack Attack episode's celebrity cachet comes from Casey "Goddamn Death Dedication" Kasem, indicative yet again of the *Saved by the Bell* team's preoccupation with their own '50s and '60s childhoods. *Blossom*'s "Rockumentary" has David Faustino, Martha Quinn, Neil Patrick Harris, and, um, Don King.

Blossom has a cold, and so she falls asleep and has her pop idol dream. Specifically, though, Blossom has fallen asleep watching *Madonna: Truth or Dare*, and so her dream is in fact a parody of the infamous documentary. When Blossom dreamed of being a music icon, she dreamed of being Madonna. That's 1991 in a nutshell.

Madonna was at the center of music in the '80s and '90s. Some have been as big a figure in popular culture as my fellow Michigander, but nobody has ever been bigger than Madonna. In 1990 she went on her Blond Ambition tour, which was controversial even before it began because Pepsi dropped its sponsorship on account of the "Like a Prayer" video. It turns out Madonna was just fine without the cola company. Alek Keshishian was hired to do a traditional concert film, but it became as much, or more, about backstage life on tour. The backstage elements were presented in black and white, which became the iconic visual imagery of *Truth or Dare*, while the concert footage was still in color.

Truth or Dare became the highest grossing documentary film until *Bowling for Columbine*. It's considered a significant milestone in the depiction of homosexuality on screen, and also in Kevin Costner calling stuff "neat." Naturally, a documentary centered on Madonna became fodder for parody. "Wayne's World" did it on *Saturday Night Live*. Julie Brown (the redhead from *Earth Girls Are Easy*, not to be confused with Downtown Julie Brown) did a full-on mockumentary, *Medusa: Dare to Be Truthful*. Then, there's "Rockumentary."

I imagine a lot of people who were watching this family sitcom focused on a teenage girl had not seen *Truth or Dare*. Madonna was a provocateur. There is a scene in *Truth or Dare* where cops in Toronto threaten to arrest her for lewd behavior. Even so, I imagine millions of people who had never seen *Truth or Dare* still got the reference in "Rockumentary." The black and white, the headset microphone, it was all of a tableau.

With all due respect to Blossom, she had nothing on Madonna as a cultural figure. Madonna is the reason "Rockumentary" is a defining TV episode for the 1990s. She gave us *Truth or Dare*, which gave us "Rockumentary." Also, "Rockumentary" is pretty fun! It turns out *Blossom* was teeming with notable '90s figures showing up in cameos as well. That puts the show up the alley of this book, and in turn up my alley for good measure. To my surprise, checking out *Blossom* for this book made me want to see more of the show. As a wise man once said, "Whoa!"

Columbo: "No Time to Die"

Columbo is an excellent "wallpaper" show. Before it had an unexpected pandemic resurgence, I was in on *Columbo*, as I was in on *The Rockford Files* and other assorted procedurals of yore. Even these days, when I need to watch something while I, say, exercise, quite often I throw on a *Columbo*. Peter Falk's defining work was a '70s staple, with the first seven seasons airing on NBC throughout the decade. Then, in 1989, ABC brought Falk and Lieutenant Columbo back. This run was even more sporadic, particularly the final 14 specials, which aired between December 1990 and, seriously, January 2003. The ABC run is spotty at best. I rarely watch them, though I will say that some of them are good. Not "No Time to Die," though. "No Time to Die" sucks.

Why am I writing about the dirt-worst *Columbo* episode? Well, obviously a portion of that is the fact that this is a book about '90s TV. I can't just pontificate about the episode where Falk's good friend John Cassavetes plays a murderous conductor, because it aired in 1972. On top of simple calendar issues, though, the unfortunate reality is that "No Time to Die" is the most '90s episode of *Columbo* and a rare example of the show trying to capture the zeitgeist. In doing so, the show also threw away everything that made *Columbo*, well, *Columbo*.

If you aren't familiar with the trappings of *Columbo*, a quick primer. Episodes start not with Columbo, but with the murderer. They are usually a notable face, such as Ray Milland or Leonard Nimoy. We watch a crime be committed, see how they try to cover it up, and then only at this point does Columbo, Los Angeles's top homicide detective, show up. Instead of being a "whodunit," *Columbo* is a "howcatchem." The movie-length episodes (*Columbo* was not a weekly show, but a frequent movie-of-the-week entrant) would focus on Columbo unraveling the killer's crime, and invariably we would see how the detective figured it out. Like 90 percent of the time the murderer was an arrogant rich person who offed their blackmailer, but that's cool. It was still fun.

This is the format of *Columbo*. "No Time to Die" completely threw that format out of the window when it aired on February 15, 1992. That's just part of why it is the worst episode, though. It is entirely anathema to the ethos, style, and tone of *Columbo*. Also, it feels like a sweaty attempt to ride the coattails of a massive pop culture phenomenon from one year earlier.

"No Time to Die" is an adaptation of *So Long as You Both Shall Live*, a novel by Ed McBain, one of the many pen names of prolific author Salvatore Lombino. Columbo is at his nephew's wedding when his bride-to-be, a famous model named Melissa, is kidnapped by a deranged psychopath played by Daniel McDonald. His plan is to marry her and then murder her. Columbo is left to race against the clock to save his nephew's fiancée from this madman. Half of the episode is spent with Columbo as he tries to figure out the case, and the other half deals with Melissa being held captive while this dude does spooky-TV-killer stuff to her. It suuuuuuucks.

One of the primary charms of *Columbo* is watching Falk as Columbo doing his thing. It's about the folksy nature, the genial-but-probing questions, the "just one more thing" of it all—that's what makes Columbo so effective, but also so entertaining. Usually, Columbo spends a lot of time with the killer, and the best episodes have the best interactions between criminal and cop. The fun of *Columbo* is watching him outwit two Martin Landaus. This is a show that, at its best, is about Donald Pleasence as a wine aficionado being like, "Hey, you got me Columbo. Well done. You're a smart dude and I respect you," and Columbo being like, "Honestly, I genuinely appreciate that, and if you weren't a murderer, I bet we could have been friends."

Columbo doesn't get to be folksy in "No Time to Die." He doesn't interact with the would-be killer at all. All the stuff with Melissa is tawdry and feels warmed over and banal. It's not a *Columbo* episode. It's a bad *CSI* episode. Or, rather, a bad riff on one of the biggest movies of 1991.

Acknowledging McBain's novel as the source material, it feels clear to me this adaptation was born out of the cultural cachet of *The Silence of the Lambs*, a hit movie also based on a trashy crime novel. This was not the first time one of Thomas Harris's Hannibal Lecter novels had been turned into a film. Two years before *The Silence of the Lambs* came out as a novel, the first Lecter novel, *Red Dragon*, was turned into the film *Manhunter*. It has largely been forgotten. *The Silence of the Lambs*, though, stamped its spot in the cultural lexicon.

One assumes nobody was expecting *The Silence of the Lambs* to hit like it did. The film was a February release, and that month is usually part of "Dumpuary," the name given to January and February because it is when movie studios tend to "dump" the films they see as distressed assets and damaged goods. You toss them out into theaters and wash your hands of them. *The Silence of the Lambs* had Jonathan Demme as a director and a notable cast, but it has the trappings of a trashy thriller. Demme gave filmgoers the ramped-up version of that, though. The film made $272.7 million worldwide, making it the fifth highest grossing movie of 1991. For an R-rated movie, that's huge. When it's made on a reported budget of $19 million, that's incredible.

This wasn't the end of the success of *Silence of the Lambs*, though! It is one of only three films to date to win the "Big Five" at the Academy Awards: Best Screenplay, Best Actor, Best Actress, Best Director, and Best Picture. The impact of this movie on the zeitgeist and on cinema in the 1990s is difficult to overstate. All that from a film built around the premise of an FBI agent turning to one serial killer to catch another serial killer. That latter serial killer? They abduct women for their nefarious wants.

Does that sound familiar? "No Time to Die" feels, 100 percent, like an attempt by ABC and *Columbo* to do their own *The Silence of the Lambs*. That is in spite of the fact this is completely against what *Columbo* is fundamentally. It showed. "No Time to Die" is a bad episode of TV, but the sweaty attempt to draft behind *The Silence of the Lambs* with no regard to what makes *Columbo* so enjoyable is why I hold this episode so fully in contempt. *Columbo* sold out. Maybe the idea of "selling out" is itself a vestige of the '90s, but what am I if not a vestige of the '90s? Let's dump "No Time to Die" like it's *Nothing but Trouble*, a disastrous film that came out one day after *The Silence of the Lambs*.

The Ren & Stimpy Show: "Stimpy's Invention"

The first three original Nicktoons debuted the same day: August 11, 1991. *Doug* was a reflection of the Nickelodeon audience. He was an everyman, but a kid, in line with the primary viewership of the network. *Rugrats* was ... for 10-year-olds who were nostalgic for being four? For tweens who wanted to feel like, "Man, I'm glad I'm not such a naïve child any longer"? I don't know. *Rugrats* is the most overrated Nicktoon. Then, there was *The Ren & Stimpy Show*, which delivered something prized by many kids: gross humor.

Ren & Stimpy was akin to *Beavis & Butt-Head*, and not just because it was an animated double act. These were shows that, in the eyes of a little kid, carried cultural cachet through being seen as transgressive. You weren't "supposed" to be watching content like this. In a certain home, it might be a little tricky to watch *Beavis and Butt-Head*, since that aired on MTV. *Ren & Stimpy*, though, was on Nickelodeon. It was the network explicitly *for* kids. Maybe the gross-out humor and child-friendly bawdiness could slip past attentive parents.

The show was created by a trash person whom I don't feel like writing about, and I don't have to because he bears no particular relevance on *Ren & Stimpy* being a defining element of the '90s. Yeah, the dude created something distinct and popular but he sucks and I don't care about him. Honestly? I don't even like the show. Not being a fan of gross-out humor, especially lazy gross-out humor, I have no affinity or fond feelings related to the aggro chihuahua and the doofus cat. That's not to say it's all bad, and I am not trying to excoriate the show in some act of bravado and posing. There's some funny stuff from the show. Powdered Toast Man is an entertaining concept. Mr. Horse has a few good moments. Then, there's "The Happy Happy Joy Joy Song," which is at the center of "Stimpy's Invention."

If there is one thing most people know from *Ren & Stimpy*, it's "The

Happy Happy Joy Joy Song." Airing as the final episode of the truncated first season of the show, "Stimpy's Invention" was, unsurprisingly, a fraught production. It took roughly one year to complete, with plenty of delays and fights and production notes in the mix. This was at the crux of *The Ren & Stimpy Show*. If you read about the production at all, sometimes it feels like a wonder that any episode from the first couple of seasons made it to air in completed form.

Stimpy, smarter than usual (as he is usually one of the dumbest TV characters ever), has been crafting inventions, which invariably make Ren angry. Thus, Stimpy decides to create a "Happy Helmet" that will force Ren to be happy. It works, but at the cost of Ren's psyche. At a certain point, Stimpy decides to put on "The Happy Happy Joy Joy Song" by Stinky Wizzleteats. The two dance to it until Ren, in an act of manic joy, smashes himself in the head with a hammer until the Happy Helmet breaks.

"The Happy Happy Joy Joy Song" is funny. It's a strong comedy song with an earworm of a chorus that evokes the idea of being annoying without actually being annoying, and there are some non-sequitur bits of business in the mix that do make me laugh and strike me as genuinely clever. *The Ren & Stimpy Show* was a defining show for kids of the '90s, and "The Happy Happy Joy Joy Song" was the defining moment of said show. Content-wise, it is the lasting legacy of the Nicktoon. Otherwise, what I remember is the overarching sense of grossness, but how that made it "cool." I say that as somebody who as a kid wasn't particularly into gross-out humor. Even so, I always wanted to see *The Ren & Stimpy Show*, because that meant something to me. It was my conception of what "edgy" was. I was not the only one.

These days, the only one of the three original Nicktoons I have much patience for is *Doug*, which is more just a "pleasant" show. It has a slice-of-life vibe I appreciate, even if it is rarely funny. You know, there may not even be anything as funny as "The Happy Happy Joy Joy Song" in the entire run of *Doug*. Ultimately, though, *The Ren & Stimpy Show* is a testament to the power of facile toilet humor, particularly to children. Is there value in that? Probably, but that doesn't mean it has to be palatable. Much in the way *Time*'s Person of the Year can be a figure of controversial significance, however, *The Ren & Stimpy Show* can be the defining cartoon that debuted in the 1990s.

Barney & Friends: "When I Grow Up..."

I hate you. You hate me. Let's team up and kill Barney. With a knife, and a gun, and a bullet to his head. Aren't you glad that Barney's dead? With that child's equivalent of a street joke, me and my fellow preteens really stuck it to ... a plush dinosaur designed to help preschool children learn? Mr. Narrator, this was Bob Dylan to me.

When *Barney & Friends* debuted in 1992, I was slightly too old for it. The show would go on for 14 seasons and 268 episodes, ending in 2010. It was a PBS show aimed at the youngest of children in an attempt to educate and to provide these tots with general good vibes. Barney was a big purple dinosaur, but he looked like a friendly stuffed animal come to life. He and his compatriots, some other people in dino suits, some puppets, some other adult characters, and a rotating cadre of kids, would impart big-picture lessons through songs, hugging, and simplified storytelling.

"When I Grow Up..." is about the idea of jobs. Shawn, one of the kids on this episode, is afraid to have a job when he grows up. Barney, though, teaches the kids that jobs aren't anything to be afraid of, and in fact they can be fun. This ... is a weird thing to teach kids who are a decade away from stocking shelves in a liquor store or shoveling popcorn at a theater, much less doing somebody's taxes or writing books about '90s television. By the time a kid is actually able to get a job, they aren't going to be afraid of it. This seems like a flimsy premise, more an excuse for Barney and company to play pretend. It's easy to fill time with some make-believe surrounding the jobs that kids can conceptually wrap their heads around.

As a small child, I watched *Sesame Street*. It was the educational TV I had at my disposal. I never had contempt for *Sesame Street*, but I don't recall it ever being treated with ardor by kids my age. There was never a *Sesame Street* backlash. Barney, though, was the enemy. It had to be known, if you were a kid my age. Barney sucked. Barney was lame. Much humor was derived from ridiculing the friendly purple dinosaur. Violence was perpetrated upon him in song. The movie *Mafia!* took a shot at Barney. In hindsight, I don't know why, other than the fact it was a facile joke in a mediocre parody. They also made an El Nino joke. It was not a Whit Stillman comedy. At the time, though, I loved that *Mafia!* made fun of Barney.

By dint of being just a bit too old for Barney, and also by dint of Barney becoming the most popular show for preschoolers, Barney was met with derision by me and my elementary school brethren. The popularity part definitely mattered there. As a kid, I would grit my teeth through the Nick Jr. shows when I was home from school, but I didn't have contempt for *Allegra's Window* or *Gullah Gullah Island*. I just didn't like them, because they were made for kids who were a few years younger, and so they were simplistic and slow and had less edge than a perfect sphere. When you're watching *Rocko's Modern Life*, Allegra's adventures just don't cut it. Barney, though, was ubiquitous. He was popular. Also, his show was boring and bad to me. I didn't dislike Barney because that was the thing to do. I had younger siblings. *Barney & Friends* was on. It earned my negative feelings, and we sophisticated fourth graders liked to make that known.

This, of course, happened before *Barney & Friends*, and it happened after as well. The only people who like shows like *Barney & Friends* are the exact target demographic. If you are slightly older than a show's audience, you are seeing the seams in it in a way you have never really done with TV before. Also, you recognize it as for being for "little kids," which is very much not what you want to be. If you are a parent, you also probably hate these shows because if they aren't holding an eight-year-old's attention, what thirtysomething has any hope? Amongst my contemporaries I have heard much contempt meted out for *Calliou* and *Peppa Pig*. The only ones who escape the orbit of the tedious shows for preschoolers are teenagers and those in their early twenties who lack children and are not friends with anybody with kids yet. When my sister liked Barney, I hated Barney, my mom probably hated Barney, and anybody five to 10 years older than me had zero feelings about Barney.

I am sure that at some point when I was but a tot some show was trying to teach me about jobs. I learned about doctors and cops and, I don't know, maybe a chef because chefs have distinctive hats and the jobs kids learn about are pretty prop heavy. "When I Grow Up…" did the same thing, but because Barney was doing it, that was a problem to kids who were just a smidge too old for that. "Tell me something I don't know, you stupid purple dinosaur," they thought to themselves before watching *Goof Troop* or whatever. As an adult, I hold no ill will against Barney, or his friends. He was just a soft, smiley Tyrannosaurus rex trying to get by. Although, now that I think about it, was his continual insistence that I loved him gaslighting? New take: Barney is canceled!

The Arsenio Hall Show: "June 3, 1992"

It's not cool to play a B-minus quality cover of "Heartbreak Hotel" on the saxophone. I believe that to be true. And yet, when Bill Clinton did that very thing on *The Arsenio Hall Show* in June of 1992, it made him, in the eyes of many, the coolest person to ever run for president of the United States. It was a defining moment in the Clinton campaign, and that November, Clinton would win the presidential election, overcoming George H.W. Bush and Ross Perot. OK, so making that sax performance was actually cooler than anything Bush or Perot had ever done.

A key part of that Clinton sax performance is "on *The Arsenio Hall Show*." Appearing on Hall's late-night talk show helped give the governor of Arkansas cachet. There is a general feeling that Clinton's stop by Hall's program helped make him more likeable to both young voters and to minority voters. This was not a begrudging appearance for either Hall or Clinton, or at least that was the feeling that emanated from their interaction. Hall was signing off on Clinton, and that couldn't have hurt. Sure, it's stupid to vote for a politician because a TV personality you enjoy likes him or her, but people cast votes for a lot of stupid reasons!

It's not shade to say that Clinton is a more important figure in history than Hall, but this is a book about '90s TV, and there isn't much else to say about Clinton's appearance. He showed up wailing on his sax. He was wearing sunglasses and he looked silly. Clinton got to pitch himself to the audience a bit and fielded a few questions from Arsenio. Also, Arsenio was wearing such a big suit. It was so baggy.

Part of why it made sense for Clinton to appear on Hall's show, though, was because Hall had managed to do something significant. He had made Johnny Carson sweat, and possibly helped push Carson out the door of *The Tonight Show*. Now, he had been the defining late-night host for decades, and retirement may have happened even if somebody hadn't successfully challenged him. As things like the "Carsenio" sketch from *Saturday Night Live* would indicate, though, there was a feeling in the air that Arsenio had surpassed Carson, at least with younger audiences.

Hall had guest hosted FOX's *The Late Show* in 1987 after Joan Rivers had gotten the boot, and he did well enough that he earned a shot at his own syndicated late-night show. *The Arsenio Hall Show* debuted on January 3, 1989, and he really carved out his own spot in late night. Here was a guy in his early thirties brimming with fresh energy. Carson was about to hit retirement age. He was, literally in many cases, your father's late-night host. Plus, Arsenio was a member of a racial minority in America, which certainly made him stand out, in addition to making him an important figure in television history.

Interestingly, Carson had signed off from his final *The Tonight Show* only a couple weeks before Clinton's appearance on *The Arsenio Hall Show*. That helps solidify just how much of a passing of the torch this was. Hall was the new king of late night … but it wouldn't last very long. Being syndicated came back to bite Arsenio. Jay Leno's *Tonight Show* debuted on May 25, 1992, and Leno was able to start generating his own audience. Of course, Leno's appointment as the host of *The Tonight Show* had led David Letterman to leave NBC, and he was given his own talk show to compete with Leno. Letterman's show was a CBS show, so many local CBS stations either dropped Hall's show or aired it later in the night. *The Chevy Chase Show* on FOX was short-lived, but FOX had insisted all affiliates air it, which pushed *The Arsenio Hall Show* from its time slot. If you wanted cool and hip, MTV debuted *The Jon Stewart Show* in 1993, and it was only 30 minutes. No padding necessary.

On April 18, 1994, Hall announced he was done with his show, with the final episode airing on May 27. That was two years and two days after *The Tonight Show with Jay Leno* debuted. It was also less than two years after Arsenio probably helped Clinton win the 1992 presidential election. That was not just Clinton's moment. It was Clinton *and* Arsenio's moment. People remember it as "when Clinton was on *Arsenio*." Again, though, why would cool young people vote for a guy because he played an Elvis song on the saxophone? Maybe Hall's blessing was all it took. Or maybe I am underestimating the power of a 45-year-old man wielding a sax in 1992.

Clarissa Explains It All: "Total TV"

My favorite of the '90s Nickelodeon shows is *The Adventures of Pete & Pete*, and I could have happily written about it in this book. I could have justified it, sure. Michael Stipe played the ice cream man Captain Scrummy in one episode, after all. My second-favorite of the '90s Nick shows, however, is *Clarissa Explains It All*, and Clarissa Darling was decidedly more of a '90s kid than either Wrigley brother, or any of the kids in Wellsville. A big part of that is that Clarissa was more of a consumer, and one of the things she liked to consume was television.

Clarissa is known for her fashion sense, and she is a true '90s style icon to be sure, but she was also big into computers and TV. Television often played a role in *Clarissa Explains It All*, something that was effectively never the case on *The Adventures of Pete & Pete*. In fact, in the second-ever episode of the show, "No TV," the plot centers on Janet, Clarissa and Ferguson's mom, instilling an anti–TV set of rules in the Darling household. The third episode? It's about Clarissa wanting to be a TV journalist. Then, there is the second-season episode "Total TV."

In a way, "Total TV" is the inverse of "No TV." Clarissa needs to do a science project, and she decides to watch TV for 24 hours straight for the project. It proves more difficult than she imagined, of course. This is an episode of TV entirely about the main character, a teenage girl, consuming television. It's the sort of thing that would have a lesson in it in many shows, especially now. That wasn't really the vibe of *Clarissa Explains It All*, though. This is one of the Nickelodeon shows from the '90s where cigarettes will just be casually smoked on occasion. Clarissa had a friend who smoked, and she was just like, "Gross!" and that was that.

Look, I feel the idea of wanting to watch a full day of TV as a kid in my bones. Once I got a TV in my bedroom as a kid, I would semi-frequently try and stay up all night watching television, usually Nick at Nite. It feels like kids of the '90s may have been the last "raised by TV" generation. I find this lamentable. Watching a bunch of TV as a kid in the '90s was great. Sure, you had to watch what was on, but by 1992, you had cable channels to consume in the mix. That includes Nickelodeon, of course.

There is another reason to highlight "Total TV" as a defining bit of '90s television, though. This episode aired as part of a new Saturday-night lineup called SNICK. Yes, on August 15, 1992, "Total TV" helped kick off SNICK, the Nickelodeon block aimed toward older kids. For the occasion, *Clarissa Explains It All* got new opening credits and end credits as well. If you were too old for Nickelodeon but not quite old enough to be going out on a Saturday night, you had SNICK to turn to. That first SNICK block consisted of *Clarissa Explains It All*, *Roundhouse*, *The Ren & Stimpy Show*, and *Are You Afraid of the Dark?*, a classic collection of '90s Nickelodeon programs.

I bet there was some Saturday evening in the summer where I watched SNICK and then tried to stay up all night watching TV. Maybe I was even successful. Sure, trying to spend 24 hours watching television messed with Clarissa's mind, and even as a lover of TV that is probably not an advisable thing to do. In 1992, though, "Total TV" was speaking to me in a major way, as it spoke to many television-loving kids of the time.

Murphy Brown: "You Say Potatoe, I Say Potato"

There have been a few quotes about being vice president of the United States that speak derisively about the position. John Adams reportedly called it the "most insignificant" office imaginable. John Nance Garner, vice president under Franklin Delano Roosevelt, infamously called his job "not worth a bucket of warm piss." You may have heard it as "warm spit," but apparently people were just cleaning it up for many years. I, however, offer authenticity. I offer "warm piss." It feels like these days, people who never ascend beyond being vice president of the United States still manage to become known figures, though not always for the best reasons. Dick Cheney's machinations got him a biopic from Adam McKay that served as a warning of things to come. That is to say, a warning that he was about to make an awful movie in *Don't Look Up*. Then, there is the saga of Dan Quayle, forever tied to Murphy Brown and the word "potato."

Quayle was a senator for his home state of Indiana who was tapped by George H.W. Bush to serve as his vice presidential candidate when Bush, who was himself the sitting veep under Ronald Reagan, decided to try to ride Reagan's coattails into office. Bush trounced the overmatched Michael Dukakis in 1988, which meant running for reelection for 1992. This year did not go well for Bush, or for Quayle.

Murphy Brown was already a massive hit by 1992. The show had debuted in 1988, and in 1992 Candice Bergen would win her third Emmy for Outstanding Lead Actress in a Comedy Series for playing Murphy, the recovering alcoholic news journalist working for "FYI," a newsmagazine show on CBS. That third Emmy was for "Birth 101," the finale of the fourth season. Brown goes into labor on air, and the episode culminates with her having her son Avery. It was also the culmination of a storyline that began in the season premiere, when Murphy finds out she is pregnant thanks to her ex Jake. Jake doesn't want any part in being a father, so Murphy decides to go it alone as a single mom.

This did not sit well with Quayle. On May 19, 1992, just one day after "Birth 101" aired, Quayle gave a speech at the Commonwealth Club of California he titled "Reflections on Urban America." In the speech, he blamed violence such as the Los Angeles riots on a lack of family values, and explicitly called out *Murphy Brown*. He said, "It doesn't help matters when prime-time TV has Murphy Brown—a character who supposedly epitomizes today's intelligent, highly paid, professional woman—mocking the importance of fathers, by bearing a child alone, and calling it just another 'lifestyle choice.'" A month later, while on the campaign trail, Quayle was at an elementary school in Trenton, New Jersey, where he corrected a 12-year-old's spelling of "potato" by changing it to "potatoe." Of course, "potatoe" was wrong, and being outspelled by an elementary school student isn't a great look for the vice president.

Take those two things, mash them together, and you get the season 5 premiere of *Murphy Brown*, "You Say Potatoe, I Say Potato." The two-parter sees Brown dealing with being a mother, but in the second half of the episode Quayle really enters the picture. Within the world of the show, Murphy is in-universe attacked by Quayle for her lack of family values for being a single mother.

My politics do not align with Quayle's at all. I think his pearl clutching about the TV character Murphy Brown being a single mom is silly. His misspelling of potato was a bad look. All that said, the thing about this episode of TV is, well, it's not good. The comedy feels so lazy. *Murphy Brown* had this thing served up on a platter to them, and "You Say Potatoe, I Say Potato" largely drops the ball.

I watched *Murphy Brown* as a kid, though I could not have told you anything about it and I only watched it because my mom did, I assume. What I did recall was a *Family Guy* cutaway joke of a *Murphy Brown* episode that is just the characters speaking gibberish with political references dropped in. When *Family Guy* is talking trash about you for lazy reference comedy, you really need to look at yourself in the mirror. It's like sitting next to Wade Boggs on a flight and him telling you that you might want to cool it on the beers.

"You Say Potatoe, I Say Potato" makes the *Family Guy* gag feel fairly accurate. It's not gibberish peppered with references, but it is flat lines of dialogue that rely on dropping names as a "joke." You can make good jokes about John Sununu and Paul Tsongas, but referencing them does not a joke make. The fact that this was the culmination of all this controversy is disappointing. There is really no point to watching "You Say Potatoe, I Say Potato." Reading up on the controversy is sufficient, and a better use of your time and energy. I mean, it's a two-part episode! That's a lot of banal humor to sit through.

As I previously noted in this book, while Quayle was out there gaffing it up, Bill Clinton was appearing on Arsenio Hall's show. "You Say Potatoe, I Say Potato" aired on September 21, 1992. That November, Clinton would defeat Bush, and Quayle's political career effectively ended. He ran for president leading up to the 2000 election, but he lasted all of five months before dropping out. *Murphy Brown* would air 10 seasons during its initial run, ending in 1998. The show returned for an 11th season in 2018 during the rise of reboots, but lasted only 13 lackluster episodes. Turns out neither of these vestiges of the late '80s / early '90s had legs.

Quantum Leap: "Lee Harvey Oswald"

The last chapter of this book was centered on a two-part episode that featured somebody, in that case Murphy Brown, who had a beef with a member of the executive branch of the US government, in that case Dan Quayle. This chapter is also about a two-part episode featuring a private citizen with an issue with a politician, though he went about things a bit differently. To begin its fifth and final season, *Quantum Leap* swung big. They delved into the assassination of John F. Kennedy.

Quantum Leap starred Scott Bakula as Dr. Sam Beckett, a physicist who not only involuntarily travels through time, but in doing so finds himself in the body of somebody else. Thus, the hook of any given episode involves Sam figuring out whose body he is in and what he needs to do to make his next "leap." For the bulk of the show's run, *Quantum Leap* didn't dip into real history. Then, for the final season, they decided to go all in on history by having Sam leap into the body of Lee Harvey Oswald. Over the course of a two-hour episode (later broken into two one-hour episodes subtitled "Leaping on a String" and "Leaping to Judgment"), Sam finds himself as Oswald in different times and different locations, all leading up to a certain November day in Dallas.

The assassination of JFK really left an impact on culture, and particularly on baby boomers who experienced it as children. Kennedy's murder is the one assassination of an American in high political office that doesn't feel old timey. It happened in the era of film, of television, of modernity. I have seen the Zapruder film. I have seen a photo of Leon Czolgosz in the movie *Slacker*, but a lot of people probably can't tell you the name of William McKinley's assassin, or that William McKinley was even president. Kennedy is a different story, and also one that has become needlessly thorny.

The sixth highest grossing film in the world in 1991 was *JFK*.

Although, fascinatingly to me, it wasn't in the top 10 of the year-end box office domestically, which means international filmgoers were really into Oliver Stone's film about the Kennedy assassination. *JFK* was a big cultural event. This is evidenced by the fact that it was parodied by both *Seinfeld* and *The Simpsons*. It's also deranged and bombastic, fitting given that Stone is himself a deranged and bombastic man in my view. *JFK* is awash in conspiracy theories. Stone has called the Warren Commission's report, which found that Oswald acted alone, a myth, and called his own film a "counter-myth." He was, in the parlance of our times, just asking questions.

In the intervening years, many have taken the version of the JFK assassination found in *JFK* the film as the truth. Is this Stone's fault? Only if that was his intent, and the closest I've gotten to a conclusion on that front is "um, maybe?" I do not hold works of fiction to journalistic standards, or need them to be accurate, even when dealing with real people. Only when a film purports to be the truth does it have any requirement to provide verisimilitude. If you turn to fiction for your facts, the problem is with you. Make a movie where Ronald Reagan saves Christmas for all I care. You could make a movie where I beat Rin Tin Tin to death with a tire iron, and my takeaway would be, "It's weird you made me a character in your film, as I am not famous." The issue is that a lot of people turned to *JFK* as fact, and it very much is not, in ways both intuitive and empirical.

Donald P. Bellisario, who created *Quantum Leap* and wrote "Lee Harvey Oswald," was one of the people who had an issue with Stone's film. So much so, it seems to have been the catalyst for his show getting into the realm of historical fiction and using real people. I found a *Los Angeles Times* piece from 1992 about the episode wherein Bellisario spoke at length about it. He said his son, 12 at the time, had gone to see *JFK* and come back "totally brainwashed" by the film. Now, why a 12-year-old was seeing *JFK* will have to be tabled, but this experience pushed Bellisario into action. He admitted that he didn't know for sure what happened, but simply wanted to counteract *JFK* and show that it was entirely possible that Oswald had acted alone. Furthermore, Bellisario was a Marine Corps veteran who, after completing his service, went back to visit some old friends of his stationed in Tustin, California. It was 1959, and while there he got into an argument with an active Marine Corps member serving there who was combatively espousing communist rhetoric. Yes, Bellisario had a chance encounter with the real Oswald in his life.

Dealing with fraught events and real people, "Lee Harvey Oswald" is on the melodramatic side for *Quantum Leap*. Interestingly, the actor playing Oswald is a young Willie Garson, a character actor you might recognize, possibly from *Sex and the City*. They manage to get out of it in the end in a fairly satisfying way. Sam leaps into Clint Hill, a US Secret Service agent present that day who climbed atop the limousine to shield the body of Jacqueline Kennedy. What the episode presupposes is that in the original timeline, both John and Jackie died, but Sam was able to save Jackie.

When you think of '90s pop culture, often you think of the Gen X of it all. But boomers were key figures as well, often creatively speaking. Stone is one of those boomers, although born in 1946 he is on the cusp. He is a key figure in the world of conspiracy, and remains so. *JFK* has had more impact on minds than "Lee Harvey Oswald," though Bellisario tried his best. Of course, this particular element of the '90s is still being felt today. The rise of the internet has only made conspiracy theories flourish and fester at an exponential rate. I even heard that some pop culture writer beat Rin Tin Tin to death with a tire iron.

Martin:
"Forever Sheneneh"

Martin Lawrence was part of the surge in the late '80s and early '90s of standups being given their own sitcoms. Lawrence, who turned his standup success into a nice run on *Star Search* and then into hosting *Def Comedy Jam*, was in the mix with the Jerry Seinfelds and Tim Allens of the era. Now, maybe *Martin* isn't remembered as well as *Seinfeld* or *Roseanne*, but his FOX sitcom got big ratings at first and ran five seasons and 132 episodes. His show may be recalled less among '90s comedies because it is set aside as a "Black Sitcom." It could be that Lawrence himself has become something of a persona non grata to many. He had multiple run-ins with the law in the 1990s and is part of that motley crew of former hosts banned from *Saturday Night Live*. Or, well, maybe *Martin* just wasn't that good.

The show centers on Martin Payne, a radio host on WZUP in Detroit, though later he follows in the footsteps of *Newhart*'s Dick Loudon and becomes a public-access TV host. Notably, *Martin* does not feature a protagonist that is a wife-and-kids family man or a single guy about town. Payne has a girlfriend, Gina, who later becomes his wife. She is the levelheaded one, allowing Lawrence to be an outrageous character in the vein of his standup persona. It is worth noting that Tisha Campbell, who played Gina, sued Lawrence during the run of the show for sexual harassment, was largely not in the fifth season, and only appeared in the series finale because the producers agreed to her condition that she not share any scenes with Lawrence.

That fifth season of *Martin* is a mess, and it also largely did away with what made the sitcom stand out. Lawrence played multiple characters. That includes his own mother; a nightmarish, *Clifford*-esque child named Roscoe; a down-on-his-luck aging pimp; and, um, a white guy named Bob. Then, here is the quintessential Lawrence character from the group, one Sheneneh Jenkins.

I half recall a line from Tina Fey's *Bossypants* that if the cast and staff of *Saturday Night Live* was comprised solely of improvisers every sketch would just be guys in drag yelling their catchphrases over and over. This is 100 percent the vibe of Sheneneh. I don't know if there has ever been a broader dude-in-drag character than Sheneneh, and that is saying something. The look is baroque, the performance staggeringly broad, and the whole thing sweaty and cringeworthy. Sheneneh is "ghetto." This is the way she is described in the show, it is the conception of her by Lawrence and the *Martin* crew, it is what it is. Obviously, it's intended as over-the-top caricature, but that doesn't mean you can get away with it. I feel like Sheneneh has to register as problematic these days, but in the '90s, she was probably the most popular thing about *Martin*. I said the show was maybe just not all that good for a reason.

"Forever Sheneneh" is a showpiece for Lawrence's character early in the first season. She wins a date with Christopher Reid, a.k.a. Kid from Kid 'n Play, thanks to Martin's radio show. Notably, Lawrence and Campbell had been in the first two *House Party* movies that made Kid ('n Play) household names. Somehow, this date ends up happening at Sheneneh's apartment, which strains credulity more than the "booty" Lawrence wears when playing Sheneneh. Malt liquor is served, and jokes in the vintage of "What if the *woman* was inappropriately horny!?" happen. It's a lot of a character perhaps best consumed in small doses, if at all.

I find the humor of Sheneneh to be the lowest hanging fruit, and a little uncomfortable, though more so in terms of Lawrence's portrayal of a woman than anything racial. Now, the show has enough sensible female characters that *Martin* as a whole doesn't necessarily feel overtly sexist, but Sheneneh just doesn't hit well with me. I will note that the show, and Lawrence, both won two NAACP Image Awards, so the NAACP was chill with Sheneneh. Also, did you know that *Muppet Babies* won their Outstanding Comedy Series award twice? "Forever Sheneneh" feels like a '90s artifact not just because Kid is in it. The whole essence of Sheneneh Jenkins screams 1992. Though, as recently as 2022, Lawrence was talking about wanting to do a movie with Jamie Foxx wherein Foxx would play his *In Living Color* drag character of Wanda opposite Lawrence as Sheneneh. Well, if *Muppet Babies* can win two NAACP Image Awards, I suppose anything is possible.

Saturday Night Live: "Tim Robbins/ Sinead O'Connor"

I assume Tim Robbins was promoting his film *Bob Roberts*, which he starred in, wrote, and directed. It had come out at the beginning of September, but *Saturday Night Live* had not yet begun its 18th season, so here he was on the second episode of said season, which aired on October 3, 1992. The cold open featured Dana Carvey as Ross Perot. Hey, an election was nigh. There was a "Deep Thoughts" from Jack Handey and a "Hollywood Minute" from David Spade. After the second performance from the musical guest, Robbins played Sweet Jimmy, the world's nicest pimp. You may not remember that sketch. It *kinda* got overshadowed by that musical guest. Sinead O'Connor came ready to fight the real enemy.

Fortunately, I don't need to tell you about *Saturday Night Live* and explain its whole deal. Let's just get to it. O'Connor had been on *SNL* one time previously, at the time of her peak of fame when "Nothing Compares 2 U" was a massive hit with an iconic music video that succeeded literally by being nothing more than an unbroken close up of the singer's face. For her second appearance, O'Connor performed "Success Has Made a Failure of Our Home" and a weird, eerie a cappella cover of Bob Marley's song "War." If the vibe wasn't unnerving enough, suddenly O'Connor was yelling about child abuse; produced a photo of Karol Wojtyla, known to most as Pope John Paul II; infamously declared, "Fight the real enemy"; and proceeded to rip the photo in half. Silence. Commercial break. Controversy.

Roman Catholicism and the Catholic Church have long fit oddly into the American landscape. Back in the day, when the Irish and Italians were discriminated against as "White Ethnics," a part of that was the fact that there were higher strains of Catholicism among them. People wondered if John F. Kennedy could become president of the United States on account of the fact he was Catholic. Skepticism has long greeted the Catholic Church in America, but there's skepticism, and there is ripping up a picture of the pope. Also, there were still plenty of Catholics around to be mad that their top dude had Sinead O'Connor coming for his neck. According to the book *Saturday Night Live: The First 20 Years*, there were 725 calls in support of O'Connor, but 4,484 complaints.

O'Connor is herself a thorny figure. Her behavior before, during, and after this time was erratic, sometimes disconcerting. She's long been unwell, both in terms of mental illness concerns and a lack of sound decision-making and poor personal choices. O'Connor's behavior has been such that her assortment of extreme claims and declarations must all be taken with a grain of salt, with skepticism as it were. She's said enough provably accurate things, and provably inaccurate things, that you just never know. O'Connor changed her name to Magda Davitt, then converted to Islam and changed her name to Shuhada' Sadaqat, but still records and releases music as Sinead O'Connor. She tweeted that she hated all non-Muslims, then said she was just trying to force Twitter to shut down her account. It's been quite the journey for Sadaqat. I still love her cover of "Nothing Compares 2 U." You want to talk defining '90s moments? That music video is one of them. And yet, even that pales in comparison to her decision to rip up a photo of Wojtyla without telling anybody on the defining sketch comedy show in the history of the world.

Here, though, is a case where the passage of time has been kind to O'Connor. The Catholic Church is an evil organization. I am not talking about it as a religion, but as an organization, although its dogma is also abhorrent. Even in 1992, the misogyny, the homophobia, the colonization paired with anti-contraception rhetoric wreaking havoc in developing nations, it was all evident. What wasn't, though, was what would become the defining black mark against the Church, Wojtyla, and the Vatican bigwigs who would follow in his footsteps. When O'Connor punctuated her version of "War" with "child abuse," we now know exactly what she was talking about. She grew up in Ireland, a country where the Catholic Church held a ton of sway, the kind that helped fuel sectarian violence that ruined lives and destroyed families. Her contempt for the Catholic Church, and for the man known as Pope John Paul II, was palpable. It is now entirely understandable. O'Connor was striking a blow against her enemy. She was right to do so. Did you know they canonized that dude? The Catholic Church is wild.

Saturday Night Live spent two weeks reeling from the fallout of O'Connor's ripped photo heard around the world. The next week, Joe Pesci's monologue was largely about what O'Connor had done. He even held up the photo, now taped back together, which honestly totally sucks. Jan

Hooks, who had left *Saturday Night Live*'s cast to be on *Designing Women*, returned to throw on a bald cap and play O'Connor in two separate sketches in the episode after that, hosted by Christopher Walken. In 1992, it felt like the consensus opinion was that Sinead O'Connor was wrong to declare Pope John Paul II the "real enemy" and to rip up a photo of him. There is a lot that Ms. Sadaqat has said and done I can't get behind, but time, and the revelations it has laid at our collective feet, has made this one I can definitely support. She took a stand against an evil man at the head of an evil organization. That being said, doing an a cappella take on Bob Marley's "War" is still a weird decision that I don't get. You can't win them all.

Postscript: Writing a book takes time. The world changes while you are in the process of putting a book together. When I wrote this chapter, Sinead O'Connor was alive. Now, she is dead. People tend to sand the rough edges off people the second they are no longer with us. I will not do that. Everything complicated about O'Connor when she was alive remains complicated now. Her death at 56 brought a tumultuous life to a close. Call her Sinead O'Connor. Call her Magda Davitt. Call her Shuhada' Sadaqat. She got into some fights she shouldn't have. She also fought the real enemy.

Baywatch: "Rookie of the Year"

I hope you enjoy tonal whiplash! A couple of days after Sinead O'Connor ripped a photo of the pope up on *Saturday Night Live*, "Rookie of the Year" aired as the fourth episode of the third season of, perhaps, the dumbest show in the history of American television. *Baywatch* was popular. It was a cultural phenomenon. It was also just so, so, so dumb. There is no substance here. *Baywatch* is not hiding any secret nuance. It's the show where people run around on the beach in red swimsuits. *Baywatch* made stars because, well, there are some people out there that folks really enjoy seeing run around in red swimsuits.

Originally, *Baywatch* was a failure. The show about lifeguards and their intertwined lives began as a vehicle for David Hasselhoff, as he was a couple years off of *Knight Rider* when *Baywatch* debuted on NBC in 1989. After one season, though, NBC canceled the show. In 1991, Hasselhoff and a few of the producers rallied and got the show into first-run syndication, and this time it worked. It wasn't smooth sailing, necessarily, and cast members were lost. Even the second season was a little dodgy, leading to more cast changes for season 3. This time, it took.

The plot of "Rookie of the Year" doesn't matter. Plots to *Baywatch* episodes are, at best, adequate. Invariably, somebody needs to be saved from drowning, as these are lifeguards. Then, there is the rest of the stuff that gets worked into the mix, such as lost pirate treasure, serial killers, and other plotlines that strike one as absurd, particularly when done in such a ham-fisted manner. "Rookie of the Year" is on the generic side. There's a storyline about the lifeguards competing to see who is the best, and then there is a secondary story about two new lifeguards who decide to move in together. See, one new lifeguard had been added in the two-part season premiere, and then another new lifeguard was added in the third episode. They are C.J. Parker and Stephanie Holden. They are played by Pamela Anderson and Alexandra Paul.

I would say, give or take a Yasmine Bleeth, Anderson and Paul are up there with Hasselhoff in terms of being the names associated with *Baywatch*. Or perhaps I should say the faces associated with the show, or even the bodies, to be frank. People didn't tune into *Baywatch* for the storylines, or because they cared about the characters. Few individuals watched "Rookie of the Year" wondering if C.J. and Stephanie could make it work as roommates. Stephanie was introduced as a woman from Mitch's past, and I can imagine some people did care about that, because if the modern internet has taught us anything, it's that a lot of folks have an unhealthy relationship with "shipping" characters. And hey, maybe Hasselhoff and Paul would make out in their red swimsuits.

You watched *Baywatch* because you wanted to see dudes in trunks and/or women in those weird high-cut one-piece swimsuits from the early '90s running on the beach in slow motion. Pam Anderson was a huge star in the '90s. It wasn't because she could act, because she really couldn't. She was the quintessential '90s sex symbol. Anderson had been a *Playboy* cover model, but if that was a bit too risqué for your tastes—or if you were too young to get your hands on a copy that was not pre-owned—maybe *Baywatch* was more palatable. Paul was a 5'10" former model who had watched an attempted movie career fizzle. *Baywatch* was water finding its level for Paul. It was where she fit in.

There is no critical merit to *Baywatch*. As a work of fiction, as a narrative program, it is a failure. Anderson and Paul would leave the show after season 7, and even in that season Paul was just recurring. Bleeth had been added to the cast for the fifth season as Caroline Holden, but she too was recurring by season 8, and after that she left the show. The writing was on the wall, the show moved to Hawaii for a couple seasons, and even Hasselhoff, who clung onto the show for dear life, dipped out for the 11th and final season. By the end of the '90s, some of the "value" in *Baywatch* was gone. The internet was in more homes, which increased access to the kind of material that scratched the itch *Baywatch* did, and then some. Swiftly, *Baywatch* became entirely a punchline, though it was always to a degree a punchline, and the same went for the cast members. Sure, you may have enjoyed watching Anderson, Paul, Hasselhoff, and the rest running in slow motion on the beach, but that did not turn them into sacred cows above reproach. C.J. Parker was not an interesting character, and Anderson was not a good actor, but episodes like "Rookie of the Year" could still deliver what viewers in the '90s were looking for. And you know what? That's totally fine. Let's not pretend the popularity of *Baywatch* was about anything but what the show is synonymous with. It was about red swimsuits, and who was filling out said swimsuits.

Where in the World Is Carmen Sandiego? "Bad Day on Broadway"

I really despised the movie *Pitch Perfect*. It's one of those movies where nobody acts like a real person, but the film isn't heightened so it just feels jarring. Also, it's not funny. And yes, I don't really have patience for a cappella music. That is, unless you are Rockapella, and I'm watching *Where in the World Is Carmen Sandiego?* in the 1990s. The words "sticky-fingered filcher from Berlin down to Belize" remain in my brain thanks to an educational game show that actually managed to be entertaining.

Playing the computer game *Where in the World Is Carmen Sandiego?* was definitely a big part of my childhood. This was when computers were for games, so I'd be playing *Treasure Mathstorm* or a battle chess game or *Carmen Sandiego* when I wasn't playing video games or playing with toys. I rose up from gumshoe to capturing the nefarious Carmen Sandiego, a stylish master criminal and jetsetter. The computer game debuted in 1985, and then the TV game show version on PBS debuted in 1991, running through 1995. Catching crooks joined forces with learning geography, and it was fun. I still have strong knowledge of flags of the world and national capitals, and *Carmen Sandiego* definitely played a role in that.

The host of the show was Greg Lee, though with all due respect to Lee, he's third banana to Rockapella and The Chief, as played indelibly by Lynne Thigpen. The Chief is the head of "ACME Crimenet," and she was the one who took the three gumshoes competing on the show through the paces. She was part announcer, part sidekick, part narrative character on a game show and an indelible piece of '90s pop culture to people of a certain age. Thigpen's performance, and style of speaking, was a big part of that. Also, shout-out to Carl Tart for his dead-on impression of Thigpen's Chief.

Through answering a series of geography questions, one of the three

Greetings, gumshoes! The Chief (Lynne Thigpen) and presenter Greg Lee need help catching the criminal mastermind Carmen Sandiego (PBS).

gumshoes would capture the V.I.L.E. villain, get the stolen loot back, and then go to the final round. There, the contestant would compete on a giant map of the world. The gumshoe would get a call from the crook telling them what continent Carmen Sandiego was on. They would then get 13 locations on said continent, with red dots representing the spots. The contestant would have 45 seconds to correctly place markers on seven (eight starting in season 2) spots on the map. If they won, they were promoted to sleuth and won a trip to any spot in North America.

To keep kids entertained while learning, there was a lot of business to *Where in the World Is Carmen Sandiego?*. It wasn't like *Jeopardy!* or one of those streamlined game shows. The V.I.L.E. criminals all had distinct personalities and, often, pun-based names. Vic the Slick, for example, or Eartha Brute. In season 2, they added an alien named Kneemoi, a reference to Spock himself, Leonard Nimoy. Also, the stuff the crooks would steal was wild. The Mona Lisa, sure, but also the Loch Ness Monster, or the La Brea Tar Pits. "Bad Day on Broadway" is an episode from the second season, which revamped a few things after learning lessons from the first season. The show you remember is the one that began with season 2. In this episode, Double Trouble—twins who sound like Jack Nicholson, like to party, and also have heads that look like if Mac Tonight had kids with a caricature of Arnold Schwarzenegger—steal the Tony Awards. Like, straight up, they steal the Tonys. Yes, sometimes a V.I.L.E. crook would steal a concept.

"Bad Day of Broadway" is your typical episode of *Where in the World Is Carmen Sandiego?*, an edition of a game show. The quality of any given episode ultimately comes down to how the game played out, and obviously as an adult watching middle-school kids answer geography questions isn't as gripping. The trappings of the show remain enjoyable, though, and the theme song remains a banger. In the '90s, Nickelodeon dominated the game-shows-for-kids space, but PBS took an early computer game, turned it into an educational game show, and made it work. Carmen Sandiego stole our hearts just as easily as she stole Stonehenge or the Hollywood Walk of Fame.

The Fresh Prince of Bel-Air: "A Night at the Oprah"

Will Smith was one of the biggest celebrities of the 1990s. For a couple years there, he was in the running to be considered the biggest movie star in the world. Yeah, *Wild Wild West* kind of cut into his resume on that front, but that movie did spawn a hit song from Smith, who also had a successful music career alongside his acting career. In fact, he rose to fame as the Fresh Prince, alongside DJ Jazzy Jeff, which paved the way for his acting breakthrough, the sitcom *The Fresh Prince of Bel-Air*. By the third season, Smith's show was already a big hit, and one episode evoked a celebrity on the star's level: Oprah Winfrey.

Yes, the cachet of *The Fresh Prince of Bel-Air* was such that Oprah appears as herself in this episode. The Banks family gets the call to be on *The Oprah Winfrey Show*, but Will is left out, so he shows up and makes a scene, which causes a problem for his Uncle Phil, who was running to be elected as a judge at the time (he'd get the gig in the next episode, for what it's worth). Now, usually a plotline of this ilk would see a family traveling to Los Angeles for their brush with showbiz, but the Bankses live in LA. Ah, but Oprah filmed her show in Chicago, so this still counts as a major event episode in more ways than one.

Notably, this was only the second time Oprah had appeared on a show as herself (aside from hosting *Saturday Night Live*), and the first time it was on the crime drama *Gabriel's Fire*, so this was the first time a sitcom had harnessed Oprah, and her talk show, for comedic effect. Having acted before, Oprah was not out of her depth, and the ensemble on *Fresh Prince* was usually effective. Smith's youthful charisma was still intact, allowing him to act untoward but then bounce back and remain the likeable protagonist of the show built around his persona. I have no beef with "A Night at the Oprah," an episode that captures two stars somehow still on the rise in terms of cachet.

The Fresh Prince of Bel-Air: "A Night at the Oprah"

Of course, the idea of Will Smith and Oprah Winfrey as megastars and beloved celebrities is now decidedly a '90s notion. Smith saw his acting career fizzle, falling out of stardom while some of his '90s compatriots like Tom Cruise, Leonardo DiCaprio, and Denzel Washington have largely managed to hold on. He kept trying to get back in the groove, but he failed. He tried to turn his son Jaden into a movie star but failed. His personal life became fodder for tabloids and rumors. Smith did manage to finally win an Oscar, but that night ended up being the low point of his career, as opposed to the crowning achievement. When Chris Rock made a joke at the expense of Jada Pinkett Smith, Will's wife, the actor decided to storm the stage and slap Rock in the face. Somehow, he was allowed to stay and accept his Best Actor award, but he then got the boot from the Academy. It was an act of lunacy in the public eye, one that could only sully his reputation. At least when Russell Crowe threw that phone, he didn't do it on stage at the Academy Awards.

Oprah's reputation has not fallen as far, though I do feel like it has fallen a bit. With good reason, might I add. It may be controversial to say, but even during the heyday of Winfrey as a global icon with her own magazine and network, I held her in disdain. Oprah was a human misery merchant, always on the hunt for some tragedy to exploit. She couched it in faux sympathy, but Oprah always struck me as utterly craven. When she would lavish her audience with gifts, it was never more than a promotional event for the companies in question, nothing involving even an iota of generosity from Winfrey. She happily helped push Phil McGraw and Mehmet Oz to the forefront, two unctuous carnival barkers masquerading as fonts of knowledge. They are both loathsome, and in turn make Oprah loathsome.

In 1992, you may have viewed "A Night at the Oprah" as a meeting of a sitcom star with clear potential as a movie headliner and the biggest name in the history of daytime TV. Now, you might see it as the meeting of a maniac and a false prophet. Hey, at least *The Fresh Prince of Bel-Air* was a fun sitcom. It gave us "The Carlton." All *The Oprah Winfrey Show* gave us is Mehmet Oz.

The Ben Stiller Show: "With Rob Morrow"

Getting a sketch show to have legs, outside of *Saturday Night Live*, has largely proven difficult. Attempts were made several times in the '90s, to varying degrees of success. Two different sketch shows were, effectively, the "Gen X" sketch shows, attempts to capture the MTV audience or the FOX audience. MTV's *The State* was a successful version of this, and the cast was full of future familiar faces for fans of comedy and/or VH1 talking-head shows. They tried to take *The State* to CBS in 1995, but the attempt failed and ended the show. Before that, another MTV sketch show made the move to network television, and it too failed. Commercially, at least, though not critically.

The Ben Stiller Show had a brief, unremarkable run on MTV, lasting only a handful of episodes, but not owing to a lack of success necessarily. Stiller, the son of comedic duo Jerry Stiller and Ann Meara, was on the rise. He had the MTV seal of approval, and FOX tried to capture that and get some of that "cool" factor, as FOX was still in the "we're the hip network channel" era of the early '90s. Stiller made the move to network television, and *The Ben Stiller Show* was reborn. Though limited, the regular cast was a shrewd collection of comedy identities. Janeane Garofalo is arguably the face of "Gen X standup comedy." Bob Odenkirk had sketch chops, having worked at The Second City and *Saturday Night Live*. He would, soon enough, headline his own sketch show alongside David Cross in *Mr. Show*, a cult favorite to this day. Andy Dick was the chaotic one, the energetic one. He was willing to do the sweatier things, to be less "cool" for the sake of comedy. He's also apparently a maniac, as history would prove.

I selected "With Rob Morrow" as the episode of *The Ben Stiller Show* that feels defining of the '90s for a couple reasons. One, the guest celebrity was, well, Rob Morrow. Morrow was a big deal in the '90s, at least for a bit. He starred in *Northern Exposure*, a CBS dramedy that was massive at the time but has fallen from the conversation. It won Outstanding Drama Series at the Emmys! And yet, nobody talks about it. Morrow won an Emmy for Lead Actor as well, but this was the 1990s. When you were a TV star, you made the move to film, the medium that matters. Like David Caruso, Morrow left his TV show to try his hand in movies. Like Caruso, Morrow failed to generate a movie career of any note. And hey, like Caruso, he returned to TV and found success on a CBS procedural, in Morrow's case *Numb3rs*. Ultimately, Morrow would end up in more episodes of *Numb3rs* than *Northern Exposure*.

When Morrow was the guest on *The Ben Stiller Show*, though, he was still in the midst of the white-hot run of his first CBS show. Morrow was definitely a "get," a chance to hopefully bolster the ratings of the fledging sketch comedy. The second reason why "With Rob Morrow" is a defining episode of '90s television is that this episode features the sketch "The Grungies." If you know any sketch from *The Ben Stiller Show*, it's likely "The Grungies." It's a high-concept sketch, the kind you can explain entirely with succinctness, which is usually ideal for a sketch. Basically, it's *The Monkees*, but grunge. In 1992, grunge was still at the forefront. It had taken over rock music thanks to bands like Nirvana, Pearl Jam, and Alice In Chains. Seattle was cool. Flannel was in. *The Monkees* was created to piggyback off the success of the Beatles. It would have been entirely plausible at the time for a show like "The Grungies" to really exist.

Maybe Stiller and company's sketch cut that idea off at the knees. It's spot-on, hilarious riff on *The Monkees*—including a cameo from Micky Dolenz—that feels like it could be parodying an actual show about a wacky grunge band. As somebody who has watched *The Monkees* in reruns, I can appreciate the level of detail in the spoof. Speaking of that show, it had actually aired on MTV in reruns as well in the 1980s, and was successful enough that it led to *The New Monkees*, a flop of a syndicated show that only aired 13 episodes.

Of course, by airing 13 episodes, *The New Monkees* beat *The Ben Stiller Show* by one. FOX canceled the show after it had aired 12 episodes, leaving one unaired until it popped up on Comedy Central in 1995. Its death was not a dishonorable one, though. At the Emmys, *The Ben Stiller Show* won Outstanding Writing for a Variety or Music Program. The show may have been canceled, but it still took home an Emmy, just like Rob Morrow. Stiller would then go on to have the film career Morrow aspired to. He became one of the biggest comedy stars in the world, and a successful director to boot. In fact, in 1994, Stiller's directorial debut, *Reality Bites*, would come out and become a defining "Gen X" movie.

Personally, I don't like it, and it did get mixed critical reviews, but it was a hit, and it got Stiller back on track after his sketch show was swiftly kicked to the curb. Before that, though, Stiller and company managed to create—give or take Weird Al's "Smells Like Nirvana"—the defining piece of grunge comedy.

Seinfeld: "The Contest"

Onan's father had a favor to ask. Judah's eldest son, Er, had died, so Judah told Onan it was his job to knock up Er's widow, Tamar. Tamar's take on this whole thing I don't know, but this is Old Testament stuff, and the Old Testament is the most misogynistic literature you'll find this side of a Neil LaBute play. Onan didn't want to have a child, though, so he would "spill his seed on the ground," and the Judeo-Christian god murdered him for it. He had committed the "sin of Onan," as it became known. Throughout the years, the story of Onan has been used by religious sorts to speak out against contraception, "pulling out," and, of course, masturbation. Onan's problem? He was not the master of his domain.

Seinfeld is one of the two tentpoles of American sitcoms in the 1990s. Technically, it debuted in 1989, like *The Simpsons*, but it is through and through a '90s show. If I put *The Simpsons*, being animated as it is, in a different bucket, the '90s were defined by *Seinfeld* and *Friends* on the sitcom front. Both were massive hits. Both changed the way people spoke and altered the lexicon. I will get to *Friends*, of course, but to me *Seinfeld* is better, and it isn't even close. I'd call *Seinfeld* the second best sitcom of the '90s. On top of that, I always like to point out that I find *Seinfeld* admirable and respectable for a specific reason: *Seinfeld* was willing to have contempt for its main characters.

Jerry Seinfeld and Larry David famously had a "no hugging, no learning" policy when it came to the show about nothing. Jerry, George, Elaine, Kramer, and assorted tertiary characters are, by and large, awful. They aren't likeable people. They are selfish, rude, corrupt, perverse—you name it. The same is true of the main sextet of *Friends*, but *Friends* wanted you to like them. You were supposed to root for Ross and Rachel, to be happy that Chandler and Monica got together. They were, well, your TV friends. People get attached to their TV friends. By dint of being the main character

The *Seinfeld* crew (from left: Michael Richards, Jerry Seinfeld, Julia Louis-Dreyfus, and Jason Alexander) formed an iconic sitcom quartet (NBC).

of a TV show, a portion of the audience will sympathize with you and root for you. That's weird! I think *Seinfeld* is great because the characters are funny, the plots are clever, and three of the four main actors are excellent in the show. There is nothing likeable about Jerry and his friends, but that's fine. Crucially, the show knows this, and the show agrees.

People by and large despised the series finale of *Seinfeld*. On a side note, the series finale was the first episode I watched. Hey, to be fair, I was 11 when it aired. *Seinfeld* was not in the rotation when I was a kid, and I was discouraged from watching it, as it was not appropriate for me. My parents happened to be out on the town that evening in May of 1998, so with my Aunt Cathy preoccupied with my two younger siblings, I went down to the basement and watched "The Finale." I had zero frame of reference for what is a reference-heavy hour of television, but I still enjoyed it.

Seinfeld: "The Contest" 69

Now, as an adult, having watched episodes in syndication over and over, I still think "The Finale" is good. Far from the best episode, sure, but a funny, fitting conclusion to the show.

I have a theory as to why so many people dislike the series finale of *Seinfeld*. The entire thing is about how much the core four suck, and how lousy they are as people. They are literally put on trial for being jerks and miscreants. Character after character from the show's history is trotted out to hold them accountable for their awfulness. In essence, "The Finale" says, "You know these characters you've been watching for a decade? They suck." To which some viewers likely responded, "Hey, don't tell me my TV friends suck!" As Jerry and company are sent to prison for misanthropy, more or less, you were unabashedly being told by the show that you shouldn't like these people. I agree, so that doesn't bother me. In a world where *Breaking Bad* fans hate Skyler because she gets in the way of Walter White's wacky adventures, though, there are television viewers who can't reconcile being told they shouldn't like characters they have spent years investing in. If you cared about the *Seinfeld* main characters, "The Finale" may have dissatisfied you. If you cared about the *Seinfeld* main characters, you deserved to be dissatisfied by it. That's on you, dude.

This chapter is not about "The Finale," though. It could have been, of course, but I mentioned how *Seinfeld* changed the lingo. With "The Contest" it did that, but it also pushed boundaries. The season 4 episode, which aired in 1992, is about masturbation. It won an Emmy. It was named by *TV Guide* the best episode of TV ever back in 2009. "The Contest" is a seminal moment in television, and fittingly semen plays a role, though only tacitly. You see, neither the word "masturbation" nor any traditional slang term related to it is used. In 1992, that simply was not done on TV. *Seinfeld* had to get creative, and, in doing so, it probably soared to greater heights.

After a disturbing *Glamour* magazine–related self-gratification incident that landed his mother in the hospital, George vows to never again engage in that particular activity (mentally insert the "men will do anything to avoid going to therapy" meme). Of course, he never says it specifically. Owing to NBC's standards decisions, the word "masturbation" is never used once in "The Contest." That is the case even though the titular contest consists of the core *Seinfeld* four seeing who can go the longest without masturbating. Elaine puts in $150 to the three men's $100, as they believe she has an unfair physiological and sociological advantage.

In this case the "nothing" in the show about nothing is four friends seeing who can remain "master of their domain" the longest. In perhaps the biggest studio audience laugh in the show's history, Kramer throws his money down on Jerry's table and declares himself out seemingly within the hour of the contest beginning, having seen a nude woman in the apartment across the street. He later spies on her extensively in one of those *Seinfeld* bits even I find a little uncomfortably nihilistic. The overarching conceit, to the extent there is one, is revisiting the characters as they try to sleep at night, the "masters of their domains" tossing and turning, those who have succumbed resting peacefully.

Jerry's situation is exacerbated by the fact he is dating a virgin, played by Jane Leeves, who is not ready to go "all the way," in the parlance of the time, or maybe the parlance of the 1950s. Who can say at this point? Is the presence of Leeves a convenient tip of the hand in terms of what I think is the best sitcom of the '90s? Only time will tell. The time is now: Yes. Meanwhile Elaine is all hot and bothered by the very '90s reference of John F. Kennedy Jr. Notably, at the end of "The Contest," we don't know who won. It is later referenced in the episode where George becomes a hand model that he won, but it is then mentioned in the finale that George cheated in the contest.

"The Contest" does represent what made *Seinfeld* so popular, and so vital, in the 1990s. It's funny, for starters, with fresh lines of dialogue and strong performances. Michael Richards may be a problematic figure, but the man was incredible as Kramer. The idea of four friends competing to see who can go the longest without masturbating threads a tricky needle of feeling plausible, perhaps even relatable, but not exactly a commonplace notion. You could imagine people doing this in 1992 but likely didn't know anybody who actually had. The notion is salacious, but not sordid. Then, of course, there is the fact that they managed to do it without relying on shock value or vulgarity. After all, they never even said the word "masturbation." I feel like now that's a word you could have heard on *Modern Family*, much less *Family Guy*.

You can quibble about the content of *Seinfeld*. Even I'll do it, and I think it's a great show. It sat within the parameters of the culture of 1992, and it arguably pushed it in a positive direction, if anything. Regardless of how funny you find *Seinfeld*, it is undeniable that in a genre that usually desires for you to care about the main characters, here was a sitcom that did not want that, created by guys who probably thought it was weird to care about TV characters at all. They aren't even real! Michael Scott is a bad person, but *The Office* wanted you to like him. *New Girl* was kind of like millennial *Seinfeld*, but Jerry and Elaine got together and George became an entirely different, better person as a grown man, and they wanted you to love the whole gang at the loft. I like *New Girl* quite a bit. I don't like any of the characters in *New Girl* as human beings, such as it is. If *New Girl* had done an episode of TV like "The Contest," it would have probably had some thematic element like "Well isn't this really born out of how hard relationships are, and don't you feel bad that they're feeling stressed out trying to be the masters of their domains?" *Seinfeld* simply said, "Look at these a-holes." I did. And I laughed. And that's ultimately what a sitcom is all about.

Law & Order:
"Point of View"

There's something about procedurals. Once I showed the USA show *Psych* to somebody, having praised its quality. They said it wasn't all that good. I started rewatching episodes, and I kind of agreed. Now, I still thought *Psych* was solid, but it did not hold up to my perception of its quality. Trying to figure it out, I realized that when I had originally watched *Psych*, I would watch it right before I went to bed. When I watched it in reruns, it was when I lived in Los Angeles without cable and streaming services didn't have original programming yet. But some channel called Ion would show *Psych* all day Saturday. My affinity for *Psych* was built upon it being an unchallenging, breezy procedural. Sometimes, I still throw an episode on, over better shows, because it has that procedural vibe. I can't count the number of times I've put on a *Columbo* when I can't find something new to stream. Watching a procedural, even a B-grade procedural, is its own experience, and *Law & Order* is the defining B-grade procedural of the 1990s.

It seems, to the general public, that the *Law & Order* spinoff *Special Victims Unit* has surpassed the original in terms of affinity. There is probably something to unpack there, but that show debuted in 1999 and thus was not yet a phenomenon by decade's end, and also I have never really watched it because I find it unpleasant. *Law & Order*, though, was in ubiquitous reruns on TNT when I was a kid in the 2000s. If I found myself at home in the evening, in a time before streaming, *Law & Order* often ended up on my television. The show ran for almost the entirety of the '90s. It debuted in September of 1990 and ran through the rest of the decade. Also, it completed the 2000s as well. The original run of *Law & Order*, all 20 seasons of it, ended in May 2010. The show was resurrected in 2022, and Dick Wolf has so much sway in the world of television it will probably be on for as long as he is alive and wants the OG *Law & Order* on NBC.

Law & Order: "Point of View"

Law & Order is a procedural, obviously, and like many procedurals there is a crime element, a mystery element, and typically a case of the week to be wrapped up by the end of every episode, give or take a ratings grab of a two-parter. This specific procedural went something along these lines: A jogger or somebody with an early morning job like a bagel maker stumbles upon a dead body. The NYPD homicide detectives look into the case. After a couple red herrings, they nab their suspect. Then, the "Law" hands it over to the "Order," and we see the DA and their team in action, usually culminating in a trial of some sort. Rinse and repeat. It all blends together and washes over you. That is the crux of the procedural.

Why "Point of View" as the episode of *Law & Order* in this book? If this is a procedural, what makes one episode stand out above the rest? This is an episode from the middle of the third season. What makes "Point of View" so noteworthy? Well, when the third season of *Law & Order* began, the detectives on the show were Phil Cerreta and Mike Logan, played by Paul Sorvino and Chris Noth, respectively. Fortunately, I don't have anything else to say about those two actors. When "Point of View" begins, Cerreta is recovering from surgery, and Logan is frustrated with the senior detective brought in to work with him. At the end of the episode, Cerreta tells Logan he has taken another position in the department and won't be returning to his old job, so Logan needs to accept his new partner. That partner? That would be Lennie Briscoe, as played by Jerry Orbach.

To me, there are two titans of *Law & Order*, Lennie Briscoe and Jack McCoy. McCoy is the attorney played by Sam Waterston who has basically been on the show since season 5. Briscoe is definitely the detective that stands out the most, though I must shout out S. Epatha Merkerson as Lieutenant Van Buren, a staple from seasons 4 through 20. When I was watching those *Law & Order* reruns back in the day, I would always be disappointed when it wasn't a Lennie episode. He was the best character, or rather Orbach was the actor I enjoyed seeing on the show the most. "Character" is not always the strong suit of procedurals, and with so many moving parts in *Law & Order*, it provided less distinct characterization than many of its brethren. Watching Lennie work a case, though, always felt like a treat.

Sure, maybe Taylor Swift has never named a cat after Lennie Briscoe, but give me Orbach's ornery cop any day of the week. When "Point of View" aired, there were surely viewers who didn't realize Cerreta was leaving and Briscoe was stepping in. It was a changing of the guard, one that led to the best era in the show's long history.

X-Men: The Animated Series: "Days of Future Past"

Increasingly ubiquitous superheroes have dominated popular culture for a while. We'll never shake that, I reckon. The new millennium did not introduce the concept of superheroes filtering out of the pages of comic books onto assorted screens but merely took things to the next level. It's hard to imagine a child of the post–Y2K era not being cognizant of multiple superhero franchises, but to me as a kid in the '90s, I feel like the X-Men were pretty much at the forefront of introducing me to superheroes, and they were the dominant force in that realm for the bulk of my childhood. A key part of that was *X-Men: The Animated Series*, which was part of the Fox Kids lineup on Saturday mornings.

Before *Batman Forever* hit theaters in 1995, the X-Men were the superheroes I largely engaged with. I was aware of Batman, and I had Batman toys, but I had not seen Tim Burton's 1989 movie, and I had only seen one section of *Batman Returns* on TV one day in the background at a friend's house. Burton's movies weren't aimed toward kids, and any Batman animation out there was not on my radar. *Batman Forever* hit theaters before *X-Men*, the film, did in 2000, so by the middle of the 1990s, Batman and Charles Xavier and his compatriots were the twin forces in superherodom to me. Until 1995, though, it was all about the X-Men cartoon, and also the arcade game I played at the local roller rink, which, as I recall, ruled.

X-Men: The Animated Series was a straightforward, faithful adaptation of the comic books, so much so that it liberally borrowed stories from said comics. It was notable in that it was also serialized, trusting kids to show up week after week to follow storylines. The very first two episodes of the show comprised a two-part take on "Night of the Sentinels." Later during the first season, on March 13 and March 20 of 1993, we got another two-parter, this time an adaptation of the iconic comics story arc "Days of Future Past."

X-Men: The Animated Series: "Days of Future Past"

As a kid, I had never read an X-Men comic. I still haven't. Frankly, the number of comics I've read not related to Riverdale is strikingly low. Fox Kids' animated series introduced me to these mutant superheroes, including the ones that were being showcased for a child audience, such as Gambit and Jubilee. Yes, as a small child I thought Gambit was cool, in fact the coolest of them all, but by the time he showed up in the films I no longer cared about Gambit. In the cartoon it was dope when he threw stuff that was supercharged. The animation style was striking, as it felt more like comics than the broadly drawn cartoon characters of other shows. Of course, now as an adult I'll take something overly cartoony over "serious" animation any day, but *X-Men* struck a chord with kids looking for something "grown up" to watch that still was a bunch of drawing doing stuff.

"Days of Future Past" is a story that would later be adapted into an *X-Men* film. The cartoon's take on the story diverges in introducing Bishop as a time traveler from a dystopian future instead of having Kitty Pryde be involved, and also, naturally, the cartoon's plot involves a lot more Gambit. If you take anything away from this chapter, it should be kids in the '90s loved Gambit. After the first part aired, you knew you had to be there the next Saturday morning to see how the story concluded, the better to consume cereal and toy ads. Hey, it's not like we had anywhere to be on a Saturday morning as a kid in 1993 anyway.

I have seen adults my age in recent years talking about rewatching *X-Men: The Animated Series* and still enjoying it. For millennials, it may have refound its footing as the definitive take on the mutant superheroes. FOX may have just been looking for some colorful characters to keep kids watching on Saturday mornings, but they managed to create lifelong X-Men fans in the process.

The Young Indiana Jones Chronicles: "Young Indiana Jones and the Mystery of the Blues"

In the 1980s, the world was treated to three films starring Harrison Ford as Indiana Jones. Well, we were "treated" to two of these movies and then also had to endure *Indiana Jones and the Temple of Doom*. Eventually, Ford would return to the role, but not until well into the 2000s. The 1990s were devoid of Indiana Jones movies, but not of Indy entirely. Without any Jones on the big screen, we got him on the small screen for a series of globetrotting adventures.

As you may recall, *Indiana Jones and the Last Crusade* begins with a vignette starring River Phoenix as a younger Indiana Jones. George Lucas figured he could take that concept and turn it into a TV show, and in the early '90s Lucas had not yet squandered any and all creative goodwill, so he got the chance. *The Young Indiana Jones Chronicles* was created by Lucas and aired on ABC as a show intended to educate kids through Indy's adventures. It was learning-through-adventuring in the vein of *Wishbone*, but with Indiana Jones—or at least a version of him.

Stories in *The Young Indiana Jones Chronicles* would vacillate between featuring an impish preteen version of Indiana and a young adult version more akin to Phoenix's portrayal. The latter Jones was played by Sean Patrick Flanery, an actor who has been in a lot of stuff, arguably none of it good. Befitting an adventure-of-the-week show designed to educate kids, Indiana would meet a ton of famous people. This is certainly the case in "Young Indiana Jones and the Mystery of the Blues," which is set in Chicago in 1920. It's a feature-length episode, basically a two-parter, in which Flanery's Jones learns about jazz from Sidney Bechet in an episode that

The Young Indiana Jones Chronicles: "The Mystery of the Blues"

also features Ernest Hemingway. Oh, and Indy's roommate is Eliot Ness. That's the kind of stuff you can pull in a show like this, but imagine if *Raiders of the Lost Ark* had featured Jones meeting a ton of famous people. Well, had it just been Lucas, that may have happened, but I can't imagine Steven Spielberg standing for that.

Speaking of famous people in "Mystery of the Blues," oftentimes episodes of *The Young Indiana Jones Chronicles* featured a present-day (i.e., 1993) version of Indiana Jones played by George Hall. Basically, nonagenarian Indy would have a memory jogged, which would fade into the adventure of the episode. Hall is not in "Mystery of the Blues," however. Instead, a middle-aged Indiana Jones bookends the episode to tell the story. He's played by … Harrison Ford. Yes, Ford deemed to do Lucas a solid and appear on an episode of *The Young Indiana Jones Chronicles*. This was in 1993, when movie stars did not appear on television, save for occasionally to do a cameo on a massive TV show. Yeah, Ford probably spent an hour, tops, shooting his stuff, but even so, it was a real coup.

To me, that speaks to the fact Ford seems to love playing Indiana Jones. It seems to be the only thing he loves other than flying planes and (allegedly?) smoking weed. Ford has always seemed to have a love-hate relationship with his other iconic franchise character, Han Solo, and seemed to desire to kill off Han as quickly as possible. Meanwhile, Ford returned to play Indiana Jones in *Dial of Destiny* at the precipice of turning 80. That speaks to his affinity for playing Jones, but I think him popping up in "Mystery of the Blues" speaks to it even more. Unfortunately for Lucas, getting Ford to stop by couldn't give his series the boost it needed. *The Young Indiana Jones Chronicles* cost a lot of money to make, and the ratings were not great. It was canceled after 28 episodes, which were followed by four movies made for The Family Channel.

On paper, *The Young Indiana Jones Chronicles* made total sense. The character had name recognition, of course, but he also had a backstory that justified episodic adventure. Alas, the execution just wasn't there. It turns out it helps to have star power in the mix as well. Flanery was no Ford. Some fine directors worked on the show (including the likes of Joe Johnston, Nicolas Roeg, and Mike Newell), but none of them are Spielberg. Apparently kids didn't care about seeing college-aged Indiana Jones rooming with Eliot Ness.

Beverly Hills, 90210: "Something in the Air"

We all have pop culture blind spots, even the kind of people who write books about pop culture. These days, it is truly impossible to watch all the TV and see all the films you would like to enjoy. Even in the '90s, this was immensely difficult, if not impossible. Then, you know, there's the simple fact you don't want to watch *everything*. All of this is to say that prior to writing this book I had never seen a second of *Beverly Hills, 90210*. To me, Luke Perry is the guy from *Buffy the Vampire Slayer*, a movie that is better than the show it inspired. Ian Ziering is the dude from *Sharknado*. Not only is Tiffani Thiessen solely Kelly Kapowski, but even Tori Spelling is Violet Bickerstaff from *Saved by the Bell*. That being said, I still knew exactly what episode of *Beverly Hills, 90210* I wanted to write about. Though I didn't know the name of the episode, I knew how to begin my search. It all started with three words: Donna Martin graduates.

Beverly Hills, 90210 was a prime-time soap for teens that aired on FOX for a decade. It was a fish-out-of-water story, at first, with twins Brandon and Brenda Walsh moving from Minneapolis to Beverly Hills, the wealthy city adjacent to Los Angeles. The show followed the kids at the center from high school to college and beyond. The third season ended with the kids graduating from high school, but before the two-parter "Commencement," there was "Something in the Air."

Donna Martin, played by Tori Spelling, daughter of producer Aaron Spelling, was drunk at the prom, and that gets her in hot water. Side note: In *D2: The Mighty Ducks*, Greg Goldberg pretends that he is the nephew of Aaron Spelling so that he and his friends can check out a store on Rodeo Drive, a street in Beverly Hills. That movie is temporally congruous to *Beverly Hills, 90210*, but I have to wonder how many people in the target audience for *D2* were aware of who Aaron Spelling was. Perhaps

An amalgamation of teens from Beverly Hills. Jason Priestley is at the center. Starting with the woman whose head is touching his and going clockwise, we have Jennie Garth, Ian Ziering, Luke Perry, Shannen Doherty, Gabrielle Carteris, Tori Spelling, and Brian Austin Green (FOX).

that was one of the "jokes for the parents," though it is a pretty tame one if so. Anyway, Donna Martin is going to be banned from the commencement ceremonies for being smashed at the prom, and her friends won't have it.

Donna's friends stage a walkout protest, and their message is clear: Donna Martin graduates! Donna Martin graduates! The protest, and the chant, permeated into the cultural lexicon. Case in point: I, a guy who has never seen this show, not only knew the phrase "Donna Martin graduates" but had some sense of the plot machinations. There is a website that solely is a video of that scene, ripped from an airing of "Something in the Air" on Soapnet, available to watch at any time. Even prior to social media creating the rise of memes, there were moments from pop culture that rose above the fray. They became touchstones for people who had never even seen the show, or the movie, in question.

I don't know anything else about Donna Martin. I didn't even know she was the one played by Spelling until researching *Beverly Hills, 90210* and "Something in the Air." But I knew her friends wanted her to graduate, and I knew they chanted about it. This is how the defining cultural moments of the '90s happened. It's the moments that weren't forgotten the second you turned your TV off.

Beavis and Butt-Head: "Scientific Stuff"

In the early 1990s, MTV was still mostly a music channel. Music videos were a driving force to get people to watch the network. *The Real World* came around in 1992 but didn't really take off until 1994, which I will get to later in this book. What else was there? Well, there were these two idiots who liked to sit on their couch and watch music videos. Somehow, they became two icons of '90s pop culture, even though they were animated. *Beavis and Butt-Head* is maybe the dumbest thing to become a massive cultural touchstone, and I mean that as a bone-deep compliment.

MTV bigwigs saw Mike Judge's short *Frog Baseball* and thought to themselves, "This is the kind of dude we want making programming for us!" I should note that *Frog Baseball*, in all of two minutes, introduces us to Beavis and Butt-Head and shows them making fun of Suzanne Somers, playing baseball with a frog, and then chasing down a poodle and (off screen) beating it with a baseball bat. We used to make things in this country. This, somehow, forever remained the essence, the ethos, of *Beavis and Butt-Head*. They were the face of blissful idiocy in the '90s, the depraved id of the teenaged boy writ large. Also, there were music videos.

Truly, describing *Beavis and Butt-Head* is as simple as saying two idiot teenagers have dumb adventures where they do stupid stuff and say gross things, and then in most episodes they also watch a bunch of music videos and make comments over them. These are largely lost to history, with the licensing rights to said videos long gone. There were a few episodes of *Beavis and Butt-Head* before the second season debuted on May 17, 1993, with "Scientific Stuff," but this is where the show proper really begins. It also proved notable, and not because they showed music videos like "Epic" by Faith No More and "Weird Science" by Oingo Boingo. No, "Scientific Stuff" introduced the world to Daria Morgendorffer.

Worried that Beavis and Butt-Head's sophomoric horndog idiocy could prove overpowering if unchecked, Daria was created to serve as a foil to the duo. She was a smart girl who didn't put up with the boys' nonsense. While Daria's personality, and voice, took some time to develop, from the get-go some of "Daria" is there, and in "Scientific Stuff" she turned Beavis and Butt-Head's stupidity into a science experiment presentation. That's something the Daria of *Beavis and Butt-Head* would certainly do, but perhaps not the Daria of *Daria*. Yes, in 1997, Daria Morgendorffer got her own show, one with its own comedic sensibilities.

Daria takes the titular character out of the world of Beavis and Butt-Head, nobody from their show has anything to do with *Daria*, and plops her into Lawndale for a more typical high school sitcom. Here, Daria was the star. She was sardonic, smart, and wry. Daria has a couple friends, but mostly dislikes the other kids around her, and most adults. The animation and tone of *Daria* is different from *Beavis and Butt-Head*, with actual character development and emotional substance. I think *Daria* is such a good show, the best show MTV has ever done. The relationship fans of *Daria* have to that show compared to *Beavis and Butt-Head* is definitely different. People like Daria. They think she's cool. To some, Daria is an inspiration. Although, in adulthood, the unchecked anxiety of adulthood exemplified by Jake, Daria's father, should resonate a bit more. Nobody sees Beavis or Butt-Head as a role model, but Daria is an icon to many. People want to be the smartest person in the room, not the idiots making that smart person frustrated.

While *Daria* is a better show than *Beavis and Butt-Head*, and also a piece of defining '90s pop culture, it simply could not live up to the impact of *Beavis and Butt-Head*. They made a *Beavis and Butt-Head* movie for a reason. Everybody from kids to adults liked *Beavis and Butt-Head*. It was one of those shows, as a kid, you want to see, because you've heard it's risqué, though that wouldn't be the word you used. Maybe you would call it "bad," but only because you internalized that vernacular from a concerned parent. There is a bit of raunchiness and some gross-out humor to Beavis and Butt-Head's antics, but a lot of parents probably simply feared that the titular morons would be a bad influence on an impressionable child.

I admire the sublime stupidity of *Beavis and Butt-Head* more than I enjoy the quality of the show, especially now that watching it with the music videos is a dicey proposition. Even *Daria*, which I have on DVD, can't be what it was in the '90s, as all the original music was scrubbed out. "Scientific Stuff" was part of the legitimization of *Beavis and Butt-Head* as a staple of MTV's lineup, and also spawned another future icon of the network. Three of the most recognizable faces of '90s MTV? Those would be Beavis, Butt-Head, and Daria. No frogs were harmed in the writing of this chapter.

Cheers: "One for the Road"

I am of two minds for how much to write about *Cheers*. On the one hand, this is one of the biggest shows of all time. *Cheers* was a cultural phenomenon. People still talk about will-they-won't-they relationships as "Sam and Diane" scenarios. Many consider *Cheers* the best sitcom ever. On the other hand, *Cheers* is a quintessential '80s show. The show aired into the '90s because it ran for 11 seasons and 275 episodes, but it debuted in 1982. It feels ingrained in the 1980s. I am far from the first person to postulate that the cultural idea of a decade is not defined by the calendar, but by events. I would argue that "The 1980s" ended in 1993, based on two events that happened in the first half of that year. First, Bill Clinton was inaugurated as president of the United States that January, taking over for the totemic '80s figure of George H.W. Bush. Second, on May 20, the series finale of *Cheers*, "One for the Road," aired.

If I were writing a book about 1980s television, *Cheers* would be at the center of it. Since you are reading a book about TV, I bet you at least have a working knowledge of *Cheers* and probably have seen some of it. It's set at the titular bar and focuses on the staff of said bar and a few barflies. If I had to guess, and I do have to guess because I don't have this information and maybe nobody does, but roughly 80 percent of the show took place at Cheers. People loved it. Ted Danson and Shelley Long, the aforementioned Sam and Diane, became stars. Both tried to get film careers going as a result, with Long going as far as to leave the show. Neither quite made it work, but Danson at least always had *Cheers*. George Wendt hasn't walked into a bar since, oh, 1983 without hearing people yell "Norm!" and slide him a beer. I know he has said he hasn't paid for a beer in decades. Also, did *Cheers* give us a spinoff that became the best sitcom of the '90s? Only time will tell. The time is now: Yes.

My personal history with *Cheers* is unusual. I saw a couple episodes on Nick at Nite back in the day, but it wasn't in the regular rotation on there when I was a kid. Then, in adulthood, I won the first season on DVD so I decided to give the show a shot. I thought the first season was so good. In particular, and this is far from a hot take, I loved Sam and Diane, both together and separately. Danson and Long were so good on the show. Diane Chambers quickly became one of my favorite sitcom characters. Then, the second season happened. It's quite good, but it is a step down from the first season. Specifically, they messed up the character of Diane, which was a bummer. I made it to the third season, which featured the introduction of Kelsey Grammer as Frasier Crane. Late in the season, there is an episode called "Cheerio, Cheers." Written by Sam Simon and directed by James Burrows, two sitcom icons, it's a great "Sam and Diane" episode, but it ends with Diane having left America with Frasier, saying goodbye to Sam. It also features the first appearance by Nicholas Colasanto in a while, in what turned out to be his last appearance on the show.

I watched "Cheerio, Cheers" and thought to myself, "This would have been a perfect series finale." I knew Long was going to leave the show and be replaced by Kirstie Alley as Rebecca. I also knew Colasanto, always a

Rebecca (Kirstie Alley) and Diane (Shelley Long) joined forces for a special *Cheers* event. Bottom row, from left: John Ratzenberger, Tom Berenger (not a cast member), Kirstie Alley, Shelley Long, and George Wendt. Top row, from left: Ted Danson, Rhea Perlman, Woody Harrelson, and Kelsey Grammer (NBC).

delight as the dim coach, passed away. Instead of dealing with all that, I decided to make "Cheerio, Cheers" my personal series finale for *Cheers*. That made visiting "One for the Road" for this book odd for me. But any book about the defining TV episodes of the '90s had to include it.

Yes, I would say that *Cheers* is a "1980s show" and that "One for the Road" ended "The '80s" as we know it. That May night in 1993, though, was a massive cultural event. The episode ran 98 minutes, which is legitimately feature length. People were in for the long haul, though. More than 40 million households tuned in. Only two episodes of series television (i.e., not including *Roots* episodes) have been watched by more people: the last episode of *MASH* and the last episode of *The Fugitive*. After dedicating the '80s to watching *Cheers*, people were ready to say goodbye to an era.

"One for the Road" is 98 minutes of television. A lot happens. Diane returns. What everybody remembers, though, is the end. Sam is alone in Cheers. Somebody knocks on the door. Sam says, "Sorry, we're closed" and exits. Our time hanging out at the bar was over. We didn't have to go home but we couldn't stay there. Although, pretty much everybody watching was at home, and they probably stayed there. It was late by the time "One for the Road" ended. A defining sitcom drew the curtain with a defining last line delivered by a defining sitcom character. More people tuned in to watch that than anything other than a Super Bowl since the turn of the millennium. Episodes of television aren't cultural events on the level of "One for the Road" anymore. That's something that has ended, like "The '80s" ended with *Cheers*. All the free beers for George Wendt in the world couldn't bring it back.

Late Show with David Letterman: "August 30, 1993"

For decades, the late-night talk show game was basically just *The Tonight Show*. Johnny Carson was *the* guy, but, as mentioned in the *Arsenio Hall* chapter, Carson hung it up at the beginning of the 1990s. Suddenly, networks smelled opportunity, and David Letterman smelled a chance to one-up both his former network and a former compatriot of his. The "Late Night Wars" began on August 30, 1993, when the *Late Show with David Letterman* debuted on CBS.

Starting in 1982, Letterman began hosting *Late Night* on NBC, which aired after Carson's *Tonight Show*. While Carson was an old showbiz pro, Letterman brought anarchy and irreverence to late night. When Carson decided to retire, it created a buzz. Who would replace him and step in as host of *The Tonight Show*, a massive gig at the time? Honestly, you could argue it was the biggest job in television, and it was assuredly the dream gig for most people in comedy. Carson wanted Letterman to replace him, and Letterman wanted to replace Carson. Instead, NBC went with Jay Leno, who was philosophically everything Letterman wasn't. Leno was a try-hard, status-seeking, people-pleasing comedian. He was inoffensive, and he wasn't afraid to sweatily politick for the gig.

Letterman wasn't about to stick around and host *Late Night* and have it air after his contemporary Leno's show. CBS had basically been out of the late-night talk show game since 1972, when it parted ways with Merv Griffin. An attempt to give Pat Sajak a show began in 1989 … and ended in 1990. Letterman, though, was a proven commodity, and he was available. CBS signed Letterman to a three-year deal to host the *Late Show with David Letterman* opposite of Leno's *Tonight Show*. Letterman would get a chance to go toe to toe with his newly minted nemesis.

The monologue that first night was heavily focused on Letterman taking pot shots at his former employer, specifically the comedic bits he was told he could no longer legally perform. Some of it seemed petty, such as saying Calvert DeForest could no longer portray the character Larry "Bud" Melman, leaving him to go by his real name for the rest of his run. Letterman's buddy Bill Murray was the first guest, a wise choice given that Murray was a superstar, had an easy rapport with the host, and was game to goof around. Billy Joel served as the musical guest. Twenty-three million people tuned in.

The *Late Show* would beat *The Tonight Show* in the ratings for two years, until Leno had Hugh Grant on to talk about his solicitation arrest. Leno was also helped by NBC's quality prime-time offerings such as *Seinfeld* and *Friends*, compared to a flagging CBS lineup. Then, you know, both shows would go on and on, because late night was about the churn. Commercially, Leno did have himself a nice run there. From a critical standpoint, it was never close.

I never had any interest in Leno. Anything I ever saw from his show was a total shrug at best. To me, there are two geniuses of the late-night realm (Stephen Colbert is a comedic genius, but his stint in late night has always been a sad "Muhammad Ali fighting Larry Holmes" experience), and they are Conan O'Brien and Dave Letterman. Although, shout-out to Craig Ferguson for doing the best celebrity interviews in the history of the medium. Conan was "my" late-night host. He was the one I "discovered" and watched regularly from adolescence into adulthood. I watched him on *Late Night*, then *The Tonight Show*, and followed him to *Conan*. O'Brien's absurd genius fit when he was writing for *The Simpsons*, a cartoon, but he somehow managed to carry that into late night.

The first late-night host I was a fan of, though, was Letterman. My dad watched Letterman, and as a kid who loved to stay up and watch television, sometimes I saw some of the *Late Show* and was always glad to do so. Sure, some of that was the small child thing of "I'm watching a show for grown ups!" and I doubt the smirking irony of Letterman fully landed with me. When Letterman would do bits like throwing stuff off a building or seeing how many people in Spider-Man costumes could fit into a Jamba Juice, he did that with a wry distance from the whole affair. It was dumb, it was in his mind a waste of time, and that's why he loved it. I just liked seeing stuff get thrown off a building. The same holds true with the Top Ten List, which I would fight to be able to stay up for (the celebrity interviews meant nothing to me, because in my mind the comedy stopped there). I didn't grasp that a good third of them were intentionally lazy, and I would be puzzled when the number-one entrant would barely feel like a joke, not realizing that was the point. It didn't stop me from reading the book of Top Ten Lists my dad had.

Now, thanks to YouTube, I have been able to go back and watch clips from the early days of the *Late Show*, and even *Late Night* and Letterman's failed morning show. This is where Letterman's true genius is obvious. Somewhere, as time went on, more real apathy emerged to replace his faux apathy, but that's the churn for you. Letterman never seemed to have the manic craving for attention O'Brien has, which is evident in the documentary *Conan O'Brien Can't Stop*. It makes sense to tie these two together, as Letterman leaving *Late Night* left the door open for Conan to replace him. Both guys also happened to get shafted by Leno, and facile as it may seem, perhaps I do begrudge Leno for that, the inveterate hack standing in the way of two geniuses with integrity. Comedic integrity, at least. Letterman's personal life is another story. The story here, though, is that night in August when millions of people tuned in to see the Late Night Wars start in earnest. In my mind, at least, the winner is clear.

Melrose Place: "Much Ado About Everything"

Aaron Spelling had his prime-time soap for teens with *Beverly Hills, 90210*, but he wanted more. Could he replicate the success of that show with one geared toward adults? How do you replicate the environs of a high school for adult characters? Hey, how about an apartment complex? Boom: *Melrose Place*, the trashy prime-time soap that tallied seven seasons, 226 episodes, and one plotline on an episode of *Seinfeld*.

Technically, *Melrose Place* is a spinoff of *Beverly Hills, 90210*, but it's maybe the most extreme example of a backdoor pilot I can recall. The series began with Kelly Taylor from *Beverly Hills* dating the bad-boy biker Jake Hanson, one of the eclectic residents of an apartment complex on Melrose in West Hollywood. Jake debuted on the final two episodes of the second season of *Beverly Hills*, and then Kelly and a couple of her compatriots came over to the first few episodes of *Melrose Place*, and then with the new show established, *Melrose Place* got to be what it always was, which is a show that had nothing to do with *Beverly Hills, 90210*. The crossover storyline was really Aaron Spelling saying, "I want more money so watch my new show!"

When *Melrose Place* began, it was a soapy but episodic show about the lives of these assorted characters. It wasn't working, though, so they decided to turn it into a proper prime-time soap in the vein of a *Dallas* or *Falcon Crest*. That meant, like, five affairs per character, but it was also highlighted by the introduction of the soapiest character of them all: Amanda Woodward. She was played by none other than Heather Locklear. While Locklear was not part of the original cast of *Melrose Place*, she became the defining actor from the show, and Amanda the defining character. That wasn't supposed to be the case, but when the producers decided the soapier the better, they realized what they had in the cutthroat de facto villain of the show. After all, what's a soap opera without a campy villain?

"Much Ado About Everything," the season 2 premiere, is when *Melrose Place* became in earnest the show it is in the collective memory of '90s TV viewers. Amanda has bought up the apartment complex, integrating herself into the lives of all her tenants, which would be followed by further integration through affairs with most of them. Notably, and weirdly, Locklear was billed as a "special guest star" for every episode of *Melrose Place* from this point on. I am not sure if that was a contractual thing or an ego thing. Either way, it just adds another layer to the bombastic soapiness of the show. There's a reason why Jerry Seinfeld was afraid to admit to his girlfriend he watched *Melrose Place*. It was low art, even by the standards of 1993 television.

Obviously, though, there was an appetite for this type of low art. Not everything needs to be heady, clever, or emotionally engaging. People watched *Baywatch* to see Pamela Anderson in a bathing suit running on the beach. They watched *Melrose Place* for all the sordid sneaking around, the hyperbolic storylines, and to root against the villainous Amanda Woodward. It didn't debut until the year 2000, so it isn't in the book, but when I watched *Jackass* in junior high and then began every Monday saying to my friends at school, "Did you watch *Jackass*?" it wasn't for the high art of it all. Sometimes low art is trash, sordid, revolting, and offensive. Sometimes, high art is that too. Deep down, in a place he didn't want to talk about at parties, Jerry Seinfeld didn't want people to know that he was up to date on all of Amanda's machinations, and who was having sex with whom at the apartment complex on Melrose. And he enjoyed every second of it.

Animaniacs: "Episode 15"

Warner Bros. cartoons long embraced anarchy. While the early Disney cartoons were built on, um, tedium I guess, Warner Bros. brought up the madcap lunacy of Bugs Bunny, Daffy Duck, and their brethren. Could you imagine a Mickey Mouse cartoon with the vibe of a Wile E. Coyote and Roadrunner cartoon? By the '90s, though, *Looney Tunes* characters were passé (unless they were dressed up in hip-hop attire on the back of tacky jackets), but Warner Bros. doubled down on not much animation, but anarchy ... and they did it with the help of Steven Spielberg.

The year 1993 was staggeringly successful for Spielberg. He had *Jurassic Park*, which became the biggest movie of all time. Also, *Schindler's List* finally won him Best Director and Best Picture. That same year, his production company Amblin Entertainment teamed with Warner Bros. to bring *Animaniacs* to television. In fact, it was technically framed as *Steven Spielberg Presents Animaniacs*, though I have never known anybody to call it anything but *Animaniacs*, and I bet even Spielberg would call it that. Previously, Spielberg and Warner Bros. had collaborated on *Tiny Toons Adventures*, which was effectively "Looney Tunes Babies." It ran from 1990 until 1992, with *Animaniacs* picking up the next year and technically running from 1993 through 1998 in its initial run. I say "technically" because *Animaniacs* was one of those kids' cartoons of the '90s where the first season is overstuffed and then the episodes air sporadically from there. Case in point: the first season of *Animaniacs* consisted of 65 episodes that aired from September 13, 1993, through May 23, 1994. The next four seasons consisted of 34 episodes total over four years.

Episodes of *Animaniacs* didn't have names, as each episode was comprised of titled segments. As was the case with cartoons for kids in the '90s by and large, rarely was there an attempt to fill a full half-hour of TV (minus the commercials) with one plot. Typically, we would get two or three segments per episode, and I chose "Episode 15" because it is comprised of two segments, one each for the two tentpoles of *Animaniacs*. One is, of course, featuring the titular Animaniacs, Yakko, Wakko, and Dot. That trio featured in 138 segments, which is significant given that there were only 99 episodes in the initial run. The second most common segment headliner was actually Slappy Squirrel, but with all due respect to Slappy, after Yakko, Wakko, and Dot, you think of Pinky and the Brain.

It was wise, perhaps crucial, for *Animaniacs* to be built around segments, because the characters on the show are very "game based." That is to say, they have a shtick, they play out said shtick, and then it is time to move on. Yakko, Wakko, and Dot, the Warner siblings, were kayfabe locked in the iconic Warner Bros. water tower in the 1930s, but escaped in the 1990s to wreak havoc and sow chaos. They are an id-based trio, basically Bugs Bunny crossed with the original iteration of Daffy Duck (the one Joe Dante has such an affinity for). In the Warner siblings segments, they come across a "straight" character or two to play off of, they proceed to be annoying and aggravating, and then the segment ends before we, the audience, are annoyed by them as well. That's a delicate balance to nail, but *Animaniacs* manages to do it, say, 70 percent of the time.

Pinky and the Brain, meanwhile, are two lab mice. The Brain lives up to his name, and is bent on world domination. Pinky is dumb. It's a classic double act. Pinky's stupidity, and the Brain's hubris, get in the way of the latter's attempts to take over the world, leaving everything back at the status quo, vital for non-serialized shows, specifically cartoons. Pinky and the Brain segments are formulaic, but that is often the case in cartoons aimed at children. Hey, procedurals for adults are formulaic too. There is a difference between "formulaic" and "repetitive."

"Episode 15" is only two segments, perhaps owing to the scope and ambition of the two stories. The segments are also thematically linked. Yakko, Wakko, and Dot are abducted by aliens, and then annoy the aliens so much they are de-abducted. Meanwhile, Brain plans to trick people into thinking aliens have invaded to get them to flee. Brain is voiced by Maurice LaMarche doing an impression of Orson Welles, making this story a clear parody of Welles's famous *War of the Worlds* radio broadcast. If you want an emblematic episode of *Animaniacs*, this is it. Pinky and the Brain proved so successful they got a spinoff show, which later worked Elmyra from *Tiny Toons* into the mix.

As a kid, I watched *Looney Tunes*, which I found spotty, but I tended to enjoy Wile E. Coyote and Roadrunner. A lot of kids blanch at watching anything "old," however. As a child whose favorite show when he was six was *Dragnet*, obviously that did not apply to me. If *Looney Tunes* reruns struck a kid as "old," they could get that anarchic style of comedy from the new *Animaniacs*. This was, even more than *Tiny Toons*, the *Looney Tunes* for kids of the '90s. While you probably needed to enjoy the Warner siblings to enjoy the show, there was otherwise an assorted cast of characters that would pop up along the way, providing variety to Fox Kids viewers. There's always a standout in an ensemble, though, no matter how egalitarian you try to be. For *Animaniacs*, that turned out to be a couple of laboratory mice who were rarely, if ever, on the same wavelength of thought.

Saved by the Bell: The College Years: "The Poker Game"

Saved by the Bell is not the only show in this book to be featured along with a spinoff. It may be surprising, however, that *Saved by the Bell* is, in this way, in the same realm as *Cheers*. As I discussed in the "Jessie's Song" chapter, *Saved by the Bell* was not a good show. It was popular, though, and a cultural touchstone for kids of the '90s. I doubt many people are going to quibble with *Saved by the Bell*, and specifically that episode, being in this book. *Saved by the Bell: The College Years*, though? Not only is it worse than the original, a show that already lacked for quality, but it didn't even make a cultural impact. Why "The Poker Game" for this book? Well, a lot of it comes down to a guest star.

There was no fallow period between *Saved by the Bell* and its spinoff. In fact, the final episode of the original show aired Saturday night in prime time on May 22, 1993. It was followed by the pilot of *The College Years* airing right after. The guys—Zack, Slater, and Screech—made the move from Bayside High to Cal U, but they were the only ones in the pilot. After the pilot, though, there were a few months before the next episode aired, now moved to Tuesday nights. This move indicated that *The College Years* was not kid stuff like the original. No more Saturday afternoons. This was prime time, baby! The cast was also changed, however. There were initially three new women in the cast: Alex, Leslie, and Danielle. After the pilot, Danielle was axed, with Tiffani Thiessen stepping in as Kelly Kapowski. One assumes the producers, and NBC, feared *The College Years* would fail without Zack and Kelly's romance. Leslie was the one who suffered from this. Alex, a warmed-over Jessie, served as Slater's love interest (he had a type). Leslie was originally in line to serve as the new gal for Zack, but with Kelly back, Leslie was just … around.

Saved by the Bell: The College Years: "The Poker Game"

The iconic *Saved by the Bell: The College Years* cast, including everybody's favorites Alex and Leslie. From left, in oh-so-very-'90s style, are Kiersten Warren, Mario Lopez, Tiffani-Amber Thiessen, Mark-Paul Gosselaar, Anne Tremko, and the late Dustin Diamond (NBC).

The titular plotline of "The Poker Game" is classic sitcom stuff. Zack and the guys want to have a poker game in the dorm, so they set up Mike, the RA, on a date. What about the ladies, though? Their storyline involves them taking a karate class together and all falling for the instructor, John Hammer. They all try to win his affections. Those are both such well-worn sitcom premises. Suddenly the girls are taking a karate class, and they all find the instructor attractive, and then karate never comes up again once the episode is over. John Hammer, though, stood out to me as a kid, and he's the reason I decided to include "The Poker Game" in this book. Hammer is played by Dan Clark. You may know him better as Nitro from *American Gladiators*.

Yes, the *Saved by the Bell: The College Years* chapter of this book is effectively a backdoor pilot to a discussion of *American Gladiators*. It had more impact on culture than *The College Years*, perhaps as much as *Saved by the Bell* proper. As a kid, both shows were regular watches of mine. Finding a single episode of *American Gladiators* to cover proved tricky, but it was a defining show of the '90s, and there isn't really any other show of this ilk, other than pale imitators. Athletic men and women from around the country, regular folk like you and me, would compete against one another, but via competition with the gladiators. Some of the events ruled. I'm talking Joust, Assault, and the trippy fun of Atlasphere. Then, of course, there were the memorable gladiators from the show, like Zap, Gemini, and, naturally, Nitro.

Clark was perhaps the most famous of the gladiators, in part because of how long he was on the show, and in part because he actually did some acting. Not good acting, though. Clark was muscular, and he had a ponytail, but he didn't bring much else to the role of John Hammer, karate instructor. Which, to be fair, meant he fit in to a tee with *Saved by the Bell: The College Years*. This show truly was worse than *Saved by the Bell*, and not really bad in a fun way either. It was utterly forgettable, so much so you may not know that Patrick Fabian, Howard Hamlin from *Better Call Saul*, played Professor Jeremiah Lasky on *The College Years*. But I never forgot about the karate storyline, and that's because Nitro was in it. *American Gladiators* was not forgettable. Those Atlasphere balls were not forgettable. *Saved by the Bell: The College Years* was canceled after a 19-episode first season. It was a failure critically and commercially. *American Gladiators* taught me who Larry Csonka was. Dan Clark brings these two shows together. Nitro is a defining figure of '90s TV, more than the actresses who played Alex and Leslie for sure.

Diagnosis: Murder: "Murder at the Telethon"

When I think of '90s television, I think of the shows for kids, and also the defining shows of the era that have stood the test of time. I would be remiss, however, if I did not recognize that defining television shows also served another demographic, one that remains vital to television ratings in the modern era. I speak of TV shows for older folks. AARP TV, as it were. Now, having been raised by TV, and specifically raised by *The Simpsons*, when I think of television craved by elderly audiences, my mind goes to *Matlock*, which indeed aired into the '90s. In addition to Andy Griffith's show, though, another icon of '60s television had a show in the '90s where he solved mysteries. In 1993, Dick Van Dyke's *Diagnosis: Murder* debuted.

Yes, *Diagnosis: Murder* began airing in 1993, at least in episodic form. It began with a backdoor pilot on *Jake and the Fatman* in 1991 before three TV movies aired, the first of which is clunkily titled "Diagnosis of a Murder." I was floored to find out that *Diagnosis: Murder* didn't air its first season until 1993, and even more surprised that it ran all the way to 2002. Van Dyke was born in 1925 and was a sitcom legend, so it's not like he had to work, but he did, for more than 100 episodes. Even into his nineties, Van Dyke has remained a consummate old-school showman, and *Diagnosis: Murder* existed as a showcase for the actor—and also a chance to engage in a bit of nepotism. Van Dyke's character on the show has a son who is a homicide detective, and he just so happens to be played by Barry Van Dyke. Now, Barry did find some work here and there on projects not involving his father, but aside from a 24-episode stint on *Airwolf*, his substantive work came on his dad's shows.

This show is in a long line of "I have this job, but I also solve crimes" procedurals, with Van Dyke's Mark Sloan being a medical doctor who lends his expertise to help the police with murder investigations. At least a doctor doing this has more plausibility than, say, a mystery writer.

Diagnosis: Murder also harkens back to the '90s style of TV, with minimal fealty pledged to continuity. Perhaps the best example of this is the fact that, without explanation, the setting of the show moved from Denver to Los Angeles. I'm not saying the characters, all of them, moved from Colorado to California. One day, viewers tuned into *Diagnosis: Murder* and Mark and his son were living in a beach house in Malibu.

It certainly feels like *Diagnosis: Murder* has a core audience built upon baby boomers who had grown up watching *The Dick Van Dyke Show* in the 1960s, or frankly even their parents. There is even an episode where Dr. Sloan comes across Rob Petrie at a radio station. "Murder at the Telethon," in addition to being ensconced in a bygone era due to it being centered around a telethon, is rife with the "That's familiar!" vibe of catering to a certain nostalgic TV viewer. Dom DeLuise plays a comedian who is murdered while hosting a telethon for the hospital Sloan works for. The episode also features appearances from Dick Martin, and multiple Van Pattens (Dick and Joyce). Even behind the camera, television history was represented, as Potsie from *Happy Days* himself, Anson Williams, directed "Murder at the Telethon." Williams is actually a behind-the-scenes Zelig for this book, having directed episodes of *Beverly Hills, 90210*, *Melrose Place*, and *Baywatch*, plus several other shows yet to get their chapters.

CBS, at least in my lifetime, has had the reputation as the "older viewers" channel, and *Diagnosis: Murder* does not dissuade me from that assessment. Van Dyke's long-running procedural is reflected in all the *NCIS* shows and all the other CBS programs nobody you know under the age of 50 watches. Though "murder" is right in the title, this is actually a fairly breezy show, which makes sense even with Van Dyke in "dramatic" mode. There is a considerable amount of lightness, and even comedy, in the show.

Yeah, when I think of '90s TV, my mind will

Dick Van Dyke (and his mustache) as Dr. Mark Sloan (and his mustache) (CBS).

start rattling off shows from Nickelodeon or TGIF. There's a good chance that you, the reader, know *Diagnosis: Murder* as a show your grandparents watched, if you knew it at all. By the '90s, members of the first generation to grow up with television as a consistent presence were looking to familiar faces with comfort shows. Those who were twentysomethings when *The Dick Van Dyke Show* debuted were now fiftysomethings, and Van Dyke was back to keep them entertained. Sometimes, he'd even bring along DeLuise and the Van Pattens for good measure.

Lois & Clark: The New Adventures of Superman: "Pheromone, My Lovely"

Superman is not an interesting superhero. I liked *Captain Marvel*, admittedly mostly because of all the '90s stuff, but as soon as that movie ended I stopped being interested in the titular character. Once she realized her full power, she became too powerful to be interesting. That is the issue with Superman. The dude is too powerful, meaning his baddies also have to be overcranked power-wise or have to go through machinations to eliminate his power. In the '90s, a Superman show came around, and it had an intriguing idea: Clark Kent is more interesting than Superman is, so why not focus on him?

It's right in the title of *Lois & Clark: The New Adventures of Superman*. Sure, they got "Superman" into the subtitle, but the opening salvo comes in the form of Lois Lane and Clark Kent. The premise effectively is that Clark Kent isn't Superman's alter ego, but the other way around. Sure, almost invariably, Clark has to throw on his costume and do some superhero stuff, but Lois and Clark, and their romantic relationship, takes center stage. And hey, if that theoretically helped them keep their budget down, even better!

Lois Lane is played by Teri Hatcher in what was her breakout role. A few months before *Lois & Clark* debuted in 1993, Hatcher had played Sidra in *Seinfeld*'s "The Implant." She is one of the iconic one-off romantic interests in that show's history, in a storyline built entirely off her breasts and the spectacular nature thereof. Clark Kent is played by Dean Cain, who sucks. As a human being, not as Clark Kent, I should clarify. He's … adequate on *Lois & Clark*. Also, I just learned he was legitimately a good football player at Princeton. During the first season, the show was stuffed with the *Daily Planet* crew, including not just Perry White, not just Jimmy Olsen, but also Cat Grant. Even Lex Luthor was in the mix! After the first season, Grant was booted, and Luthor became an occasional guest star.

The romance between Lois and Clark is the heart of this show, and love is in the air in "Pheromone, My Lovely." Or, rather, horniness is in the air. Either way, I'm being literal. The plot of this episode has '90s vibes in its bones—and a guest appearance of Morgan Fairchild as the villain, which also carries '90s flavor. Fairchild plays Miranda, a chemist who is fired by Luthor and creates a perfume she calls "Revenge." As Beyoncé might put it, when Revenge is sprayed upon you, you find yourself crazy in love. The *Daily Planet* crew go gaga over one another, save for the immune Clark. Luthor then recruits Superman to help stop Miranda before she sprays all of Metropolis with a hyped-up version. Sadly, Miranda succeeds, and the rest of the run of *Lois & Clark* is just everybody in Metropolis running around making out. I'm kidding, of course, but that would have been pretty amazing.

Later in the '90s, Austin Powers would unabashedly be horny, and openly yearn to make others horny. This was also a parody, spoofing James Bond, and the sexual mores of a bygone era when folks were taking advantage of the new freedoms. The '90s really threads a needle in making "Pheromone, My Lovely" viable on network TV. They could be a bit more forward than a decade or so prior on television, but it happened well before the modern era, where every show is either super horny or seems to hate human sexuality. "Pheromone, My Lovely" just goes, "Wouldn't it be funny, and a little sexy, if everybody at the *Daily Planet* were all horned up because of a perfume? And also shouldn't Morgan Fairchild be the villain?" That all tracks for 1993.

Weirdly, given Superman's status as the iconic superhero, *Lois & Clark* is the definitive version of Superman from the 1990s. There were no Superman movies. There was a cartoon that ran from 1996 through 2000, but I don't really remember it. Apparently there was a *Superboy* live-action show, but that truly had no footprint. I remember *Lois & Clark*, though. I knew who Teri Hatcher and Dean Cain were. When *Desperate Housewives* debuted, I had seen Hatcher on *Seinfeld*, but I probably still thought of her as "the woman from *Lois & Clark*." Specifically, the ads. I never watched the show as a kid. That being said, now as an adult, I like the idea of focusing more on Clark than Superman, and would prefer to spend more time hanging with Lois and the rest of the crew at the *Daily Planet*. Now, if I could do that without the involvement of Dean Cain, then we'd have something.

Home Improvement: "The Eve of Construction"

I am going to discuss the TV show *Home Improvement*, trust me. There will be conversation about "The Eve of Construction." I came into this project already knowing a lot about this show. I have the Superchunk lyric "Detroit has a skyline too" tattooed on my forearm. The Motor City is literally in my skin. First, though, allow me an aside to discuss the Super Nintendo game *Home Improvement: Power Tool Pursuit!*

Few video games amuse me conceptually more than *Power Tool Pursuit*. As a family-oriented sitcom, *Home Improvement* does not lend itself to being adapted into a video game, even if the opening credits did have a somewhat video game flavor. Indeed, the game has little connection to the show. Binford, the company that sponsors Tim "The Toolman" Taylor's show "Tool Time," is naming a new power tool after him. They are stolen, so Tim must go through assorted platform levels to find them. Baddies in the game include dinosaurs, mummies, and robots, all of which have zero to do with *Home Improvement*. There is no instruction manual, but only a fake manual that reads "Real Men Don't Need Instructions." Now that I have the Café Nervosa cookbook from *Frasier*, *Power Tool Pursuit* is my number-one dream piece of cultural ephemera I'd like to have. Alas, a version with the box is like 300 bucks on eBay.

"Real Men Don't Need Instructions" certainly is an on-brand joke for a *Home Improvement* game. It succinctly summarizes the comedic persona of Tim Taylor, and also Tim Allen. Allen once had two pursuits in life: standup comedy and making it snow. When the latter landed him in prison, Allen left it behind and got heavily into standup, which worked out quite well. Rarely do cocaine dealers get their own sitcoms. *Power Tool Pursuit* was released in 1994, the same year the episode "The Eve of Construction" aired. This is a fitting year to be covering *Home Improvement* as, no joke, Allen was one of the biggest stars in the world that year.

Home Improvement: "The Eve of Construction"

The third season of *Home Improvement*, the one that included "The Eve of Construction," was part of the 1993-94 TV season, and it finished number two in the ratings. Since it was behind *60 Minutes*, I'd effectively argue it was truly the most popular show on TV. Allen released his book *Don't Stand Too Close to a Naked Man*, which also became a number-one bestseller. The actor also starred in *The Santa Clause*, which was the number-one film in the domestic box office for two weeks in a row. If podcasts had existed, Allen probably would have had one, and it would have topped the charts too.

Allen's Taylor is kind of a '50s idea of a "man's man," in that he loves cars, tools, sports, and "more power." Effectively everybody else plays off him by being sensible, be it his wife Jill, his TV co-host Al Borland, or his wise-but-obscured neighbor Wilson. There are also the Taylors' three boys: Brad, Randy, and Mark. They aren't interesting for most of the show's run. Honestly, I kind of dig the last couple seasons of *Home Improvement* more than the previous offerings because the precocious kid era is over, Brad is college aged, and Mark is a Goth. Regardless, the Taylors have it good, living in a massive house in a Detroit suburb, with Tim being able to have his own TV show in spite of the fact that he lives in Michigan.

"The Eve of Construction" is a quintessential *Home Improvement* episode, right down to the B story about Brad being a snooze I don't care about. Tim and Al are building houses for Habitat for Humanity, but Tim refuses to work with Jill, because "married couples shouldn't work together." Thus, Jill join's Al's team, so Tim, determined to "win" philanthropy, gets a bunch of athletes for his squad. That includes big-time '90s names like John Elway and Evander Holyfield. Jimmy Carter, Mr. Habitat for Humanity and history's greatest monster, also appears. Tim learns a lesson in the end, as he always does. Of course, this is a sitcom, so the lesson is never internalized for future reference.

This formula drove *Home Improvement* to massive success, commercially if not critically. If you weren't there, it may seem strange, but Allen was truly one of the biggest figures in pop culture in the '90s. His sitcom ran from 1991 through 1999, eight seasons and more than 200 episodes. Throw in not only *The Santa Clause* but *Toy Story*, and the argument is clear. People did impressions of Tim Taylor. The rest of the cast is forever associated with *Home Improvement*. This show falls in the "popular but not acclaimed" category. It picked up a few Emmy nominations but never won, and the bulk of them went to Patricia Richardson for playing Jill. Allen had figured out a persona that tapped into something. Yes, people watched *Home Improvement* because it was on, but there was more to it than that, and a reason why *so many* people watched, and Allen was able to find success elsewhere. He did it. He had more power. If I could figure out how to turn grunts into text, I would.

Space Ghost Coast to Coast: "Spanish Translation"

What is the most influential TV show of the 1990s? You might think *Seinfeld* off the top of your head, but the legacy of *Seinfeld* has actually been surprisingly lacking. The show was perhaps *sui generis*, with only Larry David carrying on its voice and ethos in *Curb Your Enthusiasm*. *Friends* certainly had a legion of imitators. That being said, *Friends* did not invent the idea of the hangout sitcom, or the concept of "Hey, how about we hire a bunch of good-looking actors and have their characters hook up?" It stands at the apex of its subgenre, but the ubiquity of said subgenre tamps down its influence. No, to find the most influential show of the '90s, we have to look to the lone locust of the apocalypse … and a ghost telling Susan Powter he loves Mexican food.

Space Ghost Coast to Coast is the show in question. Yes, the absurdist talk-show parody is in my mind (and heart) the show that has cast the biggest shadow of influence on the pop culture that followed. It all began on April 15, 1994, with "Spanish Translation." Well, it actually all began on September 10, 1966, when the first episode of the Hanna-Barbera cartoon *Space Ghost* debuted. That show featured two cartoons about the superhero Space Ghost, and also one about Dino Boy and his caveman friend Ugh. It was forgettable, airing all of 20 episodes. Then, Space Ghost was saved from obscurity.

Cartoon Network, looking to expand to an adult audience, tasked Mike Lazzo to come up with something. He and his cohorts took the character of Space Ghost, which through Cartoon Network they had access to, and recontextualized him. Also, they reused a lot of animation because it was cheap. *Space Ghost Coast to Coast* may have been massively influential, but it did not break the bank.

The superhero was now hosting a talk show emanating from Ghost Planet. His enemies Zorak and Moltar were now his bandleader and producer, respectively. Space Ghost's guests were real people, who would appear on a monitor on the set. In the real world of TV production, a member of the crew had dressed up in a Space Ghost costume and interviewed the celebrities. Those answers would then be used to build the episode, allowing them to construct a narrative—and also to take a celebrity's words out of context for the sake of comedy.

Space Ghost Coast to Coast trafficked in the absurd. Continuity was irrelevant. Death was impermanent, as Zorak could be blasted into oblivion (or spanked smartly with Space Ghost's Spank Ray) time and time again. And yet, the show rarely fell into the trap of "weird for the sake of weird" that others who try to tap into the absurdist, "stoner" comedy world often do. Were there growing pains? Absolutely, and when I revisit the show usually I choose an episode from the third season or later. That first episode, though, was where it all began. The guests were musical brothers the Bee Gees, comedian Kevin Meaney, and Powter, a motivational speaker forgotten to the march of time. She wanted us to "stop the insanity," but she could not stop the zeitgeist from moving on.

On September 2, 2001, Adult Swim debuted as a new programming block on Cartoon Network dedicated to older audiences. It has effectively grown into a sub-network these days. Lazzo was in charge. Among the first shows in the block was *Space Ghost Coast to Coast*, still going strong. *Harvey Birdman, Attorney at Law*, *The Brak Show*, and *Aqua Teen Hunger Force* are all, to some degree, spinoffs of *Space Ghost Coast to Coast*. *Sealab 2021* is spiritually a spinoff as well. Without *Space Ghost Coast to Coast*, Adult Swim would likely not exist. It was a proof of concept and an inspiration all rolled into one.

We don't get *Rick & Morty* without *Space Ghost Coast to Coast* (which, to some, will be a demerit against Tad Ghostal and company) or several other beloved, absurdist shows. The rise of absurd, Dadaist comedy on television, and beyond, can all be traced back to the decision to take a forgotten '60s superhero and turn him into an ineffective talk show host. I say "beyond" because how much of what is popular on the internet, humor-wise, is in the vein of *Space Ghost Coast to Coast*? Vine was laden with absurdist humor. How much of TikTok involves recontexualizing other media in a way that derives comedy from it? This proliferation began with *Space Ghost Coast to Coast*. To the surprise of everybody, Susan Powter was present at the birth of a revolution.

"Spanish Translation" is not great television, all things considered. Comedy pilots are often hit or miss, and Lazzo and company were reinventing the wheel on a shoestring budget. It is vitally important television, though. Did *Friends* launch something akin to a new network? The idea of "Adult Swim comedy" is a real thing, and the father of that is Space Ghost. The day *Space Ghost Coast to Coast* debuted, TV as a medium genuinely changed. Man, I bet Dino Boy feels like a real chump right about now.

Frasier:
"My Coffee with Niles"

It's time. To me, *Frasier* is the best spinoff ever (if we don't count *The Simpsons*). It's also the top sitcom of the '90s (if we don't count *The Simpsons*). While it was not quite as culturally impactful as *Seinfeld* or *Friends*, *Frasier* was no slouch in terms of ratings and acclaim. It ran for 11 seasons and 264 episodes. It won 37 Emmys. Kelsey Grammer and David Hyde Pierce won four of them apiece. Rightfully so. They are both incredible on the show. Frasier and Niles Crane are genius sitcom characters, and they aren't the only quality characters from the show. It won Outstanding Comedy Series five years in a row. I quibble with none of it. I love *Frasier*. The show is a clever farce. It can do smart comedy and silly comedy. *Frasier* made so many cerebral quips, but one of the best episodes features Niles thinking he's high and Martin actually being high. I could espouse the wonderful things about *Frasier* for minutes on end. In fact, before I get to "My Coffee with Niles," here's a few quick hits. John Mahoney rules! Jane Leeves rules! Peri Gilpin rules! Every time Bebe Neuwirth shows up as Lilith I'm hyped! *Frasier*!

Maybe all those exclamation points are ill suited to this chapter about an episode that is mostly just two guys in a coffee shop talking. "My Coffee with Niles" is the first season's finale. It serves as something of a recap of the whole season, and it is also very '90s in that it is a riff on *My Dinner with Andre*. I feel like every sitcom writer saw *My Dinner with Andre*, but nobody else did. For years, up to and including an episode of *Community*, sitcoms have been referencing the 1981 movie that is 99 percent Wallace Shawn talking to Andre Gregory. It's a bad movie. *My Dinner with Andre* is so boring. I didn't even finish it. I have, however, watched plenty of sitcom episodes referencing, or riffing on, *My Dinner with Andre*. "My Coffee with Niles" is a more explicit homage than most.

Frasier rules. From left: Peri Gilpin, David Hyde Pierce, Jane Leeves, Kelsey Grammer, and an ebullient John Mahoney enjoy some coffee (NBC).

The plot is right there in the title. Frasier and Niles are having coffee at Café Nervosa having an in-depth conversation about life, with the other main characters popping in briefly. Mostly, though, it is two of the top-20 sitcom characters in history having a funny, thorough, sometimes emotional conversation. I love it. It's one of the 10 best episodes of the show, and it couldn't be simpler. We're treated to two great characters having one great conversation, a bottle episode by way of a season finale. What a bold idea, and what successful execution.

Letting a season's worth of life moments come to a head is the crux of why "My Coffee with Niles" works. Niles is continually trying to get Frasier to answer the question of whether or not he is happy. Meanwhile, Frasier is trying to get Niles to admit his romantic feelings for Daphne. When *Frasier* begins, notably, the titular character has left Boston for his hometown of Seattle, fresh off his third divorce at that. He has a new job doing talk radio, and also is maneuvering around the fact that his dad is living with him after being shot in the line of duty as a police officer. "My Coffee with Niles" is almost symphonic. The 23 episodes that preceded the season

Frasier: "My Coffee with Niles"

finale (they made so much TV back in the '90s) were almost like threads that were now being knitted into a sweater.

I could never write a book about the defining episodes of '90s television and not include *Frasier*. In terms of '90s sitcoms, it has to be included in the pantheon, or on the Mount Rushmore, as it were. I can't think of four shows that are ahead of *Frasier* in terms of defining sitcoms. "My Coffee with Niles" is a classic episode of a classic show. It also happens to reference a movie, albeit one from the '80s, that '90s comedy liked to riff on. I didn't need to watch "My Coffee with Niles" for this book, but of course I wanted to. I was excited to. It's so well crafted. Want to see the pinnacle of '90s television? Watch "My Coffee with Niles." And then watch any episode with Lilith, who rules. I feel like Frasier, the character, would scoff at excessive exclamation points, but tough luck to that fictional guy. I love *Frasier*! It's the best sitcom of the '90s!

Dinosaurs: "Changing Nature"

It feels like the cultural legacy of *Dinosaurs* is more curio than anything else. At the time it debuted, *Dinosaurs* definitely entered the zeitgeist. It just didn't stay there very long, and for a while, it felt totally forgotten. *Dinosaurs* was the kind of show you referenced for esoteric appeal. Then, suddenly, things began to bubble up, not unlike a tar pit. Now, "Changing Nature" is the focal point of any *Dinosaurs*-related conversation. Years after the fact, it became a defining piece of '90s pop culture in a "Did that really happen?" way.

Before the rise in interest in "Changing Nature," I could not have told you anything about the series finale of *Dinosaurs*. By then, I had given up on the show. *Dinosaurs* reportedly originated as an idea from Jim Henson (deceased by the time the show debuted), and the Jim Henson Company played a role in bringing the show to life. It's a family sitcom focused on the Sinclairs, who are anthropomorphic dinosaurs in a world of anthropomorphic dinosaurs. Soon after the ABC show debuted, *The Simpsons* did a bit about how much the Sinclairs were like the Simpson family, and when you go back and watch *Dinosaurs* with that in mind it's wild. *Dinosaurs* does feel at least somewhat like a rip-off of *The Simpsons*. Animation may be built on plagiarism, but not live-action shows built on animatronics and puppetry.

The one significant difference between the Simpsons and the Sinclairs is that, while Maggie doesn't speak, Baby Sinclair just won't shut up. At the time, *Dinosaurs* was "that show with the baby" to the wider world. Baby Sinclair was the breakthrough character, and, like many breakthrough characters, he was just so damn annoying. Swiftly Baby threatened to overtake the show with his grating voice and penchant for spouting catchphrases. "I'm the baby, gotta love me" was one of them. "Not the mama" was another. Baby was too much for me even as a kid. As an adult, I loathe 90 percent of Baby's screen time.

Dinosaurs: "Changing Nature"   111

Although, frankly, looking at the screen at all can be a chore with *Dinosaurs*. These characters look so weird. They are unnerving, creepy, and deep in the Uncanny Valley. I find the look of the characters on *Dinosaurs* deeply unpleasant. There is a *Twilight Zone*-esque episode where Earl Sinclair—the patriarch—is struck by lightning and becomes a tree, but with Earl's face. This is one of the two cursed images of my childhood that haunted me in my youth. The other, of course, was when Bog and Quagmire were trapped in a peanut butter and jelly sandwich in a *Monkey's Paw*-style scenario on *Eureeka's Castle*. So it is entirely possible I did not watch "Changing Nature" when in aired on July 20, 1994, because I had given up after the tree thing.

"Changing Nature" is unusual for a sitcom series finale in that the last note of the episode is, "Hey, all these characters are going to die." Not in an "everybody dies" sense, either. When not engaging in Baby-related ratings plots, *Dinosaurs* liked to touch on modern topics through the lens of dinosaurs, often with a satirical point about modern times. This is a TV episode, from 1994, worried about climate change, and the potential for disaster if you don't consider the environment. In short, a series of decisions made by the big businesses of Pangaea bring about the beginning of the Ice Age. Earl apologizes to his family for his part in changing the climate, but as he avers that dinosaurs will survive this, the snow falling outside the Sinclair home tells us otherwise.

Yes, in the world of *Dinosaurs*, the dinosaurs killed themselves off with hubris and environmental recklessness. The parallels to human endeavor are not exactly subtle. This is why, in modern times, "Changing Nature" has had a resurgence in the culture firmament. One, it's an ostensibly goofy sitcom that tacitly killed off the entire cast in the series finale. "Not the mama" and "no future" coexisted in *Dinosaurs*. Then, of course, there is the ongoing rhetoric related to climate change and the impact humans have on the globe. Now, maybe pointing to an episode of *Dinosaurs* is a weird way to make a point about taking care of the environment, but you can certainly do so.

When discussing TV episodes that define the '90s, one can consider the episodes that were defining *then*, but also the ones that define the decade *now*. "Changing Nature" was not the former. It made such a meager impact that seven never-before-seen episodes were worked into the mix in syndication starting in 1995. These days, "Changing Nature" is at the forefront when it comes to *Dinosaurs*. Even people who have never seen another episode know "Changing Nature." The show was willing to pull the trigger on an episode devoid of hope. It was willing to make us consider the reality that Baby Sinclair may never live to see adolescence, much less adulthood. Well ... maybe the extinction of the dinosaurs wasn't all bad.

The Real World: "Getting Dropped"

In Rob Tannenbaum and Craig Marks's seminal oral history of MTV, it is accurately posited by many that the debut of *The Real World* was the pivot point in taking the channel built on music videos into the channel that would, in time, effectively abandon music videos. That first season, set in New York, debuted in 1992. But while the first couple seasons of *The Real World* may have been influential, they weren't game changers. It wasn't until the third season, in San Francisco, that *The Real World* became culturally significant, and not just in terms of entertainment and ratings.

Like many people, I had my couple of seasons of the reality TV pioneer (though not originator) that I watched. Unsurprisingly, they aired while I was in junior high. The Hawaii season had everything you want/expect from *The Real World*. I'm talking pixelated nudity, toxic romantic relationships, problematic drinking, homophobia—the works. I then watched the New Orleans season, which gave us "C'mon Be My Baby Tonight" and literally nothing else I remember. The San Francisco season, which aired in 1994, was before I was of age for something like *The Real World*, but I still know the score, because it brought to the forefront arguably the two names still most synonymous with the show: Pedro Zamora and David Rainey, forever known as Puck.

Pedro was a key cultural figure in the '90s, and not merely because he was on *The Real World*. He wasn't "reality show" significant, but actually significant. Pedro was openly gay, and he was also openly dealing with AIDS. Before even being cast on *The Real World*, Zamora had begun lecturing to educate people on HIV, AIDS, and safe sex. Being on *The Real World* was a chance for him to take his message to a wider audience. And hey, if it gave MTV a chance to have an openly gay guy living alongside an ardent Republican (Rachel Campos) and a self-styled bad boy (Puck), even better for the network!

The Real World: "Getting Dropped"

Puck is a progenitor of the "villain" role so popular in reality shows. Hell, he enters the house having just been arrested for drunk driving. Immediately, Puck is off-putting to the cast, save for Rachel, who was into him at first. I figure her thought process was, "Hey, a white guy filled with hate! My dream man!" While Puck's interactions with Pedro were the most fraught, basically nobody liked him, as he did a lot of "obnoxious roommate" stuff, like sticking his fingers in other people's peanut butter and such. Eventually, though, Pedro is the one who takes things to the next level.

"Getting Dropped" starts with something of an intervention for Puck, but it's about him not being a jerk. When that fails, Pedro tells the rest of the house that either Puck goes or he does. This famously, as the title of the episode indicates, leads to Puck being evicted from the house. While he would continue to appear in the show, Puck got the boot from his living situation. "Getting Dropped" is, to me, the defining episode of not just *The Real World*, but '90s reality TV.

Sadly, Pedro would die before 1994 was even over with. He was 22. Among fans of reality television, he made a lasting impact. If you ask people to list *Real World* cast members, Pedro and Puck are going to be mentioned early by nearly everybody. Did they become overly simplified as archetypes? Sure, but that's the crux of reality television. They also, however, got to be deeply human in their different ways. In 1994, Pedro Zamora got to be an out gay man on television, and he even got to have his commitment ceremony with Sean Sasser on television. Puck, well, he got to be cultural shorthand and an example of a certain brand of reality character. But what reality show didn't want their own Puck afterwards? *Survivor* wanted Pucks. The *Real Housewives* franchise is built upon distaff Pucks. Both Pedro and Puck have lasting—though decidedly different in kind—legacies.

My So-Called Life: "Why Jordan Can't Read"

Among the 99 shows covered in this book, you will find a lot of shows that went the distance. That tracks logically, of course. Shows that make a cultural impact often get long runs, and in turn shows with long runs have an easier time making a cultural impact. Plus, shows stick around because they get ratings and acclaim. Many shows in this book aired many more than 100 episodes, sometimes more than 200. Then, there are the occasional programs here because they were fiascos. *Cop Rock* helped to define the '90s because it was an infamous disaster, one that still has legs into this decade. Not every show is a big hit or a total flop, however. There is always room for the "canceled too soon" show. *My So-Called Life* is one of those shows. It is perhaps the quintessential one-season wonder of the '90s.

The other show I could see getting mentioned on that front from the '90s is *Freaks and Geeks*. It's not in this book, though, because I don't feel it defined the '90s in any way. One, it debuted in September of 1999, so it barely aired in the '90s. Also, *Freaks and Geeks* was more of an after-the-fact discovery, so it would fit better in a discussion of 2000s shows. Then, there's the fact that it is a period piece set in the '80s. *My So-Called Life* is of the moment. It screams "the '90s" to me in a way *Freaks and Geeks* does not. But this isn't a chapter about why there is no chapter about *Freaks and Geeks*. It's about the teen drama from the '90s that teenagers felt in their bones.

Claire Danes stars in *My So-Called Life* as Angela Chase, and she serves as the narrator as well. Angela is a 15-year-old at a high school in a fictional suburb of Pittsburgh. The show, which originally aired on ABC, manages to thread the needle of being melodramatic but also feeling like a slice-of-life show. Many episodes are about "issues," but they don't feel like "very special episodes," a vestige of the '80s in my mind. "Why Jordan Can't Read" is an example of that.

My So-Called Life: "Why Jordan Can't Read"

The titular Jordan is Jordan Catalano, Angela's crush. He is played by none other than Jared Leto, a thorny cultural figure, but also an Oscar winner. The issue with Leto, such as it is, is not so much talent but his weird intensity. Angela thinks Jordan might be dyslexic; this is the issue of the episode, but it isn't handled in an overwrought fashion. There's as much oomph given to Angela thinking Jordan's band's song "Red" is about her but then finding out it is about his car. Hell, Angela's parents even get a storyline about Patty thinking she may be pregnant, the emotions Patty and Graham feel about the possible pregnancy, and their reaction when it proves to be a false alarm.

Now, I can't convey the nuance of the storytelling within a brief synopsis, but *My So-Called Life* was a critical gem, even at the time. Many critics specifically spoke to how realistic the show felt. The "teenage experience" was captured in a way that resonated with adults and actual teens. Even though the show only lasted one season, it was nominated for four Emmys, and Danes won a Golden Globe. Now, the Globes long loved themselves an ingénue they could plant a flag on, but that doesn't mean Danes wasn't great on the show. There's a reason why she has had such a successful career as an adult.

Yes, there were those who loved *My So-Called Life*. The problem was that in 1994, a small-but-passionate fan base was not going to cut it, especially on network television. ABC did the show no favors, as it aired opposite *Martin* and *Living Single* on FOX, and *Mad About You* and *Friends* on NBC. Those are four shows all being covered in this book. If you are an adult tuning into TV on a Thursday, are you going to check out the new drama about moody teens, or watch a sitcom that targets your demographic? Notably, *My So-Called Life* was the subject of an online fan campaign, which in the mid–1990s was unheard of. There was more working against the show than the ratings, however. It is known now that Danes didn't want to keep doing the show, and her hesitancy made it easier for the network to pull the plug.

The passion of the fans did do one thing for *My So-Called Life*, which is that it got reruns shown on MTV in the '90s. There, it was discovered by more fans, which is how it became a staple of '90s culture, as well as a common example of a show that was "brilliant, but canceled." Angela Chase is an iconic example of a TV teenager, even though she only had 19 episodes to make an impact with. Don't forget about Jordan Catalano, either. Sure, part of that is the fact Danes and Leto became stars in adulthood. In "Why Jordan Can't Read," though, you can see why *My So-Called Life* is not merely a blip on their respective resumes, but what some still consider their best work.

Silk Stalkings:
"The Mud-Queen Murders"

I miss when shows like *Silk Stalkings* existed, but also I would never watch a show like *Silk Stalkings*. Do you know what I mean? Does such a thing as "sensual television" exist these days? You know, basic-cable sexiness? This is conceptual branding, not my opinion of these shows necessarily. Of course, that sounds like maybe I am protesting too much. Maybe that's why shows like *Silk Stalkings* no longer exist. Or maybe it's because stuff like "The Mud-Queen Murders" makes it hard, if not impossible, to get behind shows like *Silk Stalkings* other than for laughs.

Silk Stalkings had quite the ride. When I dove into researching the show and I saw it was created by Stephen J. Cannell, I did a double take. Cannell created shows like *The A-Team*, *21 Jump Street*, and the legitimately good *The Rockford Files*. What was he doing getting down and dirty with a show like *Silk Stalkings*? Well, the show debuted on CBS. It was part of a forgotten block called "Crimetime After Primetime." In lieu of a late-night talk show, CBS began airing crime shows late at night, shows with names like *Dangerous Curves* and *Sweating Bullets*. Then they hired David Letterman, and the block was nixed. *Silk Stalkings* moved to USA, where it got even trashier under the watchful eyes of a basic cable audience.

The show was about two detectives who solved sexual "crimes of passion," almost always perpetrated by rich people in Palm Beach, Florida. Now, just because these were sex-based crimes, don't envision a show with a *Law & Order: SVU* vibe. Some of the crimes were certainly unpleasant and sordid, and it seemed like every few episodes a serial killer popped up. They didn't want to let all the crime get in the way of a fun, sexy time though. Nuance was not welcome, nor was it necessary.

While the "two detectives" format stuck through the eight (!) seasons of *Silk Stalkings*, the detectives in question ended up changing. "The Mud-Queen Murders" aired during the run of the original two detectives,

Christopher Lorenzo and Rita Lee Lance. Lorenzo was played by Rob Estes. Estes left the show and found himself with regular roles on *Suddenly Susan* and *Melrose Place*, so that worked out. Rita Lee Lance was played by Mitzi Kapture. Yes, Mitzi Kapture. If that sounds like the made-up name of a character who might be on *Silk Stalkings*, she was born Mitzi Gaynor Donahue. After *Silk Stalkings*, Kapture spent a season on *Baywatch* and then played a seductress on *The Young and the Restless*, so, you know, she knew where her bread was buttered.

Let's not stand on ceremony. What's "The Mud-Queen Murders" about? It's about a mud wrestler who gets murdered. The end. That is, however, also able to perfectly encapsulate *Silk Stalkings* as a show. You have mud wrestling, a quasi-sexy escapade of a bygone era that would still show up in pop culture in the '90s. Then, you have a murder. Sex, violence, and a woman named Mitzi Kapture. Oh, and an appearance from Gilbert Gottfried, who was on *USA Up All Night* at the time. Another vestige of the '90s, *Up All Night* was a late-night movie show that would legitimately run through the night, usually airing from 11 p.m. to 5 a.m. In the vein of Elvira or Svengoolie, the movies would be punctuated by commentary and skits featuring the hosts. The films were of the cult classic and B movie variety. They would show a lot of "sexploitation" movies, but cut out anything too sexually graphic for basic cable. So yeah, *Silk Stalkings* and *Up All Night* ran in the same circles.

You watched *Silk Stalkings* if you wanted to watch something a little sexy and a lot trashy. It wasn't pornographic, of course, but in the '90s, people seemed to be more open to the idea of a bit of sexually provocative content. My feeling nowadays is that when people want trashy TV, they tend to go to the realm of reality shows, where they can watch real people with real unacknowledged problems with alcohol yell at one another. This is more palatable than "The Mud-Queen Murders." The internet is packed to the brim with pornographic content—impressive for a boundless, immaterial concept—while it feels like any television show that broaches sex is about how sex makes the characters feel bad. Increase Mather will have his revenge on Rhonda Shear.

I am not here to say *Silk Stalkings* was good. I also won't be loudly championing the idea of more mud wrestling on crime dramas anytime soon. But *Silk Stalkings* is a deeply '90s show. Before the idea of "TV-14" existed, it was doing "TV-14 sexual content" on CBS, and then especially on USA. Sometimes Lorenzo or Lance would be stalked by a secret admirer. Sometimes a ballet dancer would be murdered and the suspects would be two identical twin ballet dancers, one his wife, the other his mistress. Sometimes Gilbert Gottfried would show up. What was will never be again.

Picket Fences: "Rebels with Causes"

Hey. How are you? We can be honest with each other at this point. You've read this far into the book (unless you immediately jumped to the *Picket Fences* chapter). I'll let you in on something. This book is about 99 TV episodes that define the '90s, and 99 different shows make up those 99 episodes. There were, however, more than 99 shows of significance in the 1990s. So, on a few occasions, I chose episodes for this book because they allowed me to talk about multiple shows. In fact, some shows made that quite easy for me. For example, *Picket Fences*. "Rebels with Causes" is a crossover episode, baby!

David E. Kelley is one of the most successful creators in TV history. He's up there with Stephen J. Cannell, Dick Wolf, and Greg Daniels. There were times when three or four shows he created were on television simultaneously. When Kelley's critically acclaimed, but ratings challenged, *Picket Fences* was in its third season, his medical drama *Chicago Hope* debuted. To try and goose the ratings of both, each show was given a crossover episode to air during its season. *Picket Fences* got first crack, and that episode is "Rebels with Causes."

Picket Fences is as close as Kelley came to channeling the spirit of another noted creative David, Lynch, because the premise of *Picket Fences* is, effectively, "What if a small town was really weird?" As in, the mayor being convicted of murder and then spontaneously combusting. Rome, Wisconsin, is a strange town, to be sure, with residents who are unusually forthright about risqué, even taboo topics given the small-town, midwestern nature of the city. It's almost as if it's not a real town, but the creation of a Princeton-educated lawyer whose dad was a professional hockey player with a penchant for melodrama rivaling the most bonkers of soap operas. Kelley also created *Ally McBeal*. Strap in for that chapter when it arrives.

Even *Chicago Hope* couldn't just be chill. I'll give any medical drama doctors having affairs with patients. It's television. We have at the center of *Chicago Hope*, at first at least, Mandy Patinkin as Dr. Jeffrey Geiger as a hotshot cardiac surgeon. That's great! Also, he's an emotional wreck because his wife drowned their infant son. That's ... excessive! *Chicago Hope* managed to be a bit more of a ratings success (it lasted six seasons and 141 episodes) and almost as much of a critical success as *Picket Fences*.

Truly, *Picket Fences* was a darling of awards blocs, specifically the Emmys. The show won 12 acting Emmys, and it won Outstanding Drama Series the first two times it was eligible. While the town as a whole was featured, it helped drive the drama that the central family, the Brocks, happened to be headed by the town sheriff, Jimmy, and his wife, the town doctor Jill. That gives you a legal drama, a crime drama, and a medical drama all rolled into one, plus exploding cows for some reason. Kelley has never been one for nuance. He's the inverse of Coco Chanel. Right before his show airs, he adds one more thing to it.

In "Rebels with Causes," the crossover action happens not in Rome, but in Chicago. Dr. Brock goes with defense attorney Douglas Wambaugh to Chicago Hope Hospital because he's worried about his heart. There, Dr. Brock gets to clash with Dr. Geiger, what with him a hotshot surgeon and her a small-town doctor. Of course, if Kelley, who wrote the episode, was going to bother with a crossover, he was going to throw a little extra seasoning on the dish. Wambaugh is diagnosed with multiple sclerosis.

Crossovers were commonplace in '90s TV. Sometimes it was to create an event to lure eyeballs to the screen in the days when you saw something air live or had to wait for a rerun. Other times, it was to try and give a ratings boost to a new show, or to a flagging show. Interestingly, and possibly uniquely, "Rebels with Causes" does both. Maybe *Picket Fences* viewers would see the *Chicago Hope* characters and give the medical drama a shot. If you were already a *Chicago Hope* fan, perhaps you would tune into *Picket Fences* to see Dr. Geiger and company, and maybe you would stay around for more. The 13th episode of the first season of *Chicago Hope*, "Small Sacrifices," returns the favor. There is no trip to Rome, however, as instead Wambaugh heads back to Chicago Hope. Also in this episode a mugger with a fetish for biting off fingers submits to a procedure to have a flautist's finger removed from his stomach, only for the staff to find multiple fingers. Look, I'm getting back to Kelley later in this book. Let's not bother unpacking all that now.

Sister, Sister: "Get a Job"

The Olsen twins didn't have the lock on twin stars of the 1990s. Hey, when we first met Mary-Kate and Ashley, they weren't even appearing on screen together, instead sharing the role of Michelle Tanner on *Full House*. In time, the Olsens would get their own movies, and their own TV show, and if you are of a certain age you likely remember Mary-Kate and Ashley as part of the cultural landscape. That being said, the Olsens never really had a successful TV show of their own. They did have a successful pizza-based rap, but that's a story for another day. No, in the realm of television, the Olsens take second place to Tia and Tamera Mowry.

The Mowry twins became stars thanks to their sitcom, *Sister, Sister*, which ran for six seasons and 119 episodes. Instead of sharing a role—to be fair, the Olsens started playing Michelle as literal babies and were hired to work around child labor laws—the Mowrys got to work together and engage in some classic twin antics. Unless you are David Cronenberg, when you see identical twins, you think "antics." That was at the heart of this family sitcom aimed toward a younger audience. It began as a TGIF show on ABC, after all. In the pilot, Tia Landry and Tamera Campbell run into each other at the mall and are reunited. Tamera's adoptive father, Ray, agrees to allow Tia and her adopted mother, Lisa, to move into his suburban home so the twins don't have to be separated again.

With the sweaty business of the pilot out of the way, Tia and Tamera could get into teen mischief, twin hijinks, and especially teen twin wackiness. "Get a Job" is a paramount example of what you would expect a show like this to be. Plus, it features Tahj Mowry, younger brother of Tia and Tamera, as the characters' cousin. He would eventually get his own sitcom, *Smart Guy*. The Mowrys were running things in the '90s.

This plot is obvious, but in a charming way. The twins are cajoled to get jobs, because getting a job is a staple of sitcoms centered on teenagers.

Ray gets them jobs at his limousine company, but then a handsome guy offers the girls a job at Rocket Burger, a fast food spot. What are two twins to do? Oh, how about one twin pretending to be both twins at the limo service, and one twin pretending to be both at Rocket Burger. Spoiler: That's not sustainable.

If you told me there was a TGIF sitcom about identical twins, my first question would be, "How many episodes are about one twin pretending to be the other twin?" I mean, literally in the next episode after "Get a Job," a guy unknowingly asks both Tia and Tamera out on dates. *Sister, Sister* didn't mess around. In one episode they pulled off both the "job" episode and also did a twin ruse for good measure. That's efficiency in storytelling! "Get a Job" does not reinvent the wheel. It is a perfect reproduction of the wheel.

The second season of *Sister, Sister*, the one wherein "Get a Job" aired, was the last as part of the TGIF lineup. Don't worry. All was not lost. The show simply moved to The WB for the final four seasons. *Sister, Sister*, as well as *Smart Guy*, ended in 1999. This was the end of the era of the Mowrys. Their acting careers effectively came to a conclusion with the end of *Sister, Sister*. They've done some acting since, but none of note. Tamera has had a slightly better career, having served as a co-host of *The Real*, a syndicated talk show in the vein of *The View* that I honestly had never heard of. "Slightly better" does not equate to "good." At least the Mowrys got to mine their twindom for sitcom success. Would Tia or Tamera have had a career without the other one? That's unknowable, but it kind of feels like they wouldn't have. Then again, Patty Duke didn't need an actual identical cousin. Shout-out to Tajh, though. He did it without a twin.

Living Single: "There's No Ship Like Kinship"

First, to answer the obvious question, yes, I hear *"Living Single"* to the tune of the Living Spaces jingle every time I see the name of the show. We wrap up the year 1994 with "There's No Ship Like Kinship," which aired 10 days before Christmas that year. Pennies were being put in old men's hats and such, but while that was happening, the crew over at *Living Single* were having some interpersonal issues—and getting a visit from a huge '90s celebrity.

I think it is apt to classify *Living Single* as a "Black Sitcom." This designation is a two-way street. That is not merely to say that the primary cast of a show is comprised of Black actors, but that, through marketing and demographic positioning, a show is nudged toward a predominantly Black audience. This creates a sense of "for me" and "not for me" that drives an audience in whatever direction. *Living Single*, in the beginning, is focused on six single Black people sharing the two halves of a Brooklyn brownstone. On one side you find four ladies, on the other two gentlemen.

Now, if you had asked me to tell you what *Living Single* was about prior to me writing this book, I would have said, "It's that show about Queen Latifah and her lady friends hanging out." I had no idea about Kyle and Obie over in their apartment. To be fair, the season 1 DVD of *Living Single* features only the four women. The image on HBO Max (I will never call it by the abbreviated name) is of the ladies as well. They were the selling point, with Queen Latifah at the forefront. She is, without a doubt, the biggest star from the cast. As such, there were surely people in the 1990s who thought to themselves, "That show is for a Black audience" or, "That show is for a female audience" or, "That show is for Black women."

As a kid, I watched shows like *Kenan & Kel* and *The PJs*. Hell, I watched *My Brother and Me* even though it was terrible and was the show that led me to realize some professional actors are bad at acting. I also watched old sitcoms like *Laverne & Shirley* and *The Mary Tyler Moore Show* and modern shows like *Murphy Brown*. If you put a show in front of me as a kid with a largely Black cast or with female leads, I'd watch it. If you told me or hinted to me that a show was for Black people or for girls, though, I'd think to myself, "Well, I guess I'm not supposed to watch it then." In adulthood, I realize such designations can be rather facile, though occasionally apt to some degree. *Living Single*, though, is just a show about a bunch of single adults in New York City. There have been, oh, a million shows like that?

"There's No Ship Like Kinship" focuses the attention on *Flavor*, a magazine for young urban professionals. It's run by Khadijah, Latifah's character, and her cousin/housemate, Synclaire, is her receptionist. In "There's No Ship Like Kinship," an old friend of Khadijah's, Sheri, comes to work at *Flavor*. Sheri starts to hang out more and more with Synclaire, however, which leads to jealousy and friction. It made perfect sense to me to include *Living Single* in this book as a successful sitcom centered on Black women, and '90s star Queen Latifah, but the actress who plays Sheri is the reason why this episode was selected. Sheri is played by none other than Rosie O'Donnell.

Though her standup career was already going and she had been in *A League of Her Own*, Rosie's peak was just around the corner. She played Betty Rubble in 1994's *The Flintstones*, sure, but in 1996 she was given her own daytime talk show. This was when Rosie O'Donnell became a household name, a true challenger in the quest to be the face of daytime television. She was "The Queen of Nice." She shot Koosh balls into the crowd. She declared Tom Cruise a "cutie patootie." Rosie would remain in the closet through the end of the '90s, not publicly identifying herself as a lesbian until 2002, just before her daytime show ended. Since then, I've only seen her on game shows (never seen an episode of *The View* to my recollection), but I will say she is quite good at *Match Game*.

For an episode of television in 1994 to feature both Queen Latifah and Rosie O'Donnell is to encapsulate the '90s right there. Latifah was on her way to bigger things as well, leaving behind an ensemble sitcom (wherein she was nudged to the front of said ensemble, admittedly) to become a legit movie star, an Oscar nominee and, like Rosie, the host of a daytime talk show. As of this writing, she is *the* Equalizer on *The Equalizer*, a show for which she also serves as an executive producer. If my sense of CBS procedurals is accurate, that show will go for as long as Latifah desires.

Careers in entertainment can be long and winding. Such as it is, one could consider oneself fortunate in the entertainment industry if one's career has enough length to it to wind. "There's No Ship Like Kinship" aired three decades ago. *Living Single* ended on New Year's Day 1998, an airdate with real "I don't recall saying good luck" vibes. I don't think Queen Latifah's star has waned at all since then. There is likely an entire generation that doesn't envision her as a sitcom actor. They've never seen Rosie shoot a Koosh ball. Nobody gets to have every life experience.

The Parent 'Hood:
"Ring Around the Nosey"

On January 11, 1995, the WB Network debuted. Three of the original four WB sitcoms aired that night. The fourth would debut a week later on January 18. One of those shows, *Muscle*, didn't make it past the 13-episode first season. The parody of prime-time soaps like *Melrose Place* couldn't find its audience on the WB. The other three shows—along with *Sister, Sister*, which the WB picked up after ABC axed it—would all run five seasons and between 90 and 101 episodes. One of those shows, the one that debuted a week later with "Ring Around the Nosey," is *The Parent 'Hood*.

Did the people behind the WB think it could pull a FOX and become one of the big networks? Was that the goal? For years, decades in fact, the triumvirate of CBS, NBC, and ABC dominated American television. No network even tried to get on their level, and then FOX rolled around in the late '80s and managed to do just that. To this day, though, there are just the four networks of note. Or, perhaps, was the goal of the WB less ambitious? Did they want to serve as the second-tier of network television? Maybe the WB couldn't throw its weight around with the big guns, but it could make a go of it and stick around for decades in its own right.

That didn't end up happening. The WB and UPN merged together in 2006 to form the CW, which, to be fair, mostly followed in the footsteps of the programming that the WB had become known for. It was the network for teen dramas. The WB gave us shows like *Dawson's Creek*, *Gilmore Girls*, and *Smallville*. That was the footing it found. Before that, though, there were the original sitcoms, including *The Parent 'Hood*, which, aside from *Muscle*, had the fewest episodes of the first four shows. Do you remember the sitcom *Unhappily Ever After*? This warmed-over *Married ... with Children* clone apparently lasted 100 episodes. Also, when I call it a *Married ... with Children* clone, it was literally co-created by the guy who co-created *Married ... with Children*. I like typing out those ellipses.

Speaking of co-creators, *The Parent 'Hood* was co-created by the star, a fascinating figure by the name of Robert Townsend. Rising to fame first as a standup, Townsend is forever linked in my mind to the cult classic film *Hollywood Shuffle*, which he co-produced, co-wrote, starred in, and directed. It holds a sterling reputation as a searing satire of what it is to be an African American actor trying to make your way in Hollywood. Townsend would also pull off the director/writer/producer/star thing with *The Five Heartbeats* and *Meteor Man*. Then, um, he would direct *B*A*P*S*. Of course, if anybody prepared America for the idea that "a Black dude has to do what he can to make a living in Hollywood," it was fittingly Townsend himself.

Originally, *The Parent 'Hood* was going to be called *Father Knows Nothing*, a riff on the old sitcom *Father Knows Best*. The title they went with feels a bit sweaty and "of the moment," but on the other hand it maybe didn't have much cultural value for a show in 1995 to have a title playing off another show that ended in 1960. Townsend plays Robert Peterson, a college professor who has to step up as a parent when his wife, Jerri, reenters the workforce. From there, it becomes a "things sure were different when I was a kid" style sitcom, with Robert deciding he has to be the tough dad to the four Peterson children.

This is exemplified in the titular plot from "Ring Around the Nosey." The B-story, for the record, involves Robert being so thoroughly disturbed by the character of Mrs. Wilcox being sexually active it temporarily makes it impossible for him to be horny. I should perhaps note *Hollywood Shuffle* is effectively a sketch movie, and like many who work within the sketch milieu, Townsend is not adverse to broad, low-hanging-fruit comedy. Let's not pretend the guy is August Wilson in his spare time. In the aforementioned A-story, though, Peterson children Michael and Zaria think they can trick their parents to get their grandmother's car. Michael pretends he wants a tattoo and Zaria pretends she wants a nose ring, which surely their parents will object to, making the car ask seem totally sensible in comparison. Then, Robert and Jerry call their bluff and take them to get inked and pierced, waiting to see who blinks first.

That effectively sums up *The Parent 'Hood*, outside of noting that there were an awful lot of cast changes for a sitcom that lasted only five seasons and 90 episodes. It's not a very good show. It's heavy on broad, obvious comedy and facile observations. There are numerous C-grade family sitcoms of this ilk. This one, though, was the family sitcom that the WB introduced when the network debuted. Yes, *Unhappily Ever After* was a sitcom about a family, but I assure you that it was not a "family sitcom." Granted, I am basing that off the Wikipedia page and a bit of internet sleuthing, but *Unhappily Ever After* tried to kill off the matriarch of the family, brought her back to life by having a "network executive" appear on screen to tell her she was no longer dead, and then wrote her off anyway by having her abandon the family for a lesbian lover. There's a show that took some big swings, at least. *The Parent 'Hood* can't even say it did that. Not that I think Jerri should have left her family to run off with her lesbian lover. It's just that a little verve and originality would have been nice.

All That: "Da Brat"

Nickelodeon went to the sketch comedy well a few times in the early days, which makes total sense. Sketch comedy is often broad, as is comedy aimed toward kids. There's also the concern about the attention spans of children, and with sketch you pop in and get out before you wear out your welcome. Sketch comedy and Nick were a natural fit, and sketch was part of the channel's landscape from almost the beginning. The Canadian sketch show *You Can't Do That on Television* was the first real hit on the channel. *Roundhouse* was a staple of the early SNICK lineup, as the humor, and the age of the cast, skewed older. Neither is in the running for the quintessential Nickelodeon sketch show, however. That honor goes to *All That*.

Effectively designed to be *Saturday Night Live* but for kids, *All That* lived up to that in some ways. It wasn't live or 90 minutes long, but the sensibilities were similar. There were recurring characters, a load of catchphrases, clear standouts in the cast, musical guests, and a sense of humor that felt generalized, but not in a bad way. MTV's *The State* went the absurdist, Gen X route, whereas *Kids in the Hall* felt more like a creation of a world outside of our own, with a streamlined cast that always seemed deeply committed to the bit. *In Living Color* catered to a hip, diverse audience, though diversity was also a clear element of the *All That* cast. More than any other sketch show I can think of, *All That* felt like *Saturday Night Live*, but with a cast comprised of kids.

Taping out of Nickelodeon's studio down in Orlando, Florida, *All That* produced a pilot episode that aired in April of 1994, but it became a part of the Nick schedule on January 21, 1995, when "Da Brat" aired. Episodes of *All That* were titled based on the musical guest. The original cast consisted of Angelique Bates, Lori Beth Denberg, Katrina Johnson, Kel Mitchell, Alisa Reyes, Josh Server, and Kenan Thompson. The pieces that

The first cast of *All That*, a tween-age answer to *Saturday Night Live*'s original lineup. Starting in the back left to right, we have Kel Mitchell, Angelique Bates, and Josh Server. Up front, same direction, there's Katrina Johnson, Kenan Thompson, Alisa Reyes, and Lori Beth Denberg. Yes, all three girls in the front have *Blossom* vibes (Nickelodeon).

would come to make up *All That* as we know it were largely in place. Hell, there was already a recurring sketch, and this was only the second episode! Earboy had appeared in the pilot and was brought back immediately. Two more regular aspects of the show debuted in "Da Brat," including the iconic sketch birthed from *All That*. The sketch that, like many *SNL* sketches before and after, spawned a spinoff movie.

The first segment in question is "Vital Information," which was something of *All That*'s cross of "Weekend Update" and "Deep Thoughts with Jack Handey." Denberg, as herself, was seated at a desk and would deliver jokes not unlike "Weekend Update," but since episodes were taped in advance it was not a segment that commented on the news. Instead, "Vital Information" was more evergreen, and as such leaned on absurdity quite often. Denberg was often used as the straight character in sketches, or as the put-upon authority figure. She made the most sense to serve as the show's equivalent of the "Weekend Update" host. I would never say that a child had "gravitas," but Denberg came the closest in the cast. She was well suited for this role, so tapping her was a wise decision. Also, while I am here, I want to voice my appreciation for Denberg being one of the only, if not the only, panelist on the Nickelodeon game show *Figure It Out* who took the game seriously. I appreciated it as a kid, and I appreciate it more as an adult. We also used to go to the same *Simpsons* trivia event in Los Angeles. Lori Beth Denberg seems pretty cool.

Then, of course, there's "Good Burger." Mitchell emerged as an early standout on *All That*, because he excelled at the kind of sketch performance that appeals to an audience of kids. Namely, he was as broad and hammy as conceivably possible. Like Chevy Chase before him, Mitchell would throw his body around for jokes, even when not called upon. Every line was delivered at, like, an eight at the very least. Mitchell had no interest in subtlety, but it served him well. Ed from "Good Burger" is the quintessential *All That* character, and all the character is, fundamentally, is a dumb guy who is bad at his job. Mitchell, and the writing staff, just filled Ed with so many tics and quirks he leapt off the screen. There's a reason why, when Nickelodeon decided to produce a film based on an *All That* sketch, they produced *Good Burger*.

Furthermore, there's a reason why, when Nickelodeon produced *Good Burger*, the member of the *All That* cast chosen to play off Mitchell's Ed was Thompson. Thompson didn't just have the only adult performing career of note among the original cast. The dude is legitimately sketch comedy royalty. He is the longest-tenured *Saturday Night Live* cast member in the history of the show. Nobody has spent more time on *SNL* than Thompson. I'm not going to pretend Kenan was the height of nuance all throughout his sketch career (Pierre Escargot flies in the face of that), but he could do the straight role, even then, and he played exasperation well. Thompson's skilled sense of scene work and willingness to play off high-energy characters really helped balance out the Ed's of the world.

After all, there's a reason why Thompson and Mitchell were paired off not just in *Good Burger* but also on the Nickelodeon sitcom *Kenan & Kel*. For four seasons, the duo got to show off their distinct dynamic and establish themselves as two of the biggest stars Nickelodeon ever minted. Watching *Kenan & Kel* in adulthood, I was struck by a couple things. One, the show held up better than I anticipated. Two, Thompson is largely responsible for that. I am sure as a kid I was all about Mitchell's wackiness, but as an adult I appreciate Thompson's performance much more. He is funny, but he also is comedically complex, especially for a kid. Mitchell is … a trip to behold. He definitely was attempting to carry over his energy as a sketch performer to a sitcom. Watching it, though, half the time I wish there were a dial I could use to turn the energy down, say, seven notches. Mitchell is funny at times, but it's like watching Robin Williams at his cocaine-iest riffing.

As with all sketch shows, the cast of *All That* would change throughout the years. Bates's two-season tenure was the shortest, while Server lasted the longest of the original cast, going six seasons. Was it hit-or-miss? Of course, it's sketch comedy. Even "Da Brat" is a mixed bag. I never liked Earboy as a sketch. It feels like a parody of sketch comedy, but it isn't. Kids weren't going to be staying up to watch *Saturday Night Live*, though, and they could appreciate comedy played to their level. I'd call *All That* one of the biggest successes Nickelodeon ever had. The career of Thompson after the show is part of that, I'd argue, but he wasn't the only one to find success in the wake of *All That*. The show was co-created by Brian Robbins. He's now the president and CEO of Nickelodeon and Paramount.

All-American Girl: "Pulp Sitcom"

In the '90s, "diversity on television" largely meant "Black people on television." Even then, this was usually achieved in a sectioned-off corridor of television. There were "Black Sitcoms" and "Black Sketch Shows," and Arsenio Hall was the "Black Talk Show Host." Diversity meant white people and Black people being on television, often in their own shows, and that sufficed. Look to the cookie, Elaine. It turns out there are other ways in which to diversify television broadcasts, however, and *All-American Girl* was one such show.

ABC had found success in sitcoms such as *Roseanne*, *Grace Under Fire*, and *Ellen*. Funnily enough, those are three shows built around women with problematic personalities. So hey, why not throw in a fourth woman with a strong, sometimes problematic personality? ABC turned to successful standup Margaret Cho and installed her in the role of sitcom lead in *All-American Family*, a show that Cho has claimed, many years later, she was the star of and nothing more. Cho starred as Margaret Kim, a Korean American with Korean immigrant parents living in San Francisco. Do cultures clash? You bet!

Early on, much of the thrust of the show was built around Margaret being more "Americanized" than the rest of her family. This was the first network sitcom built around Asian American characters in decades, which was notable. It also got a lot of criticism for broad stereotyping and its depiction of Korean Americans. With the ratings struggling, ABC and the producers pivoted and turned the show into more of a *Friends* clone, focusing on Margaret and her friends. Then, in a Hail Mary effort, *All-American Family* turned to the last refuge of the ratings-challenged scoundrel: big guest stars.

Remember the *Fresh Prince of Bel-Air* chapter? I covered an episode called "A Night at the Oprah," which featured Will and the Banks family

All-American Girl: "Pulp Sitcom" 133

on Oprah Winfrey's show, with a cameo from Oprah herself. Well, the 17th episode of *All-American Family* is called ... "A Night at the Oprah." It's about the Kim family going to a taping of Oprah's show and hijacking it, with Winfrey playing herself. If that wasn't enough, the next episode was "Pulp Sitcom," and it featured Quentin Tarantino. Not as himself, mind you, but as a character. Never forget, Tarantino was a failed actor before he was a successful director.

Spoiler: Tarantino will come up again later in this book (I am writing about defining '90s moments, after all), so I won't delve too much into him here. This episode aired in February 1995, though, when Tarantino was riding the wave of 1994's *Pulp Fiction*. He was a celebrity director and a famous face. They called this episode "Pulp Sitcom" entirely to draft off the success of Tarantino's hit film. His hit, middling film in my opinion. In my rankings of Tarantino's movies, *Pulp Fiction* is second from the bottom, ahead of only *The Hateful Eight*.

At the time of *All-American Family*, Tarantino and Cho were dating, so bringing him in was an easy favor. Plus, at the time, I imagine Tarantino loved getting a chance to act again in a movie not directed by himself or Robert Rodriguez. He plays Desmond, a video store guy who Margaret starts dating, only to find he's selling bootlegs. Another way you could sum up the plot of this episode? "Hey! Guys! Look! Quentin Tarantino!"

The show tried one more swing after "Pulp Sitcom." In the final episode of the first season, Margaret moves in with three guy roommates, one played by Diedrich Bader. Mariska Hargitay plays the bartender at their new hangout. Only Margaret's grandmother appears from the original cast. The episode was titled "Young Americans," and the hope was to re-title the show that and truly revamp it as a new series. ABC balked at this idea, and *All-American Girl* was canceled.

It wouldn't be until *Fresh Off the Boat* that an Asian American family would be at the center of a network sitcom again. The thing with equality is that it's built on meritocracy and recognizing that treating a person as an equal means acknowledging positives and negatives. Condescension and patronization do not equality make. One's race should never be a mitigating factor in giving them a show, or casting them on a program. One's talent, though, always should be. I've never found Cho funny or talented. I have no interest in watching a sitcom with her as the lead, regardless of the premise. Nobody I am aware of is trying to reclaim *All-American Girl* as a forgotten classic. They made fun of it on *Fresh Off the Boat*. "Pulp Sitcom" is not the kind of move a successful show confident in its quality makes. *All-American Girl* is culturally significant. No broad assertions about shows with a heavily Asian cast should have been gleaned from its failure. Being significant doesn't make you good. Being an iconic director doesn't make you a good actor. I don't think of Cho as an Asian American lead who starred in a failed sitcom. I think of her as one of the many stand-ups who, ultimately, couldn't hack it as a sitcom star. In that way, she's not special.

The Critic: "Siskel & Ebert & Jay & Alice"

These days, film criticism is people complaining about Rotten Tomatoes, people complaining about IMDb ratings, people complaining about any negative review of a film franchise they are invested in, and people finding love on Letterboxd. Back in the day, though, there were notable, significant film critics. There were movie thought leaders who were genuine celebrities. Why, you could have a cartoon about a professional film critic with a TV show and it made sense in the mid–1990s. A successful cartoon of that sort? Maybe not!

The Critic came and went swiftly, but it did it with gusto. Co-created by star Jon Lovitz and former *Simpsons* showrunners Mike Reiss and Al Jean, *The Critic* centered on Jay Sherman, the host of the review show *Coming Attractions*. He was famed for his catchphrase of "It stinks!" delivered with that classic Lovitz pep. Jay was surrounded by eccentrics, from his boss Duke to his parents and beyond. Only his younger sister Margo seemed sensible in the first season. In the second season, Jay got a love interest in Alice, a Southern single mom. Every episode served up brief glimpses of films from within the world of *The Critic*, usually parodies, and even occasionally funny parodies.

The spoof films aren't my favorite bits—they seem more in line with *Family Guy* jokes—but all in all I like *The Critic*. I watched it as a kid, and I got the full series on DVD in adulthood, wherein I found the show spottier but still good. *The Critic* was a hit-or-miss show, with some delightful episodes, and some where one rewatch was enough. One of the good episodes, though, is "Siskel & Ebert & Jay & Alice." It was also part of an attempt to save the show after it already was given a second chance at survival.

Originally, *The Critic* aired on ABC. It only lasted 13 episodes, though, getting canceled before it even finished out the first season. Then, it was given new life by FOX, the home of *The Simpsons*. Hey, Jean and Reiss had worked on *The Simpsons*! Lovitz had lent his voice to the iconic animated show on multiple occasions! This could work. *The Critic* was slotted into the Sunday night block for FOX, right after *The Simpsons*. Directly before the second-season premiere of *The Critic*, the *Simpsons* episode "A Star is Burns" aired. It's about the citizens of Springfield putting together a film festival. One of the judges of the festival? None other than Jay Sherman. Yes, in an attempt to get people to watch *The Critic*, James L. Brooks, an executive producer on both shows, pitched a crossover episode. It didn't go over well with everybody. Matt Groening hated it and complained about it to anybody who would listen. I think "A Star is Burns" is funny, but it is also undeniably an attempt to use *The Simpsons* to goose the ratings of another show.

That was week one of the FOX era of *The Critic*. Week two was "Siskel & Ebert & Jay & Alice." Gene Siskel and Roger Ebert voice themselves, and in the episode the duo breaks up and both try and get Jay to be their new partner, until Jay is able to help them reconcile. Alice is referenced in the title to make it both a play on "Siskel & Ebert" and also the movie *Bob & Carol & Ted & Alice*. At their peak, Siskel and Ebert were bigger celebrities than some movie stars. To this day, with both men having passed years ago, they are still the biggest film critics ever. I think it is safe to assume that will always be true. In 1995, it was a get, and a ratings ploy, to have two film critics voice themselves. People around the country turned to Siskel and Ebert to help them make decisions about what movies to see. In a time before the rise of the internet, two dudes who got their break as film critics for rival Chicago newspapers became tastemakers, celebrities, and icons.

While "Siskel & Ebert & Jay & Alice" is funny, and while it is fun to hear Siskel and Ebert poke fun at themselves, this second bite at the ratings-grab apple did not do enough. *The Critic* ran for 10 episodes on FOX before being quietly canceled, as apparently the network dragged their feet on the official cancellation. The show ended ignominiously with a clip show that was originally intended to air a month earlier but was pushed due to the Oklahoma City bombing. The wraparounds setting up the clips involve terrorists taking Jay hostage with a bomb. That, fittingly, stinks. So did the tragic deaths of Siskel and Ebert. Sometimes "it stinks!" does sum it up nicely.

The X-Files: "Humbug"

There's a joke from an episode of *The Simpsons* from the '90s featuring FOX's programming chart for the week. The bit is that only three shows are on the chart, with the rest of the spots filled in with question marks. Naturally, *The Simpsons* is there at 8 p.m. on Sundays. *Melrose Place* has a spot on Monday locked in. The one other show? That would be *The X-Files*, filling the 9 p.m. to 10 p.m. hour on Sunday nights. While *The Simpsons* was never shy about taking swipes at FOX, even the people working on it weren't going to pretend like *The X-Files* was anything short of a lynchpin in the lineup. Plus, you know, the show did do a crossover on *The Simpsons* once, one that roped Leonard Nimoy into the mix as well.

My exposure to *The X-Files* as a kid came from ads airing on FOX and that one *Simpsons* episode. I never saw an episode until a teacher showed us a couple in eighth grade for some reason. They were on the tamer side of things, in terms of the kind of weird, disgusting, graphic content that *The X-Files* occasionally traffics in. This teacher also showed us *One Flew Over the Cuckoo's Nest*, so, you know, she liked to really throw us in the deep end there. I quite enjoyed Miloš Forman's Oscar-winning movie. *The X-Files* was kind of whatever. Perhaps it is a take that runs contrary to the general consensus, and the FOX schedule, but I still find it to be kind of whatever. I will watch a procedural with gusto. I'm not afraid of science fiction. *The X-Files* just never hit my vibe. And yet, somehow, I had seen "Humbug" before starting on this book. Now, I didn't know it as "Humbug," but I definitely remembered it. You don't really forget an episode of TV like this.

The X-Files, for the bulk of its run, focused on FBI agents Dana Katherine Scully (shout-out to Tacocat) and Fox Mulder. They worked the odd, paranormal cases that land in the titular "X-Files." Mulder, well, he wants to believe. He's a full-on believer in the paranormal from the beginning,

I believe this is Gillian Anderson as Dana Scully and David Duchovny as Fox Mulder. At least, I want to believe (FOX).

never afraid of a conspiracy theory, and is willing to accept supernatural theories at face value immediately. Scully, meanwhile, is a skeptic. Her job in the duo is to rein Mulder in and to apply science to his conspiracies. Of course, after Mulder time and time again proves to be right and as Scully comes across aliens, monsters, cryptids, and more, her skepticism starts to strain credulity.

Episodes are placed in two categories when it comes to *The X-Files*. There are the conspiracy episodes that are part of an overarching story running through the show, pushing it forward bit by bit. This is where the Smoking Man comes in (shout-out to the Barenaked Ladies). Then, there are the monster-of-the-week episodes, which do what they say on the label. There's a monster of some sort, and by the episode's end the case is solved and everybody moves on. "Humbug" is of the latter type. Airing near the end of the second season, "Humbug" is credited as a pivotal episode for the show, as one of the best episodes, and also as one of the weirdest, grossest episodes.

"Humbug" is the first script written by Darin Morgan (no known relation), younger brother of *X-Files* writer Glen Morgan. Darin is a favorite of *X-Files* fans, because he has a reputation for being the funniest *X-Files*

The X-Files: "Humbug"

writer, and also for being willing to get weird, even by *X-Files* standards. If an episode is an odd, comedic story, there's a good chance it's Darin Morgan's work. Also, the classification of "Humbug" as funny speaks to a sliding scale. It's weird, sure, and a bit absurd, but not exactly a laugh riot.

Mulder and Scully are sent to Gibsonton, Florida, where for 28 years (slow to get down to business, FBI!) a community of former circus sideshow performers have been attacked by an unknown assailant, one even capable of murder. As is his way, Mulder quickly comes to believe the alleged Fiji mermaid is the killer, but Scully, naturally, thinks the Fiji mermaid is nothing but a hoax. It turns out Vincent Schiavelli's character is a guy who has an underdeveloped conjoined twin, but that twin can actually detach himself from his brother's body, and he has been trying to burrow into a new body to find a home. Schiavelli's character dies, his brother breaks free for good, and when the episode ends is still on the loose. Yeah.

I came to find myself watching "Humbug" because I was hanging out with somebody before she had to go to work one morning and she threw it on. Odd viewing for the breakfast hour, to be sure, but one time I came over in the morning and she had *Dateline* on, so she was a real trip. I found "Humbug" weird, without a doubt, but not good. It was not gripping, somewhat alienating, and just too strange and gross. Maybe, had I watched enough *X-Files* to place it in a context, I might have enjoyed it more, but I doubt I'd be a full convert. My contribution to the viewing was suggesting we watch "Jose Chung's *From Outer Space*," another Morgan episode I had heard was quite good and delightfully meta. It was fine.

I knew *X-Files* had to be in this book. It was a cult show that became a genuine hit, spawning two movies in the process, and eventually earning a reboot. Without a doubt, *The X-Files* is a defining show of the '90s. I just had to find the right episode. When I read that "Humbug" was considered both one of the best episodes and a major step toward the show embracing humor and absurdity, I jotted it down as the episode to cover. Then, when I saw that it was the weird episode I had seen, one of a half-dozen episodes I had ever watched, I was flummoxed. If "Humbug" is peak *X-Files*, and a defining episode of '90s TV, I don't think I've been missing out. Of course, maybe I'm just part of some vast anti–*X-Files* conspiracy.

The Tonight Show with Jay Leno: "April 11, 1995"

The year 1995 was huge for Jay Leno. I've already discussed the whole Letterman versus Leno thing in the *Late Show with David Letterman* chapter. After Letterman's CBS show debuted in 1993, he was the ratings champion for a long time, making *The Tonight Show* an also-ran after decades as the defining show in late night. It was in 1995 that Leno was able to turn things around. Now, the turning point most people cite is July 10, 1995, when Leno had Hugh Grant on and tut-tutted him for solicitation. On April 11, 1995, the guests were Bob Saget and Matthew Perry. That's a nice bit of '90s TV, sure, two sitcom stars meeting at the crossroads, Saget's *Full House* peak behind him, Perry and *Friends* still surging. Being able to name drop those guys helped in terms of picking this episode. April 1995 also came right in the heat of the era of the Dancing Itos.

Ultimately, this is not so much a chapter about Leno, the hacky face of late night in the '90s, as it is a chapter about Orenthal James Simpson and the trial that dominated television in 1995. Leno is the vessel for O.J. talk, because he is one of the two pop culture figures of the era most closely associated with the trial that wasn't actually part of the trial. The other is a comedian who is in many ways the opposite of Leno, Norm Macdonald. While the iconoclastic Macdonald was manning the "Weekend Update" desk on *Saturday Night Live* and straight-up calling O.J. a murderer to the dismay of Don Ohlmeyer, potentially getting himself fired in the process, Leno was mining the trial for every iota of (theoretical) comedy he could get from it. If it's not obvious by this point, I don't think Leno is funny, I've never found him funny, and his '90s work on *The Tonight Show* wasn't good. People will say, "He was funny in the '80s and as a standup, check that stuff out," and I have, and it's slightly better. Congratulations to Leno for making C-plus comedy at the peak of his skills.

Ensconced in his *Tonight Show* era, though, Leno was far from the peak of his powers. Now, I will acknowledge that generating content for a comedy show that puts up five episodes most weeks is probably immensely difficult. To that end, Leno and his staff found the O.J. Simpson trial a boon, though even then he relied on going to the same well over and over and on his banal comedic sensibilities. The Dancing Itos, the shorthand for Leno's O.J. era, are a sterling example of that. Lance Ito was the judge presiding over Simpson's trial. Leno and his producers threw a bunch of Asian dudes into judge's robes and had them put on fake beards and do choreographed dance moves. The Dancing Itos did not show up once. They showed up time and time again. This was how Leno made use of the Simpson trial to generate content.

Leno wasn't the only one, though, because the O.J. Simpson trial was a massive event. If you had a show that did topical comedy, the trial was fodder for months. Hell, even non-topical shows like *Seinfeld* and *The Simpsons* derived humor from the circumstances. If Robert Kardashian hadn't been a friend of Simpson, and thus a member of his legal "Dream Team," the Kardashian entertainment empire may never have happened. Of course, I would be remiss for not noting that all this happened because two people, Nicole Brown and Ron Goldman, were brutally murdered. Maybe by O.J. Simpson. Probably by O.J. Simpson. I'm allowed to surmise as much as a matter of opinion.

Orenthal James Simpson was a very famous person in 1994. He was a Hall of Fame football player, not to mention a Heisman winner at USC. He was in commercials as a pitchman. In 1978, he was in the sci-fi thriller *Capricorn One* and hosted *Saturday Night Live*, the very show where Macdonald would accuse him, repeatedly, of being a murderer. Most notably, he played Nordberg in all three *Naked Gun* movies. He was not some tertiary figure in American life that became famous because of the bloodthirstiness of many members of the public. The man was a true-blue celebrity, and because of that, he was on the path to becoming one of the most infamous figures of the '90s.

Brown and Goldman were stabbed to death, likely on June 12, 1994, and less than a week later Simpson was charged with those murders. In one of the biggest shared cultural moments ever, O.J. got in the back of his buddy Al Cowlings's white Ford Bronco and led the police on a low-speed chase. They interrupted the 1994 NBA finals to show live coverage of the chase. *The NBA Finals*. Reportedly, 95 million people saw some portion of that chase, which did for the Ford Bronco what COVID-19 did for Corona beer. Simpson turned himself in. His trial began on January 24, 1995. It ended on October 3, 1995. In between, it got wall-to-wall coverage. Name a judge who hasn't been on the Supreme Court with the name recognition of Lance Ito. Has there ever been a more famous lawyer than Johnnie Cochran? Why do we know who Kato Kaelin is?

As infamous as the crime itself is the verdict. In criminal court, Simpson was found not guilty of both murders. My personal feeling, one shared by many these days, is that the pervasive racism at the core of the LAPD so tainted the trial that O.J., whom I believe to be responsible, received a not guilty verdict. It's worth noting that Goldman's father brought a civil suit against Simpson, and in 1997 a civil court found him responsible for the deaths of Goldman and Brown. Also worth noting is the fact that in 2007 in Las Vegas he was arrested for armed robbery and kidnapping and convicted on both counts. There's also the whole *If I Did It* fiasco, which began with O.J. working on a book that "theorized" about how he would have committed the murders. Eventually, the rights to the book were awarded to the Goldman family, the title was changed to *If I Did It: Confessions of a Killer*, and on the cover the "If" is hidden as well as possible to create, well, the illusion of a different title. It was ghostwritten by Pablo Fenjves, a screenwriter and author who had been a witness in the trial and in an interview with *Slate* about the book says that he believes O.J. to be a murderer.

Anyway … Jay Leno, right? From the day of the Bronco chase to, oh, probably the end of October 1995, avoiding news about O.J. Simpson was effectively impossible. That was definitely true if you watched the *Tonight Show*. Not since Lyndon Baines Johnson had somebody gained more from a murder. Eventually, Leno would have to move on from the Dancing Itos and all that stuff, but he had already sunk his teeth into the ratings lead. His hacky, often mean-spirited comedy had won out over Letterman's mix of absurdity and cynicism. Now, the O.J. Simpson trial is a historical footnote, a piece of history you likely know even if you don't remember it. It's strange to live in a world where you remember something so vividly that so many people have no memory of. The next event of that ilk was 9/11. Someday there will be adults who don't remember the day Donald Trump was elected. Once, tens of millions of people watched a Ford Bronco cruising down the highway because Nordberg was in it. Once, Bob Saget and Matthew Perry took a backseat to jokes about a Heisman winner's murder trial and a bunch of guys dressed up like Lance Ito.

ER: "Motherhood"

I'd say *ER* is the most successful medical drama of all time. What else could it be? *Grey's Anatomy*? *ER* had real heft behind it, having been created by Michael Crichton and produced by Steven Spielberg in the wake of *Jurassic Park*. It feels like NBC almost wanted to burn *ER* off, having green-lit it as a favor to the successful author and the biggest movie director in the world. They ordered six episodes and aired it opposite *Monday Night Football*. Then, they moved it to Thursdays and it became the biggest show on TV. "Motherhood," the 24th episode of the show, was the highest rated show that aired that night, beating the likes of *Seinfeld* and *Friends*. It would eventually win 23 Emmys, one for Outstanding Drama Series, and run for 15 seasons and 331 episodes.

Instead of relying on stars, *ER* made stars. Julianna Margulies was originally only in the pilot, but became a regular, paving the way for *The Good Wife* eventually. Noah Wyle made his name on the show. Then, of course, there's George Clooney. After years of struggling to find his footing in Hollywood, Clooney was cast as Doug Ross in *ER*, and long story short he got to direct *Leatherheads* eventually. Why? Because he became one of the biggest movie stars of his generation. Clooney, though, isn't the star of "Motherhood." People often call "Hell and High Water," the seventh episode of the second season, the one where Clooney minted himself as a TV star, which was the first step to films. No, the star of "Motherhood" isn't even on the screen. He's behind the camera.

Airing on May 11, 1995, "Motherhood" was hooked to the holiday of Mother's Day. This was done in a "circle of life" sense. We have Dr. Susan Lewis helping her sister Chloe give birth, with Chloe then naming her daughter Susan. Meanwhile, Dr. Peter Benton finds out his mother has died. Dr. Ross is around, but he's not doing anything mother related. And yet, Clooney played a key role in getting the director on board. See,

Julianna Margulies and George Clooney rock some '90s hair (NBC).

there was a celebrity director on "Motherhood." His name is Quentin Tarantino.

The idea of a TV episode marketing itself based on having a big-name director was unheard of, and frankly it still is uncommon. In the '90s, though, big-time TV directors weren't popping in to direct an episode of a sitcom or a procedural or any show. Why would they? Television directors are often anonymous. The divide between television and film was stark for actors. For directors, it was a chasm. Rarely, if ever, was a director the selling point for a TV show. *ER* having Tarantino direct an episode, much less having it be a selling point, was a strange event in television history. Sure, Steven Spielberg directed a *Columbo*, but that was before he had even directed *Jaws*. Tarantino was at the peak of his powers in 1995.

I mentioned in the *All-American Family* chapter that there was more Tarantino to come. I'd call him the defining director of the '90s, but I don't think that's true when all is said and done. He was the defining director of, say, 1992 to 1996. Maybe just 1994 and 1995, to be honest. Now, this is not to downplay his notability. Even if his peak was brief, his peak was intense. There were only a handful of movie stars bigger than Tarantino in the wake of *Pulp Fiction*. That film, along with Tarantino's unabashed self-promotional tendencies, turned him into a celebrity director. I do mean *celebrity* director. Yes, Spielberg was famous, and ultra successful, but he didn't seek the limelight like Tarantino. Tarantino was, and is, that Dr. Joyce Brothers joke from *The Simpsons*. I brought my own mic!

Pulp Fiction shook up people's worlds. Most of them hadn't seen *Reservoir Dogs*, a better, more linear movie. Not entirely linear, mind you, but more linear. *Pulp Fiction* was littered with pop culture references. It was told out of order. Vincent Vega dies, and then he's back in the film. Music you think is non-diegetic turns out to be diegetic. *Pulp Fiction* is sordid. It's glib. The movie developed a passionate fan base and racked up Oscars nominations, if not wins. Tarantino earned himself a variety of imitators, and also a swiftly forming cult. Then he made *Jackie Brown* and it didn't land as a phenomenon. I think *Jackie Brown* is one of his three standout films alongside *Once Upon a Time ... in Hollywood* and *Inglourious Basterds*. Most people didn't feel the same way.

I think *Pulp Fiction* has a great story arc between Vincent Vega and Mia Wallace, a couple good Jules and Vincent scenes, and the rest is a mess. Call it uneven. I'm not a member of the cult of Tarantino. I like his movies enough to say I am overall a fan of his work, though after reading his book *Cinema Speculation* I actively dislike the man and find him a disturbed individual. Regardless, I cannot deny *Pulp Fiction* grabbing the zeitgeist in an intense, "let's reference it in *Space Jam*!" kind of way. Tarantino was the chatty, opinionated video store clerk manifested into a success story, and in 1995, people wanted to ride his coattails.

It's Clooney, Tarantino's co-star in *From Dusk Till Dawn*, who suggested he direct an episode of *ER*. Tarantino agreed. Lydia Woodward wrote the episode without Tarantino attached, and then went back and added some "grossness" to the mix for his sake. "Motherhood" grabbed the ratings, and largely got good reviews. Some say the Tarantino of it all was obvious, others that he barely made himself noticeable. Tarantino himself did say he learned a lesson in the nature of television, which is to say directors are not at the forefront.

"Motherhood" is considered by some one of the best *ER* episodes, though not necessarily in the top five or 10. If you want to watch the best *ER* episode, or a Clooney showcase, you should watch a different episode. If you want to feel the essence of 1995 in an episode of *ER*, though, obviously you have to watch the one with Tarantino behind the camera.

The Wayans Bros.: "Blood Is Thicker Than Watercolor"

Going back to *The Parent 'Hood* chapter, *The Wayans Bros.* was the first original show to air on The WB network. It was there right at the beginning, and stayed with The WB through five seasons and 101 episodes. The Wayans family's tendrils were deep into television in the '90s, with brothers Shawn and Marlon taking center stage with their own sitcom.

Shawn and Marlon may feel like the "next generation" of the Wayans family, but that's not true. Keenen and Damon may have risen to fame first, but they are the older siblings of Shawn and Marlon. Howell and Elvira Wayans just kept churning them out, having 10 children between 1956 and 1972. Shawn and Marlon are the two youngest kids of that era of the Wayans clan, but interestingly I'd say "baby" Marlon is the most successful Wayans of them all. I mean, the stuff he has been in is mostly trash, some with his family and some not. He was in *White Chicks* and *Little Man*, after all. Having said that, his movie career is the most extensive in terms of "major motion picture" releases, and *The Wayans Bros.* was a successful show as well.

Not that it was smooth sailing for the youngest of the Wayans' sitcom. The first season consisted of only 13 episodes, airing January through May of 1995. Season 2 started that September, but in between the show was revamped heavily. Lisa, Shawn's ex, was written off the show. Marlon's love interest Monique was written off after 11 episodes of the second season. Lou the (female) security guard was added to start season 2 but left after the seventh episode to be replaced by Dee, who stuck it out. Most notably, the space wherein the show operated was compressed. In the first season, Marlon works at their diner Pops' Joint in Harlem. For the second season, Marlon joins Shawn working at the newsstand in the fictional

The Wayans brothers, Marlon in the middle and Shawn on the right, played brothers in their sitcom. John Witherspoon played their father. He had to do a bit more acting (The WB).

Niedermeyer Building at Rockefeller Center. Also, Pops' Joint is moved into the Niedermeyer Building as well. That got Shawn and Marlon working together, and within close proximity to their father. They were also given a few new characters to play off of. Hey, at least *The Wayans Bros.* got a chance to retool instead of being axed. Of course, being on a brand-new network probably helped, though that didn't save *Muscle*.

"Blood Is Thicker Than Watercolor" is the third episode of the second season. While the first season was littered with the brothers coming up with get-rich-quick schemes, once they worked together at the newsstand that became less of a part of the show. This episode has a classic sitcom-style plot. The show had a lot of those, actually. In fact, let me riffle through the five-episode run that starts with "Blood Is Thicker Than Watercolor." This episode features an art critic who sees Marlon holding a paint-smeared cloth and considers it high art. Marlon then envisions himself an artist, much to the chagrin of his inner circle. It's the classic '90s joke about high art and art critics. They'll like anything! They are always mistaking something that isn't art for art! Actually, that's a sitcom staple that goes back probably to the days of *I Love Lucy*. Television, long seen as a low-culture medium, was never shy to lampoon the high-culture snobs, even when they were straw men.

So that's "Blood Is Thicker Than Watercolor" in a nutshell. Next up, a woman leaves a baby on Shawn and Marlon's doorstep, with one of them possibly the father. Then, the crew finds $100,000 in a garbage bag. Complications ensue. Next up, we have Monique (still on the show at this point) asking Shawn to pretend to be her husband when an ex-boyfriend from college is in town. Rounding out the five, it's a Halloween episode. Pops thinks the Niedermeyer is haunted. Shawn and Marlon are dubious.

All that's missing from that quintet of episodes is an old army buddy coming to town. In the final season Marlon does manage to accidentally enlist in the army. The show did makeover episodes on multiple occasions. I will give *The Wayans Bros.* this, though. In the second-ever episode, Marlon pretends to be New York Knicks guard John Starks to get into first class. Now, trying to get into first class is a time-honored sitcom tradition, but dropping Starks as a reference is a fun pull, and also a real throwback to the '90s. The fact that Marlon Wayans didn't look anything like the 6'5" shooting guard is a story for another day.

What *The Wayans Bros.* gave The WB is a sitcom. That may sound tautological, but let me explain. A network was launching its original programming, and what they got was a situational comedy, something straightforward and understandable for the audience. Nothing about *The Wayans Bros.* is reinventing the wheel. It's not meta, it's not a twist or a take on anything. No, it's just a show about two single guys in New York City who are a mismatched pair of brothers with distinct, complementary personalities, and they spent a lot of time with their "from another generation" dad whom everybody calls "Pops." There is nothing fresh in that description, and nothing fresh about "Blood Is Thicker Than Watercolor." In this instance, I don't say that as a criticism. *The Wayans Bros.* gave a burgeoning network stability. Everybody could "get" the show. After that, it was up to you whether or not you liked it. *Muscle*, a show I never

The Wayans Bros.: "Blood Is Thicker Than Watercolor"   149

imagined talking about this much in this book, swung for the fences and is now only known as the first show The WB ever canceled. *The Wayans Bros.* didn't swing for the fences. It was Ichiro, smacking opposite-field singles time and time again, until it had racked up 101 episodes and its stars made the move to film. Where they struck out a bunch. Seriously, Shawn and Marlon have awful filmographies.

Goosebumps: "The Haunted Mask"

Hands are wrung about trying to get children to read in every generation. When I was a kid in the '90s, this didn't seem like a problem. If you wanted a kid to read, all you had to do was put them within spitting distance of a Goosebumps book. In the '90s, Goosebumps books were like Harry Potter books, but with more titles available. OK, so maybe not that popular, but I've read Goosebumps books and I have never read a Harry Potter, and solipsism is its own reward.

R.L. Stine's horror series for young kids and tweens hooked many a child into reading, and also horror stories. In elementary school, we had a program called Accelerated Reader. Some books in the school library were assigned Accelerated Reader points, based on reading difficulty, and you would take a quiz after reading the book to earn those points. I was driven toward accumulating Accelerated Reader points, and thus found myself reading many a Hardy Boys book, because they gave the most bang for your buck in terms of points versus length of time they took to read. Others, though, eschewed Accelerated Reader. Why? Because Goosebumps books were available, and they weren't part of the program. My fellow kids did not care. They wanted Goosebumps books, and they also knew that they were such a hot commodity that you had to strike when the iron was hot or be left with one of the "lesser" titles to consider.

I would, instead, accrue Goosebumps books via having them bought for me by my parents, the first of which being *The Abominable Snowman of Pasadena*, one of the lighter, funnier titles. That one was never adapted for the television show, but given how popular R.L. Stine's series of books was, naturally an anthology series was a logical extension of the brand. Like *Are You Afraid of the Dark?* before it, *Goosebumps* was a Canadian production that made its way over the southern border into these United States, landing on FOX Kids. Fittingly, it debuted on October 27, 1995, just a few days before Halloween. Also fittingly, it began with a two-parter based on *The Haunted Mask*.

The Haunted Mask is one of the two iconic, quintessential titles in the Goosebumps series, the other being *The Night of the Living Dummy*. Not coincidentally, they are two of the titles that got sequel-fied in the book series. The belated Goosebumps films of the 2010s—which are surprisingly fun meta movies I didn't expect to watch, much less enjoy—lean heavily into *The Night of the Living Dummy*, making Slappy the main villain. Slappy is the defining character of the Goosebumps universe, but the defining image, I would say, is the titular haunted mask.

I was not as much of a Goosebumps lover as my childhood compatriots, established canon at this point, which was true when it came to the books, and certainly true when it came to the TV show. The thing of it is, I did not watch a single second of *Goosebumps* as a kid, and you couldn't have paid me to in 1995. It's directly because they started with "The Haunted Mask," and I saw a trailer for the episode and it went into the memory bank of cursed images for me as a kid. This was a horror anthology for kids, and it certainly worked a treat on me, so much so that I did not dare watch it out of fear.

The story of "The Haunted Mask" is horror heavy, with the show pulling no punches out of the gate. Young Carly Beth steals a Halloween mask from a store, but this mask doesn't mess around. Not only does it *meld to her face*, but it begins to take over her personality. All I remember is an image from the commercial of the girl panicking, unable to get the mask off her face, and in my preteen brain I said, "Fire this into the Sun, salt the earth so nothing may grow here again." Clearly this made-up version of childhood me was clumsy with his imagery. On the other hand, to be fair to me, the idea of putting a mask on, having it latch onto your face, and then having it start to overtake your personality is a disconcerting concept. It's *Alien* meets *The Exorcist*. I would not call that light horror. It's still an unpleasant notion, though obviously not a real possibility. Back in 1995, though, it's possible I had not checked off "haunted mask melding to your face" on the list of "impossible circumstances."

Now, as an adult, I can watch "The Haunted Mask" and think to myself, "Ahh, '90s Canadian television production values, you were too beautiful for this world." I admire *Goosebumps* starting here, dropping an hour-long episode just before Halloween, and going with a story that doesn't mess around. This is a horror anthology for kids. Make it spooky! It's not like it is an inappropriate story. Plus, it has a message, and that message is "Don't steal haunted masks." To this day, I have never stolen a haunted mask. What's striking to me now is the fact that *The Mask* came out in 1994, part of Jim Carrey's incredible year that saw him star in three hit comedies and immediately minted him as one of the five biggest movie stars in the world. I saw *The Mask* as a kid, and I remember enjoying it. It didn't spook me. Maybe it's because the film is a broad comedy. Perhaps it is because that mask seemed to take over your personality less, and more imbue you with a cartoonish version of your unleashed personality. Also, it certainly helped that Stanley Ipkiss was able to take the mask off when he was so inclined.

Horror for kids in the '90s was defined by Goosebumps. That was true on the page and on the small screen. Maybe Slappy is more my speed, but "The Haunted Mask" was the right choice for a series premiere. When it came to scares, it could deliver in a way no dummy could.

Xena: Warrior Princess: "Prometheus"

Xena: Warriors Princess is a spinoff that has outpaced the show that birthed it culturally, a rare, if not unique, circumstance. It was a swift spinoff, by the way. *Hercules: The Legendary Journeys* dropped five made-for-TV movies in 1994, but it began as a show proper on January 29, 1995. The ninth episode of *Hercules* is titled "The Warrior Princess," and it featured the debut of Xena, then a villainous character. Originally, or so the lore goes, she was going to have a three-episode arc that ended with her dying. Xena got her three-episode arc, but it ended with her renouncing her evil ways. The second season of *Hercules* debuted on September 4, 1995, the same day that the first episode of *Xena: Warrior Princess* aired. In lieu of death, Xena got a show that ran for six seasons and 134 episodes.

Both *Hercules* and *Xena* were successful for low-budget, syndicated shows, to be sure, but *Hercules* has largely been left in the past. I'm discussing both shows here, but I can have my cake and eat it too because "Prometheus," the eighth episode of *Xena*, features her old buddy Herc swinging by. The two join up to save Prometheus, one of the doper dudes from Greek mythology. You likely won't be surprised to hear that *Hercules* and *Xena* were steeped in Greek myth. As with any story that has stuck around for centuries, there are variations of the Prometheus myth. The general tale, though, is that he stole fire from the gods to give it to mankind. Zeus then set him up for eternal punishment, traditionally having an eagle eat his liver out every day. Zeus had to give him a regenerating liver to make it happen. In essence, though, the story is of a god who was kind to humanity, not traditional of Greek gods, and was tormented for it.

Prometheus has gotten a glow up recently thanks to *Oppenheimer*, based on Kai Bird and Martin J. Sherwin's J. Robert Oppenheimer biography *American Prometheus*. The subtitle of Mary Shelley's *Frankenstein* is *Modern Prometheus*. My first introduction to the name came from

Nickelodeon's *KaBlam!*, as one of the recurring segments on that show was "Prometheus and Bob," which focused on an alien, Prometheus, trying to educate a caveman, Bob, with disastrous results. While "Prometheus and Bob" was no *Action League Now!*, anything that meant not having to see the awful animation style of *Angela Anaconda* was worthwhile.

Both *Hercules* and *Xena* are substandard shows. They look cheap and rely too heavily on lackluster special effects. They are unremarkable '90s syndicated TV fodder. *Hercules*, sensibly, rarely gets mentioned at all, and effectively never positively. *Xena* gets a bit of love still, though. There are a couple reasons for this. One, *Xena* is a slightly better show, entirely because Xena is played by Lucy Lawless, while Hercules is played by Kevin Sorbo. Lawless is a decent actor. She's no Cate Blanchett, or even a Kate Beckinsale, but she can act. Also, I'm not knocking Beckinsale. Ever seen *The Last Days of Disco*? She's great in it. Sorbo, though, is a bad actor. The only cultural legacy of *Hercules* is a meme of him shouting, "Disappointed!" believed to be him accidentally reading stage directions. His reputation as a religious weirdo who stars in films like *God's Not Dead* and complains that being Christian limits his work in Hollywood doesn't help his—or *Hercules*'s—legacy either.

Xena also grabbed more of a cult classic status, in part because of a sizable lesbian fan base. Now, I imagine some of that was merely lesbians who were into a rocked up Lucy Lawless and thought to themselves, "Oh yeah, throw me against the wall, Xena," and to those ladies, I say that's groovy with me. There were also, however, a lot of individuals into the idea of Xena and her friend and sidekick Gabrielle being lovers. This is in spite of the fact that Xena and Gabrielle were not a couple in the show, which brings me to one of my pop culture pet peeves, the cult of "shipping" and those with a one-track mind for it.

Some people only care about characters getting together romantically. Two actors can't show a hint of chemistry without corners of the internet going gaga over the idea of them getting together. If the show or movie doesn't deliver, they're disappointed. They're angry. Nothing matters to these people other than romantic relationships between characters. It is all they are invested in. They only understand chemistry through a romantic lens, and to them culture exists as a vessel to give them the romantic relationships they want to see portrayed. Storytelling is irrelevant. The intent of creators doesn't matter. All they want, loudly and aggressively, is romance. *The Office* had to quickly boot characters from the show because fans wouldn't accept anybody getting in the way of Jim and Pam. People became preoccupied with the idea of Poe and Finn from *Star Wars* being a couple, even though there was no hint of that, and no intent of that in the screenplay.

I find this tedious at best, deranged at worst. It's an unhealthy prism through which to view pop culture. It's an unhealthy way in which to live your life. *Xena* spawned a ton of fanfic built around Xena and Gabrielle. People watched without any interest in the stories. It was just to give them a chance to "ship" these two characters. Does *Xena* have a cult following, or does the fanfic? "Xena and Gabrielle" exist in a way that has nothing to do with the show.

As is evident, I love pop culture, but part of what drives me in my work is that I also have a reasoned, sensible, healthy relationship with pop culture. Far too much of the ingestion of entertainment out there is being done in baffling, frustrating ways. People indulging in the kind of nostalgia where they watch a show from their childhood simply because they liked it as a kid. People emotionally invested in "shipping" characters regardless of what's going on in the show or movie series. Hell, people being emotionally invested in fictional characters at all is a bit odd. The first time I saw the word "headcanon," I wished that our American Prometheus, Oppenheimer, and his gadget had accidentally destroyed the atmosphere and turned this into a dead planet circling around an indifferent star. Prometheus stole fire from the gods, and for that, his punishment was having to deal with angry people on the internet incensed that two characters they want to see together aren't a couple.

Ace Ventura: Pet Detective: "The Reindeer Hunter"

I've already written quite a bit about Jim Carrey in this book. Hey, you can't get away from discussing Carrey when it comes to '90s pop culture, even in a book about television. His 1994 is well known at this point. Famously, that year, a promising comedian best known for *In Living Color* got to star in *Ace Ventura: Pet Detective*, *The Mask*, and *Dumb and Dumber*. Honestly, though, 1995 is a more interesting year when it comes to Carrey. He starred in the quickie sequel *Ace Ventura: When Nature Calls*, and on top of that he played Riddler in *Batman Forever*, a decent movie that paved the way for the failure of *Batman & Robin*. What is really wild to me, though, is that in 1995 all three of his 1994 movies were turned into animated series.

Now, needless to say, Carrey had nothing to do with any of these shows. They were all just attempts to strike while the iron was hot. Animation quality and effort varied. *The Mask* had the most effort put into it. It has the best voice cast, the best animation, and also ran the longest, making it to 54 episodes. *Ace Ventura: Pet Detective* lasted 41 episodes, 26 on CBS and then, belatedly, 15 more on Nickelodeon once Nick started airing reruns of the first two seasons. While *Ace Ventura* had the worst source material of these three shows by a long shot (even as a kid I couldn't finish the movie because of how unfunny it was), I get why it was turned into an animated show. A goofy guy with a bunch of animal friends? That's a swing worth taking, even if the movie is not necessarily appropriate for the morning cartoon crowd. Not that this has ever stopped production companies. RoboCop, Rambo, Beetlejuice, the list goes on.

Ace Ventura pulled a *Simpsons* and debuted with a Christmas episode. It aired on December 9, 1995, so that makes sense. Santa's reindeer have disappeared, so Ventura's first job on this cartoon is to save Christmas. Ace is friends with a monkey named Spike. The villain is named

Ace Ventura: Pet Detective: "The Reindeer Hunter"

Atrocia Odora. Ventura does the thing where he talks with his butt. It's exactly what you expect, which is to say it is like the movie, which isn't good to begin with, but worse. I wonder how much advertising, if any, CBS did to get kids to watch "The Reindeer Hunter" in the vein of selling the Christmas of it all.

The animation of *Ace Ventura* is kind of pleasant in its cheapness and simplicity, more so in the backgrounds than when a character's mouth movements don't match the words. Michael Hall's version of Ace Ventura does sound like a reasonable facsimile of Carrey's performance. The *Dumb and Dumber* voice for Lloyd is bad if it is attempting to be a Carrey impersonation, and that show also has the worst animation. There's a reason why that was a 13-episode flop. *The Mask* has the best animation by a wide margin, though Rob Paulsen just sounds like Rob Paulsen as Stanley Ipkiss and his Mask persona. None of these shows, critically, are the least bit funny.

Other than "The Reindeer Hunter," the only notable *Ace Ventura* episode is part of a two-part crossover with *The Mask*. First, "The Aceman Cometh" aired on *The Mask*, and then "Have Mask, Will Travel" on *Ace Ventura*. Both shows kept their animation style. I don't know if this was a ratings grab or a last hurrah, but it served as the latter. This was the series finale of *The Mask*, and it would have been the series finale of *Ace Ventura* if not for the Nickelodeon pickup two years later.

Carrey was arguably the biggest movie star of the '90s, but his luminance waned in the new millennium, which is far from unheard of, until he effectively stopped making movies of note. His odd behavior in the age of social media likely didn't help either. Nowadays, he has resurged thanks to playing the villain in the *Sonic the Hedgehog* movies. Having Carrey's name attached to a script may once have sufficed to get a movie green-lit, but now he plays second fiddle to a CGI anthropomorphic hedgehog. If you want to remember just how big Carrey was, though, just look to 1995, when three of his films were turned into animated series. "The Reindeer Hunter" had Santa Claus, but the selling point was Ace Ventura.

Muppets Tonight: "Michelle Pfeiffer"

The Muppets have been ensconced in pop culture for decades. Ever since the 1970s, Jim Henson's conception has always been around, showing up here and there, even after the untimely death of Henson himself. Except for during the 2000s, that is. The Muppets effectively took the 2000s off. Kermit and company—to give these felt figures inaccurate agency—dropped a couple made-for-TV movies and a special or two, but there was no theatrical film, no TV show in the mix. Part of the reason for that, I imagine, is that the '90s were not kind to the Muppets. Pretty much everything their puppet hands touched turned not to gold, but to failure. It was a rough decade for the brand, and *Muppets Tonight* is an example of that.

For reasons likely not more intricate than my general voracity for cultural consumption, I have seen most Muppets products of note but never really felt particularly enthused. The ceiling on the Muppets is, like, a B, maybe a B-plus. The first Muppets movie is pretty good, Charles Grodin rules in *The Great Muppet Caper*, and I actually thought *Muppets Most Wanted* was good. That's about it for the films, though. I watched *Muppet Babies* as a kid, but also I was a kid. It was the show that I watched before I headed off to kindergarten to learn about letters and to (metaphorically, I stress) have my left-handedness beaten out of me. The ambition of the *Office*-aping sitcom from the 2010s was admirable, but the show didn't succeed. For some reason, I watched every episode of *Muppets Now*, which is when I started pondering my relationship—such as it is—to the Muppets. I'd watch an episode, think it was fine, and then find myself watching the next one anyway. The convenience of streaming? Perhaps. Crucially, I think the original *The Muppet Show* is bad, and *Muppets Tonight* was attempting to modernize that show for a '90s audience.

The Muppet Show was about the Muppets putting on a stage show at their theater, with us seeing the show (replete with celebrity guests) and also the behind-the-scenes machinations. For the '90s, the theater was replaced with a TV studio, and their stage show replaced with a television show. Otherwise, it's the same shtick. Of course, the show needed a host, and from the extensive back catalog of Muppets, naturally they landed on ... Clifford. You know, everybody's favorite Muppet. You remember Clifford, right? The bass player for Solid Foam on *The Jim Henson Hour*? One of the most tertiary Muppets on the roster, the hope was that this show would call attention to Clifford as a character.

Michelle Pfeiffer is the celebrity guest on the very first episode of *Muppets Tonight*. The episode has a lot of track to set out. It begins with Kermit showing the new studio to the Muppets, and then they realize they have to put a show on that night but don't have a show planned. Clifford is named the host. Miss Piggy and Pfeiffer are both selected to be guests and have to be kept apart as such. A couple of recurring sketches make their debuts. "Bay of Pigswatch" is, naturally, a *Baywatch* parody, this being 1996 and all. Fair enough. Then, there's "Great Moments in Elvis History," where, well, Muppet-y versions of Elvis are involved in historical moments. In this episode, the Elvises show up at the signing of the Declaration of Independence, which somehow is mashed up with Benjamin Franklin's electricity experiments.

Muppets Tonight has that sweaty, warmed-over feeling that encapsulates '90s Muppets output. It's trying to capture the feeling of *The Muppet Show*, which again I don't think is a good show at all, but can't escape the shadow of its predecessor. That's typical of the Muppets in the '90s. This is the decade of *Muppet Treasure Island* and *Muppets in Space*, the latter of which is largely seen as the worst Muppets effort. *Muppets Tonight* did not hit with people, unsurprisingly. ABC had ordered 13 episodes, but canceled the show after it aired 10. The Disney Channel picked the show up, ran the three unaired episodes from ABC, and produced nine more offerings, though one was a clip show of the ABC era. That was that. The next thing the Muppets would try was the TV film *It's a Very Merry Muppet Christmas Movie* in 2002. Hey, when all else fails, get Christmas in the mix.

That being said, while Clifford largely disappeared, there is one lasting legacy of *Muppets Tonight*. In the second episode, where Garth Brooks was the guest, a new Muppet was introduced. He was an elevator operator and cook at the studio. His name is Pepe, and he is a king prawn. Pepe has since become an inner-circle Muppet. He's at the forefront of every 2010s and 2020s offering from the Muppets. Credit where it is due, the people behind the Muppets did an assessment of their failure and figured out what to take forward from it. Also, in terms of deserved credit, one of the pig characters in "Bay of Pigswatch" is named Spamela Hamderson. Full marks for that one.

Mad About You: "The Finale: Part 1"

Shows likes *Mad About You* were, and are, rare, and that's weird. You've got shows about single friends out there dating coming out television's wazoo. That way you get a litany of guest stars, many of them good looking, and also maybe your favorite TV friends might, dare to dream, *have sex with each other*. Then, there are the shows about marriage, but they are usually about how marriage is, in the words of Cosmo Kramer, a "manmade prison." Even these "marriage sucks" shows are usually about families, because then you can also do "parenting sucks" at the same time. There are also plenty of sitcoms about families that are kinder and gentler, from *Father Knows Best* to *Modern Family*. Shows about committed married couples and their loving, complicated relationships? Those are relatively infrequent, but *Mad About You* still has managed to fall from the limelight among '90s sitcoms, even if it was immensely acclaimed at the time.

Though the episode this chapter focuses on dropped at the end of the fourth season in May of 1996, *Mad About You* debuted in 1992. Paul Reiser and Helen Hunt star as Paul and Jamie Buchman, who are newlyweds when the show begins. They live in New York City, where Paul is a documentarian and Jamie works in public relations, which are atypical jobs, sure, but entirely plausible for New Yorkers. The show documents their relationship, and their lives, in ways both acutely observed and large scale. It was never a huge hit, but it did make a splash in terms of giving Reiser a platform for his persona while also helping bolster Hunt's stardom. She became a movie star, and an Oscar winner, during the run of *Mad About You*, and in fact the fourth season was delayed so that Hunt could finish shooting *Twister*. Hunt was the focal point of *Mad About You* adulation, being nominated for an Emmy every season of the show's original run, and winning four years in a row.

Mad About You: "The Finale: Part 1"   161

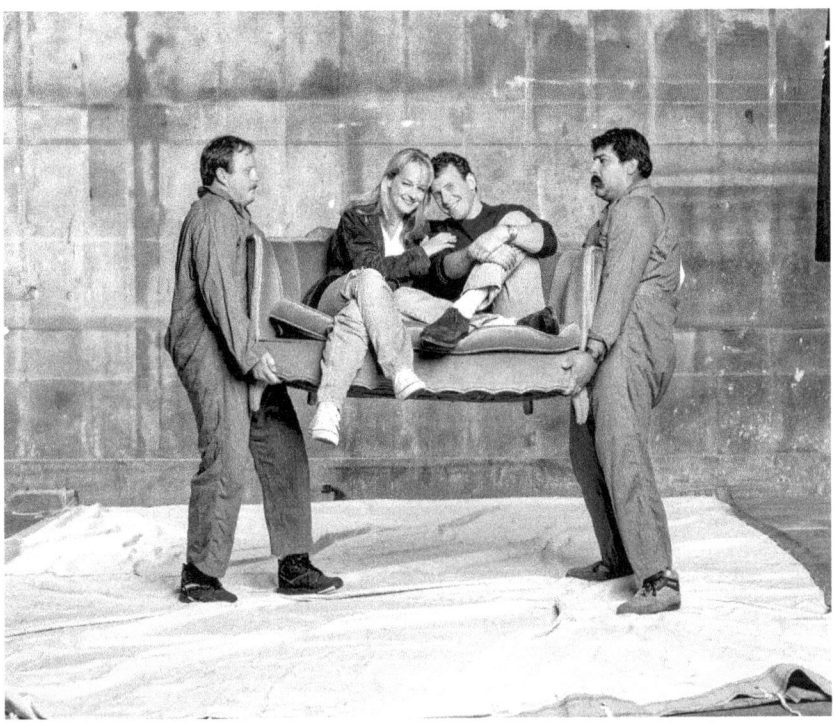

Helen Hunt and Paul Reiser pose for a thematic *Mad About You* promo shoot. Also, shout-out to the unknown actors hired to play those two movers. Whoever you are, you did the (literal) heavy lifting in this shoot (NBC).

Saying "Helen Hunt is a good actor" is not going to get you on the Wall of Fame for hot takes, and she is quite good as Jamie. Reiser is, I feel, underrated as an actor, though once he got a bit older and started popping up in stuff like *Red Oaks* and *Stranger Things* it seems the love started to pour in a bit. When Reiser is doing his thing, understandably you might not shower him with praise for his acting chops. Sure, he stands out in *Diner* as a young man, but it really seems like he's just being Paul Reiser. There is some of that in *Mad About You*, sure, but that isn't a bad thing, and he does show off his acting skills as well. *Mad About You* does largely excel on the backs of the Buchmans, and the actors who portrayed them.

Of course, I began these proceedings extolling the virtues of *Mad About You* as a show about a married couple who love each other, and then I choose an episode that sets forth the looming specter of the dissolution of the Buchmans' marriage. "The Finale: Part 1" is the first in a trio of "The Finale" episodes, but this one sets the table for the two-part event that served as the season finale two weeks later. But I am here to praise the show for the execution of this story, which is a "marriage is hard" narrative, not a "marriage sucks" narrative. The Buchmans didn't suddenly morph into the Bundys.

The overarching feel of the fourth season leans on things being tough for Paul and Jamie, at home and at work. They earned "The Finale" with their storytelling. For the bulk of the season, the Buchmans are trying to conceive a baby, with no luck. That's a strain. Two episodes before "Part 1," Paul gets fired from a job, and Jamie's boss's indiscretions cause conflict at her work as well. The next week, Jamie can't go with Paul to an awards ceremony, and he's tempted to go home with another woman. That paved the way for "The Finale" to provide its opening salvo. The cards are on the table for the Buchmans. Jamie kisses a coworker, and Paul tells her about the woman he almost went home with. The episode leaves you hanging, of course, because there is a two-part finale to whet your appetite for.

"The Finale" as a whole works because, one, the show had established the rhythms of Paul and Jamie's marriage to this point, and also provided real divorce stakes. This wasn't one of those sitcom relationship blowups where, like, two seconds of explanation about a misunderstanding would solve the whole thing. It also works because of Reiser and Hunt. They didn't leave the laughs on the sidelines, but they took the marital strife seriously.

This was not the end for the Buchmans, or for the show. *Mad About You* ran seven seasons in its initial run. "The Finale" does, however, sort of serve as an end to the show that *Mad About You* was, as in the fifth season's opener the Buchmans find out that they are expecting. By the end of the season the baby had been born and, well, that was that for the show that *Mad About You* was. Paul Reiser was no Bob Newhart, who—paraphrased anecdote alert—fielded a suggestion that the Hartleys have a kid on *The Bob Newhart Show* with words to the effect of, "That's great, but one question: Who will be playing Bob?" Of course, Reiser never expressed the same qualms about being a TV dad, or about that kind of material. His follow-up book to *Couplehood* was *Babyhood*, after all.

Now, the birth of the Buchmans' daughter, Mabel, did goose the ratings, but they swiftly fell across the sixth season. The seventh—and final—season was moved to Monday nights and is pretty lackluster. *Mad About You* wasn't a show ruined by the introduction of a kid, but they seemed to run out of steam creatively. Then, the show was part of the wave of '90s revivals, but it has perhaps the strangest story of them all, even if it had the most story to tell. *Mad About You* returned for an eighth season in 2019, and there was an obvious hook. Paul and Jamie were now empty nesters, with Mabel off at college. The problem? *Mad About You*'s eighth season aired on something called "Spectrum Originals." I still don't know what that means, and I refuse to learn. What it meant was that nobody watched it, few knew it was happening, and it might as well be retconned out of history. Not the show's history. Human history.

Mad About You did the breakup story arc and did it in a way that didn't feel like a rug pull or a cheap ploy. They earned it. The show also earned the reconciliation of the Buchmans. Helen Hunt earned her four Emmys awards. Television history, and the '90s, is littered with shows about single friends or unhappy couples. *Mad About You* did something different, even by simply focusing on characters with life circumstances that literally millions of TV viewers could relate to. What a zag.

Dexter's Laboratory: "Dexter's Rival / Dial M for Monkey: Simion"

Kids in the '90s had options for networks catering to them. Nickelodeon, of course, which was the hub for the household I grew up in. Television for kids in the '90s is synonymous with Nick, but that was my experience. Other kids were from Disney Channel homes. Sure, battle lines weren't drawn, per se, but you likely landed on one channel more than the other. There was also a third option, one I dipped my toe into occasionally. That was Cartoon Network, the home of *Dexter's Laboratory*.

I knew Cartoon Network kids, so I was aware of *Johnny Bravo* and *Cow and Chicken* and *Dexter's Laboratory*. But I never watched these shows. Before writing this book, I had watched zero episodes of *Dexter's Laboratory*. I almost shortened that as *Dexter*, but obviously that could cause confusion, thanks to a certain Showtime program about, to the best of my knowledge, a lumberjack. Never would I have imagined that the Dexter of '90s Cartoon Network would become the second most famous pop culture Dexter.

Though Cartoon Network had been around for a few years by the time *Dexter's Lab* (there's a shorthand that works, though now this aside has led to a much longer typing experience for me nevertheless) rolled around, it was the first fully fleshed-out show on the network. Prior programs were collections of unrelated shorts with no real narrative throughline. There was also, of course, *Space Ghost Coast to Coast*, but that was built heavily on reused animation and pre-existing characters. *Dexter's Laboratory* was an original show with original animation, with four "pilots," which were really test shorts, airing before the show was picked up as a proper series by Cartoon Network.

Dexter's Laboratory: "Dial M for Monkey"

Dexter's Lab was created by Genndy Tartakovsky, a beloved animator, director, and creative force in cartoons. He's also the guy behind *Samurai Jack* and *Star Wars: Clone Wars*. Dexter is a boy genius who fashions himself as something of a mad scientist, and his unnamed parents are completely oblivious. On the other hand, his good-natured older sister, Dee Dee, is aware of his secret lab, and she often ends up hindering his experiments but not with malice. This being a cartoon for kids, this plays out episode in and episode out. Also like most animated shows for children, a single story is not asked to fill out a full half-hour episode. *Dexter's Laboratory* episodes are divided into two or three segments. Early in the show's run, non–Dexter segments are included. "The Justice Friends" is a superhero spoof about three heroes who share an apartment. Then, there's "Dial M for Monkey," which features Dexter's lab pet Monkey's secret life as a superhero.

"Dexter's Rival / Dial M for Monkey: Simion" appears to have been first in production order for the first season of *Dexter's Laboratory*, but it aired fourth. This is not uncommon, and it is also likely more common in animation, and was certainly more common in the '90s. I mean, I remember episodes of the sitcom *Community* airing out of order in the first season, even though it messed with the development of storylines. With a show like *Dexter's Laboratory*, that sort of thing was not a concern. My guess is, as with the intended first episode of *The Simpsons*, there may have been animation issues, or maybe they decided not to introduce Dexter's rival right out of the gate.

The titular rival in question would become a recurring character throughout the run of the show. Mandark Astronomanov is a classmate of Dexter's, and also has a secret lab and such. Mandark is decidedly more nefarious in his goals, however, and often tries to thwart Dexter's inventions. He's also voiced by *Laserblast* co-star Eddie Deezen. Deezen is known for, shall we say, his distinct vocal tones. In "Dexter's Rival," Mandark shows up at the school and basically immediately puts an end to Dexter's scientific dreams, until Mandark develops a crush on Dee Dee, which allows Dexter the upper hand. In the second story, the "Dial M for Monkey" episode, Monkey does battle with an anthropomorphic chimp named Simion. Like Dexter, Monkey comes out on top. It would have been weird if the chimp had succeeded in his plot against humans.

There's an old-school animation look to the early *Dexter's Laboratory* episodes. I felt like I could have been watching a cartoon from the golden age of *Looney Tunes* or something. It has some nice flourishes, but the show lacks something in the way of panache. I don't feel like I was missing anything having not watched *Dexter's Lab* as a kid. But if you were a Cartoon Network kid in the '90s, it was probably because you were a *Dexter's*

Laboratory kid. Even I, too busy watching *Doug* or *Rocko's Modern Life*, was well aware of it. It was the defining original show on Cartoon Network in the '90s. Dexter is the face of afternoons spent watching Cartoon Network, presumably to the chagrin of Mandark.

Clueless: "As If a Girl's Reach Should Exceed Her Grasp"

Television shows spun off from movies rarely succeed. You take a story that works as a film, then try to adapt it in some way, shape, or form into the episodic nature of TV, and it doesn't click. They tried it with *Animal House*, *Ferris Bueller's Day Off*, *Turner & Hooch*, and more. Often, these shows die a swift death. Even the ones that don't, a *Harry and the Hendersons*, a *Weird Science*, aren't typically acclaimed. *M*A*S*H* worked a treat, sure, and the *Buffy the Vampire Slayer* show was a success in a way the film wasn't, commercially at least. *Clueless* got the TV adaptation treatment, and you may have forgotten it. That's totally fair, because it was not one of the successes.

I had to include *Clueless*, the show, though, because *Clueless* is perhaps the most '90s movie in existence. It remains beloved, and Cher Horowitz remains a style icon. I didn't see *Clueless* until adulthood, and for some reason the first time I tried to watch it I gave up. Maybe I just wasn't in the right mood or what have you, because I tried again and really enjoyed it. The film is quite good, and quite '90s, but in an ideal way. I will say, though, that when I gave up the first time it was when Cher gets held up in the Valley, and that is the worst stretch of the movie. I hate the "rollin' with my homies" moment, and for reasons I can't fully articulate the brief scene where the kids are sitting on a kitchen island and throwing themselves around like they are in a car or something is one of my least favorite movie moments ever. I loathe it. It sucks.

The film came out in 1995, and *Clueless* the show debuted on ABC, TGIF style, in 1996. Amy Heckerling, who wrote and directed the movie, created the show, and she directed and co-wrote the pilot, "As If a Girl's Reach Should Exceed Her Grasp." (The original intended pilot, "Don't

Stand So Close to Me," aired seventh.) If you had told me "As If a Girl's Reach Should Exceed Her Grasp" was the intended pilot, though, I would have fully believed you. Turning this movie into a TV show made some sense, because basically you just turn it into a high school show. Those are a dime a dozen. Basically, an episode of *Clueless* could be the movie but slimmed down to 22 minutes of storytelling. It's branding. *Clueless* was a brand, and that was the selling point. The problem, as is often the case with these TV adaptations of movies, is casting.

Stacey Dash is there as Dee, Elisa Donovan is there as Amber, and Donald Faison is there as Murray, but with all due respect, the center of *Clueless* is Cher, and Cher is played in the film by Alicia Silverstone. Silverstone wasn't about to commit to starring on a TV show in 1996. That's not what movie stars did then, and Silverstone was en route to movie stardom. She was going to be Batgirl! In a terrible movie! You have to have Cher at the center of all things *Clueless*, though, which meant recasting. Rachel Blanchard, who I recognize as Sally from *Flight of the Conchords*, stepped into the role. Brittany Murphy, Paul Rudd, and Breckin Meyer all turned up … in one-off appearances as different characters. Josh was recast, but Tai and Travis aren't even characters on the show. Well, Tai shows up, including in the pilot, but she makes three appearances total and is tertiary at best. Even Dan Hedaya didn't return as Cher's dad, with him recast with Michael Lerner. Good casting, but not the same.

This pilot episode has a fitting plot for an adaptation of a movie that was itself a loose adaptation of Jane Austen's *Emma*. Cher takes over as the advice columnist of the school newspaper, but her advice ends up causing problems for her friends. Now, Cher doesn't do as bad of a job as Jerri Blank, but her run as "Miss Buzzline" is a disaster. There is the essence of Cher: well-meaning but overly confident in her abilities. This is an ideal way to try to set the table for *Clueless* to be a TV show.

I must say, I genuinely enjoyed "As If a Girl's Reach Should Exceed Her Grasp." Right from the opening credits, which are quintessentially '90s, I was in. Sitcom pilots are usually difficult, but in a way *Clueless* had a pilot already in the form of a popular movie. It also helped that the pilot had Heckerling prominently involved. That certainly helped *Clueless* get off on the right foot. Heckerling wasn't going to have a problem tapping into the look and sensibility of *Clueless*. She created it. It was hers. Obviously, the big question is Blanchard. All in all, I thought she was good. Blanchard seems to be doing a bit of an impression of Silverstone as Cher, but why not? She's playing an established character, a popular one at that, so trying to be as "Cher" as possible makes sense. They didn't have Blanchard wear Cher's iconic yellow outfit in the pilot, but that may have been for the best. Otherwise, the comparisons may have been too strong in the heads of viewers.

Iconic outfit or not, one assumes a lot of people tuned into *Clueless*, saw that Silverstone wasn't Cher, and tuned out. This is the problem with trying to turn a movie into a TV show. Blanchard was never going to be Cher in the eyes of a portion of the baked-in audience ABC was presumably hoping for. Plus, Heckerling couldn't be hands-on to the same degree as with "As If a Girl's Reach Should Exceed Her Grasp" week in and week out on a network sitcom schedule in the 1990s. ABC canceled the show after one season.

Clueless was rescued from cancellation by UPN, but the move from ABC, and the TGIF lineup, to a secondary network came with changes. A drop in production value, sure, but also significant changes to the cast. Josh, Mr. Hall, and the now Mrs. Geist-Hall were all axed from the show. Michael Lerner left, to be replaced by Doug Sheehan as Cher's dad. *Clueless* got two more seasons and 44 more episodes thanks to UPN, but then the show was canceled once more. By then, it was May of 1999, and perhaps it was for the best that *Clueless* got canceled. The essence of *Clueless*, the milieu of this world, didn't belong in the new millennium.

If you like *Clueless* the movie, by all means give the show a shot. I know you fans are out there. There's a reason Silverstone returned to play Cher in a commercial for ... some product. I don't remember, and I don't care. My reaction was, "Hey, Silverstone is playing Cher!" and that was all my brain synthesized. Granted, that is not something you can exclaim about the show. "Hey, Rachel Blanchard is playing Cher!" doesn't hit quite the same, but don't be scared off by that. At least nobody rolls with their homies, mercifully.

7th Heaven: "No Funerals and a Wedding"

When I was in eighth grade, I had a class called "Life Skills." In the parlance of a previous era, it would have likely been called "Home Economics." It was a one-semester class and the easiest A conceivable this side of a gym class. Once a week we would go into the kitchen to cook something, but other than that, we basically did nothing. One day we sewed, and one day we learned to write a check, but I literally remember doing no other projects over the course of the semester. Mostly, we watched TV shows, specifically two TV shows. The one we watched, with no hyperbole, every week was *Degrassi Junior High*. In the mix, though, there was also *7th Heaven*, which was in the middle of its lengthy run.

7th Heaven was the longest-running show in the history of The WB, where it aired for 10 seasons. It lasted so long that the 11th and final season aired on The CW, the network born of the fusing of The WB and UPN. All in all, *7th Heaven* lasted a staggering 11 seasons and 243 episodes. The lesson: never underestimate religious people with bad taste. When you see that a film you have never heard of with no stars in it is a major box office success, it's probably catering to a religious audience. Well, specifically, a Christian audience. *Touched by an Angel* ran for 211 episodes. Even *Highway to Heaven*, an '80s show that was a little less overtly Christian but definitely was heavy on the religious overtones, ran for 111 episodes. The Ned Flanderses of the world need entertainment, and they don't care how tedious, poorly written, and inane it is. If it's sweet and reinforces Christian ideology, they're all in, baby!

You could call *7th Heaven* akin to *The Brady Bunch*, only worse and preachier. It's all about heavy-handed lessons, it's "all hugging, all learning." This is the kind of show that the Parents Television Council would laud, and they did, frequently calling it one of the most family-friendly shows on TV. Of course, it's family friendly based on the definitions set forth by the PTC's skewed version of the world. Now, if you are religious and reading this, you might be thinking, "Oh great, another atheist with an ax to grind against religion." Sorry, straw man, but that's not my issue here. Sure, I think religion is silly, and Christianity has its issues, but I hold no particular animus against religion. I've watched shows featuring religious characters, and I would gladly watch a good show that had an element of religion to it. My feeling is akin to the episode of *Seinfeld* where Jerry believes Tim Whatley has converted to Judaism for the jokes. He goes to vent to a priest about it, and the priest assumes he is offended as a Jewish person, to which Jerry clarifies that, no, he is offended as a comedian. *7th Heaven* doesn't offend me as an atheist. It offends me as a fan of television.

The show is about the Camden family, consisting of minister Eric, his wife Anne, and their seven children. To answer your question, he's actually Protestant, not Catholic. If the show has any cultural legacy aside from being "that bad religious show that was on forever" it is that one of the Camden kids, Mary, is played by Jessica Biel. "No Funerals and a Wedding" is the fourth episode of the show, airing on October 7, 1996. That title is such a sterling example of the "Wouldn't it be nice if TV was nice?" ethos of *7th Heaven*, which is a large part of why I chose it to represent the show as a whole.

For the first few episodes of *7th Heaven*, Anne's mother Jenny is a key figure, as she tells her daughter she has leukemia. The episode prior to "No Funerals and a Wedding" is about Jenny living her life to the fullest, and then she disappears into the bedroom to die off camera. While "No Funerals and a Wedding" focuses on the fallout of "Grandma Jenny" dying, it picks up *after* her funeral, because I guess a funeral is too sad? The kids deal with the death of their grandma in cheesy ways including trying to listen to her favorite song to keep her memory alive. She died, like, two days before, Ruthie. Chill a little. Then, of course, precocious 10-year-old Simon has to ask where Heaven is. Meanwhile, Eric is counseling a young married couple, and in checking out this episode for this book I realized how much the idea of a couple going to a minister for relationship counseling makes my skin crawl.

Again, though, it's in the execution. There have been plenty of good, even great, episodes of TV about death and centered on funerals. My favorite episode of *New Girl* is probably the one where Nick's dad dies. *7th Heaven* is bad television, and it would be if you removed every element of religion from it. But it was a "Christian show," and that helped goose the ratings enough for it to last long enough for the Camden kids to have kids of their own. Michael Jordan would tell you Republicans buy sneakers too.

The WB would have told you religious people watch TV too. Now, many of them have good taste and never would have been caught dead watching *7th Heaven*. If you were Christian and liked bad TV, though, The WB had the perfect show for you. Also, for the record, I don't recall picking up any life skills from watching *7th Heaven* in eighth grade.

Judge Judy: "Episode 30"

The first significant TV judge was one Joseph Wapner. Presiding over *The People's Court*, he was a celebrity, famously name dropped in *Rain Man* as a favorite of Raymond Babbitt, as played by Dustin Hoffman in a performance that, um, involved a lot of business. Between 1988 and 1990, the three winners of Best Picture at the Oscars were *Rain Man*, *Driving Miss Daisy*, and *Dances with Wolves*, and somehow the one that holds up the best is *Dances with Wolves*. Wapner's run on *The People's Court* ended in 1993 due to woeful ratings. Hearing that news, a judge rang up the producers offering to take over but was purportedly dismissed out of hand by the receptionist. That judge? Judith Sheindlin, forever known as Judge Judy, the most iconic TV judge ever.

Sheindlin actually first rose to fame before she got her own court-based television show. She began her legal career as a lawyer, becoming a prosecutor. Now, there's always reason to be skeptical of prosecutors, but Sheindlin was in New York City's family-court system, so maybe she was being chill and trying to help kids in abusive homes, but she also prosecuted juvenile offenders, so I'm not going to take a stance either way. In 1982, New York's mayor, Ed Koch, made her a family-court judge in Manhattan, and she eventually became the supervising judge. There, Sheindlin earned a reputation for toughness, which definitely sucks. I loathe self-styled "tough judges" who love the authoritative aspect of their profession. When such a judge is also phoning up producers to get on TV, call me extra skeptical.

Somehow, in February 1993, Sheindlin was profiled in the *Los Angeles Times* owing to her reputation for toughness, which later that year led to *60 Minutes* profiling her. The media megalith was falling for the fetishization of the tough lady in New York making one of the worst days in the lives of most of the people involved in the cases she presided over all about her. This led to a book deal, which gave us *Don't Pee on My Leg and Tell Me It's Raining*, which came out in February of 1996. Later that year, *Judge Judy* took to the airwaves. It would run for 25 seasons, 6,280 episodes, and make Judge Judy both a household name and just so incredibly rich.

Judge Judy (I'm just going to call her that now that we've entered that portion of her story) was effectively presiding over arbitration for people who otherwise may have gone to small claims court. It was all artifice, other than the fact that the parties involved signed binding arbitration agreements prior to showing up. The plaintiffs and defendants were paid appearance fees for being on TV, however, and any award payments Judge Judy decreed were paid by the producers. The audience in the "courtroom" were all paid extras, mostly aspiring actors. If you had a squabble going on, especially if you thought you might end up on the losing side of it, getting your case taken up by *Judge Judy* was a great option compared to actually going to court. You head in knowing that you won't have to pay any awards meted out, and you'll get paid to be there. All you have to do is put up with Judge Judy's nonsense. For producers, the show was massively cheap to make, even when Judge Judy's salary ballooned to a reported $47 million per year.

Episodes of *Judge Judy* are largely interchangeable. I chose the 30th episode of the first season, which dealt with an animal cruelty case, because Bea Arthur of all people showed up as a witness. I didn't include *The Golden Girls* in this book—it's an '80s show and its series finale isn't as significant as the one for *Cheers*—but a chance to shout out Arthur covers my bases a bit there. Even if you have never seen *Judge Judy*, you have likely through osmosis gleaned the gist of it, and her general demeanor. Within the artifice of *Judge Judy*, which is a TV show masquerading as a court proceeding, I have more tolerance for her shtick, though I still don't enjoy it. But, you know, people wanted Don Rickles to roast them, because that was his role in culture, and they wanted Judge Judy to tell them not to urinate on her calf.

I find the idea of these court shows inane, more so than basically any reality show conceivable, but I cannot deny that *Judge Judy* permeated the culture, and pretty much right out the gate. She was already famed by the time the '90s were ending. If you are going to do a show like this, I begrudgingly admit a personality like Judge Judy's is the only way to go. Otherwise, there is no "there there," as they say. I don't like Sheindlin, which is likely abundantly clear at this point. Trying to glean her personal politics, she's kind of all over the place. She is a "registered Independent," which just means that, like most judges, she feigns to be above the political fray, but as the Supreme Court has taught us time and time again that is entirely disingenuous. Sheindlin weirdly supported Michael Bloomberg in the 2020 presidential election. She voted for Barack Obama in 2008 and for Bill Clinton in 1992 and 1996, though Clinton is one of the lesser lights of the Democratic Party since it stopped being the part of the racist South, as his politics were quite moderate, leaning conservative, during his heyday. On the other hand, she voted for Ronald Reagan twice, so she can kick rocks.

Judge Judy was a hit, and it revived the courtroom genre, spawning many imitators. In fact, I'd argue it also resurrected *The People's Court*, even if they decided not to hire an aspiring Sheindlin when they kicked Wapner to the curb. *The People's Court* was revived in 1997, one year after *Judge Judy* debuted, and it ran all the way until 2023. I couldn't tell you who was the judge on that show. I couldn't tell you Judge Mathis's first name. But I knew Judith Sheindlin's full name when I sat down to write this chapter. She saved her genre, and she rose above it. Credit where it is due. It was actually raining. She was not merely peeing on our legs.

Mystery Science Theater 3000: "Revenge of the Creature"

We've grown accustomed to shows being rebooted, including shows from the '90s. *Roseanne*, *Will & Grace*, *Murphy Brown*, the list goes on. The idea of bringing a show back, at a new home or elsewhere, was not invented in the last 20 years, of course. In fact, it happened in the '90s. It's true! Look no further than *Mystery Science Theater 3000*.

I previously wrote a full book about *Mystery Science Theater 3000*, so go find that if you are so inclined, but I love the show, a true cult classic of the '90s. *MST3K* is a reminder of how much cable was the Wild West back in the day. If you aren't familiar, the premise of *MST3K* is that a man has been sent into space by a mad scientist to be experimented on by making him watch bad movies. This man only has robots for accompaniment on the Satellite of Love, and they spend their time riffing on the films. In reality, *MST3K* is about the host and a couple of puppet robots making jokes over a movie that is hopefully of the "so bad it's good" variety. It was at the forefront of this kind of appreciation of films as content itself.

Originally, Joel Hodgson was the host, and the man behind the show. It began locally in Minnesota, before The Comedy Channel, to become Comedy Central, picked it up nationally. The show took up three hours of TV time, but back in the early '90s, a network like Comedy Central was just trying to fill the schedule. Hell, The Comedy Channel's show *Higgins Boys and Gruber* might as well have been titled "Comedians Killing Time." It was a low-budget show as well, the likes of which you don't see on cable anymore. Even the cheap shows like *The Soup* don't look it. From early on, though, change was a part of the process for *MST3K*. J. Elvis Weinstein was out as one of the baddies, and the voice of Tom Servo, to be replaced by Kevin Murphy as Servo, and Frank Coniff as the new sidekick to Dr. Clayton Forrester. Dr. Forrester was played by Trace Beaulieu.

The seventh season of *Mystery Science Theater 3000* was a truncated six episodes, and it was going to be the end of the line. Mike Nelson, having replaced Joel as the human up in space after Hodgson left the show, and the 'bots turned into pure energy, and Dr. Forrester got the *2001: A Space Odyssey* treatment. *MST3K*'s tape-circulating cult of fans kicked it into gear and got the Sci-Fi Channel, now SyFy, to pick it up, however. The Sci-Fi channel was where Comedy Central had been when *MST3K* aired on that network. Beaulieu did not return, though, leaving the show to completely revamp. When the eighth season debuted with "Revenge of the Creature" on February 1, 1997, the entire cast had turned over from the beginning of the show.

Mike returned, as did Tom and Crow, but Mr. T. Robot was now voiced by Bill Corbett. Mary Jo Pehl had made some appearances as Pearl Forrester, Clayton's mother, in the Comedy Central days, but she now was the main antagonist, the one running the experiment. In time, she would pick up two sidekicks. Professor Bobo, a *Planet of the Apes* riff, was played by Murphy. Observer, a.k.a. Brain Guy, was a reference to a character from the *Star Trek* TV show and played by Corbett. Fortunately, Pearl, Bobo, and Brain Guy proved just as entertaining as Dr. Forrester and TV's Frank. Corbett's voice, while quite different from Beaulieu's, was still good for Crow. Of course, I didn't discover the show until the Sci-Fi Channel era, so when I found out about the likes of Joel and Trace, it was a stunning turn of events.

While "Revenge of the Creature" has to lay some track, the show does it smoothly. Corbett is ready to riff right from the get-go, though he also had to puppet Crow, and that took a little more time to get up to speed. The Sci-Fi Channel cut the show's budget, which was already low, and also insisted on science fiction films, which limited the potential movies they could show. *Revenge of the Creature* is an interesting choice, as it is the first sequel to the iconic Universal horror movie *Creature from the Black Lagoon*. It's far from the worst movie *MST3K* ever riffed, but provided good fodder for the jokes. In essence, it was like *MST3K* had never left. The cult show surely brought a new audience to The Sci-Fi Channel. It's the only show I have ever watched on the network, then or in the SyFy days.

Some of the best episodes in the history of *Mystery Science Theater 3000* aired during the Sci-Fi era. I'm so glad the show was able to come back, especially because it is how I found the show. Imagine a world without the "Hobgoblins" episode. I shudder to think. *MST3K* ran for three seasons on The Sci-Fi Channel, gaining even more of a cult following in the 2000s. Then I wrote my book about the beloved '90s show that was in the past and would definitely never come back and make my book out of date ... and then it came back. After a Kickstarter campaign—leaning on those adoring fans—*Mystery Science Theater 3000* returned on Netflix.

The entire cast was different, from the host to the voices of the puppets to the Mads. Finally, Hodgson was back in charge, having wrested control of his baby's legacy.

The reboot was hit or miss. I thought Jonah Ray was a solid host, and there are some very good episodes. The villains weren't as good, however, and the comedy wasn't as strong. For the second Netflix season, they only made six episodes and the premise was that you were supposed to binge it. *Mystery Science Theater 3000* didn't fit on TV in the 2010s, three hours with commercials is a hard sell, but it also didn't fit on Netflix, even with the lack of advertisements required. Then, it came back again. Now it exists on the "Gizmoplex," a subscription service that is self-funded. These episodes do show up on the various *MST3K* channels on streaming services, though. Honestly, the Gizmoplex era bums me out. It's a mess. It seems to be budgeted like it is the KTMA days again, but instead of being lo-fi it just has the look and feel of the cheap sci-fi movies they riff. The Gizmoplex and *Atlantic Rim* don't feel all that different.

Sometimes, dead is better. I appreciate the swing of the Netflix era of *MST3K*, but it didn't quite work. The Gizmoplex is something that never should have happened, creatively speaking. On the other hand, sometimes rebirth is good. "Revenge of the Creature" started a new era of *Mystery Science Theater 3000* that was as strong as the Comedy Central era. We got Pearl, Bobo, Brain Guy, Crow with a Brooklyn accent, and the chance to be exposed to movies like *Space Mutiny* and *The Final Sacrifice*. It's a cult show that could only really have found even cult status in the specific era it thrived in. What do you think, sirs?

The Simpsons: "The Itchy & Scratchy & Poochie Show"

All right, everybody clear out. *The Simpsons* is not just the defining show of the 1990s. It's not just the best TV show of all time. No, *The Simpsons* is the greatest cultural achievement humanity has ever managed. It beats not just every television show, but every film, every song, every work of literature, every painting—you name it. Picasso's *Guernica* can take a hike. *Citizen Kane* should be thankful that *The Simpsons* deigned to reference it so often. Even the Care Bears movie can't beat *The Simpsons*. Since the show has been written about so extensively, I'll likely never get to dedicate a full book to it, but I can take some time in this chapter to espouse the glories of *The Simpsons*.

Now, while I consider *The Simpsons* a work of genius, and while it has been on for more than 30 seasons and 750 episodes, truly staggering, I will admit it is only a defining show of the '90s. Seasons 3 through 9 is when *The Simpsons* earned its status as a work of all-time comedic brilliance, and all those seasons aired in the '90s. After that, the show got spottier, there are some bad seasons in the mix, and then, shockingly, in the 2020s *The Simpsons* almost rebooted without rebooting and strung together a few funny, fresh seasons. Doing that after three decades is as remarkable as anything else the show has done.

But let's talk about *The Simpsons* in the '90s. The animated sitcom focused on the Simpsons and other residents of Springfield really grabbed people, and pretty much right away. At first, Bart was the breakthrough character, as his rebellious attitude made him a favorite of children and somehow scandalizing to some TV viewers. Bart talked back to his father! He swore! He rode a skateboard! That didn't stop Bart from adorning ubiquitous merchandise, including the iconic Bootleg Bart merchandise, and pitching products such as Butterfinger candy bars. Michael Jackson insisted on writing a number-one hit for Bart, and he did in some countries! And we probably shouldn't unpack that any further at the moment!

Eventually Bart stopped being the de facto main character and ceded the center of the show to Homer Simpson, the greatest character ever created. His amazing lines of dialogue are legion. Dan Castellaneta's voice for Homer evolved over time, and once he landed on the defining voice for Homer, it took the character to the next level. There's a reason he won four Emmys for his voiceover work. Homer has more complexity as a character than Bart, and can do so much more for storylines as he is an adult man with a job, a wife, kids, and life anxieties. Of course, the quality of *The Simpsons* is not built on one character, or one family. It's built on dozens of great characters and the best joke writing any show has ever boasted, and the '90s-style animation was also quite enjoyable. There was a time in the teens, season-wise, where the animation got a little mediocre, but then HDTV hit and it picked back up.

The best season of *The Simpsons* is the eighth season, and the best episode of the show comes from that season as well. That would be "The Itchy & Scratchy & Poochie Show." Now, I am not merely writing about this episode because it is the best episode of the best show, though it helps. It also speaks to the defining nature of *The Simpsons*, though, and the complicated side of adoration and cultural ubiquity. Here, *The Simpsons*, a long-running, beloved cartoon, does an episode about what it is like to work on … a long-running, beloved cartoon.

With "The Itchy & Scratchy & Poochie Show," *The Simpsons* passed *The Flintstones* as the prime-time animated series with the most episodes. That makes it the perfect time for a little navel-gazing. While this is my favorite episode of *The Simpsons*, my favorite show, I don't recommend it as one of the first couple episodes for newbies to watch. No, it is built upon the legacy that *The Simpsons* had established, and has continued to establish since then. They are able to do this thanks to the existence of "Itchy & Scratchy" within the world of *The Simpsons*. While "Itchy & Scratchy" is not like *The Simpsons* at all, it is a popular cartoon in the universe of *The Simpsons*, one we had already seen time and time again.

Ratings for "The Itchy & Scratchy Show" have started to fall, seemingly owing less to a dip in quality and more to apathy. Trying to goose ratings, the show's producer, Roger Meyers Jr., along with Krusty and a bunch of executives, decides to add a new character. He's Poochie, the rockin' dog, a collection of buzzwords and sweaty attempts to grab the zeitgeist, and Homer ends up voicing him. Poochie proves immensely unpopular, and fans rebel. He gets killed off, Homer is out of a job, and everybody's favorite character, Roy, moves out of the Simpsons' home to go live with two sexy ladies.

"The Itchy & Scratchy & Poochie Show" is the most meta episode of *The Simpsons*, but they manage to thread the needle so well. They are able to poke fun at executives who foist bad creative ideas on creators, fans who feel they are owed something from creatives (spoiler alert: you're owed nothing), and what goes into bringing a cartoon to life. The episode is filled with caricatures of writers and directors from *The Simpsons*, which I love, but obviously isn't for those who don't adore the show. I may think to myself, "Hey, that's George Meyer," but your mileage may vary on that. Of course, it's not all meta commentary, though the one-off introduction of Roy brings me so much joy, and there are so many great jokes that don't require you to care about the thorny business of what popularity can do a show, especially with the internet on the rise. In this episode, Comic Book Guy references complaining about Poochie on the internet, and also for the first time drops a "worst episode ever" on us, which became a piece of the *Simpsons* lexicon.

What makes this episode sing is that they channeled the experience of working on *The Simpsons* into the story but crafted a story that fully succeeds on its own. It's my favorite plot of any episode, even more than "Homie the Clown" or "Homer Goes to College." Did I mention that Homer Simpson is the best character in fiction? Plus, it's just packed with funny jokes and great moments, including perhaps the best visual joke *The Simpsons* ever did, a newspaper headline about Poochie that reads, "Funny Dog to Make Life Worthwhile." Clearly, though, "The Itchy & Scratchy & Poochie Show" is also indicative of how deeply entrenched *The Simpsons* was in '90s culture. There is a reason *Simpsons* trivia nights still happen, and why it still gets quoted constantly. That all stems from the show's run in the '90s. It impacted culture more than even *Seinfeld*.

Obviously, if you have enough of an affinity for *The Simpsons*, and are feeling more enthusiastic than contemplative, you can find yourself just remembering funny bits and rattling off your favorite quotes. That is the nature of the beast. I could certainly do that with "The Itchy & Scratchy & Poochie Show." It's brilliant. It's genius comedy. It has also got a lot on its mind, so to speak. If you love *The Simpsons*, and enjoy thinking about pop culture, I imagine you also love "The Itchy & Scratchy & Poochie Show." Sure, perhaps you have to be inclined to like a joke like the introduction of Roy, but if you are reading a book about TV in the '90s, I imagine you are. From Rasta Bart to the iconic *Simpsons* arcade game to Butterfinger B.B.s, covering the overarching impact of this show on the decade of the '90s is nigh impossible, especially with only one chapter to dedicate to it. My heart was a dungeon, and *The Simpsons* used the Wizard Key. No show has ever been better. No show will ever be better. You want to understand the 1990s? You could just watch *The Simpsons*. Of course, you've already got this book, so you might as well keep reading it!

Friends: "The One with the Morning After"

If you were to put together a Mount Rushmore of '90s sitcoms, three shows are obvious choices, and then finding a fourth is a little tricky. I mean, would it be *Frasier*? *Murphy Brown*? There is no strong choice that leaps out to me, but the other three are clear: *Seinfeld*, *The Simpsons*, and *Friends*. Now, as I discussed in the last chapter, I think *The Simpsons* is the greatest show in the history of the medium. *Seinfeld* is an iconic sitcom, though among live-action '90s sitcoms, *Frasier* does top *Seinfeld* in my opinion. *Friends* is the populist favorite among, well, all '90s shows, save for perhaps *The Simpsons*. It had huge ratings, became a true cultural phenomenon, and gave the Rembrandts a legitimate hit song. Nobody was cutting their hair like Elaine, especially not with her early-season 'do. *Friends* has lived on in popularity as well. It was huge on Netflix, and I imagine it remains huge on HBO Max. Young people clamor for it in a way they don't for *Seinfeld*. Among the tentpole shows of the '90s, however, *Friends* is the one that doesn't hit for me. It's not on my personal Mount Rushmore, though I will never deny its place in the cultural landscape. For all the popularity the show managed, and for all the imitators it inspired, *Friends* is just a mediocre sitcom. To me, it's no different than *The Big Bang Theory*. Yeah, a lot of people watched it, and still do, but I can't quite parse why.

There is no premise to *Friends*, one of the ultimate hangout sitcoms. Six people in New York are friends. They are in their twenties or thirties, depending on the time in the show's run. The characters pair off romantically, have ongoing relationships that change the dynamic of the show for a bit, live in unreasonably large New York apartments, and only worry about money when it is germane to the plot. There's Rachel, Monica, Phoebe, Ross, Joey, and Chandler. All of the actors got a chance to be movie stars.

The cast of *Friends*. I know you probably don't need a rundown, but it is my professional obligation: from left we have Matthew Perry, Jennifer Aniston, David Schwimmer, Courteney Cox, Matt LeBlanc, and Lisa Kudrow (NBC).

Matt LeBlanc's Joey got a spinoff that flopped. Jennifer Aniston became one of the biggest celebrities in the world. It wasn't as well observed as *Seinfeld*, but you got to imagine good-looking celebrities having sex, and of course "shipping" probably came into the picture.

As I noted in the *Seinfeld* chapter, the most significant difference between *Seinfeld* and *Friends* is that *Seinfeld* had the courage of its convictions to make the main characters, and most of the secondary characters, unlikeable. They didn't ask you to like Jerry and the gang. In fact, they didn't like them either. The *Seinfeld* crew would do selfish or awful or unethical things for the sake of the plots, but Jerry Seinfeld, Larry David, and company were happy to wallow in it. The main characters on *Friends* were no more likeable as people, and no more ethical or altruistic, but *Friends* wanted them to be your TV friends. They wanted you to like them, to root for them, to care about their love lives. *Friends* wanted to have its cake and eat it too. It's like *The Office*. They mine Michael Scott acting awful episode in and episode out, but then they also say to the audience, "Isn't it nice Michael has found love with Holly?" and many viewers answer, "OMG yes!" Michael sucks. He's a bad person. He's completely

Friends: "The One with the Morning After"

unlikeable. I don't care about his love life, and I am not "happy" he's in a relationship.

The characters on *Friends* are entertaining sometimes, to be sure. Look, that cast was a collection of talent and charisma that is hard to come by. Matthew Perry and Lisa Kudrow know how to land a joke, and every episode has a few jokes that are worthwhile. Had *Friends* had the cynical ethos of *Seinfeld*, it could have worked. It wouldn't have been as funny and well crafted, but it would have been pretty good, all things considered. Yeah, *Friends* could be mean spirited, even compared to *Seinfeld*, and the pretty people and ooey-gooey romance maybe spackled over that to some viewers. Also, I am not here to do the thing where I point out the jokes that are problematic—gay panic was not uncommon—and pat myself on the back while I tut-tut this show from decades ago about its content. My apathy regarding *Friends* is a little deeper than that, and the unlikability of the characters stems from more than the occasional dicey joke.

"The One with the Morning After" is a sterling example of *Friends* as a cultural powerhouse, but also as a show about unlikeable people I don't care about that is clearly emotionally invested in the characters, with the hope the audience would follow suit. It worked, of course, but it usually does. Ross and Rachel were the "90s" answer to Sam and Diane, and this is a definitive Ross-and-Rachel episode. Now, Sam and Diane were better characters with more chemistry, but that's just me piling on at this point. This episode also gave us likely the most iconic quote from *Friends*, give or take a "Pivot!" and that's "We were on a break!"

It is the most banal thing you can do to say Ross sucks as a person, but you will still hear it all the time because it has become an acceptable take that you can comfortably throw out there to the world. That kind of thing is big with the boring, "I have no personality of my own, tell me what I need to say to get your acceptance!" crowd. Of course Ross sucks, but all six of the *Friends* friends suck, and "The One with the Morning After" gives us a nice peek into that, though it is mostly Ross and Rachel (and the storytelling) doing the sucking. I recognize I chose a *Friends* episode that particularly gets on my nerves, but it is a defining episode of '90s TV, and of '90s culture, so it was to me the best choice. *Friends* is a C, C-plus show, not a bad show, but this episode is an aggravating mess.

In the previous episode, Ross and Rachel decide to take a break from their relationship. You are reading this in the future, though even if you were reading this as I typed it you couldn't hear the heavy sigh that was conjured up by that sentence alone. Anyway, these grown-ass adults go "on a break," and then Ross immediately sleeps with Chloe, a woman he meets at the Xerox shop (very '90s, probably the only fun thing about revisiting this episode). As the title indicates, this episode deals with the morning after, picking up with Chloe at Ross's place. Ross gets a message that Rachel has immediately done an about-face on the whole situation and is now on her way to his place.

This is a classic sitcom episode of the "If people actually acted like rational adults, everything would have been fine." To which you might argue that then there would be no story, which is not necessarily true, and it wouldn't be a bad story. When you build a show or movie around dumb people or toxic people or what have you, these kinds of behaviors can work narratively. The problem is *Friends* doesn't treat its characters like they are in that vein, so instead we have to deal with a bunch of nonsense.

Ross tries to keep Rachel from finding out, getting Chandler and Joey in the mix there, but she finds out anyway. They fight and argue and their conversation is tedious and full of deranged behavior. Somehow this devolves into Ross begging on his knees for forgiveness, which doesn't happen, so they remain broken up and the gang, minus Ross, comfort poor Rachel. Poor, immature, unreasonable Rachel. If you watch "The One with the Morning After" and come away with a takeaway other than, "These two people are incapable of being in a healthy relationship and shouldn't be dating anyone, much less each other," I fear for your own romantic relationships, and really all your interpersonal relationships.

Of course, Ross and Rachel would get back together. They are the great (meaning large or immense) love story of *Friends*, even though Chandler and Monica get married and are less toxic as a couple and as individuals. "The One with the Morning After" is so deeply invested in the emotions of two awful, unlikeable people who are acting absolutely ridiculous, and it's not in any way, shape, or form fun sitcom style ridiculousness. The idea people could watch this and care about Ross, Rachel, or "Ross and Rachel" is beyond me. But David Schwimmer did get to say "We were on a break!" There's that.

This is a little in the armchair psychology vein, but I think the sensibilities of "The One with the Morning After," which permeates *Friends* well beyond this one episode, is part of the reason the show remains popular with young people. It's much in the way that Taylor Swift is popular with young people. Both *Friends* and Taylor Swift's music embody an unhealthy approach to relationships, but one that appeals to the selfish and narcissistic (and who is more selfish and narcissistic than teenagers?). *Friends* and Taylor Swift provide validation for one's own perniciously self-centered worldview. You are always the hero. You are always justified. You never have to change or grow. Everything must be melodramatic. Everything should be simple. Communication is for fools.

There are good episodes of *Friends*. There are great jokes from *Friends*. When Joey suggests that Ross craft himself a pair of paste pants, that bit is as funny as anything *Seinfeld* ever did. Again, though, *Seinfeld* knew what it was. It did not hide its dark heart. The series finale literally sends the main characters to prison for their awfulness. *Friends* ends with Chandler and Monica adopting twins and moving to the suburbs. Also, with Ross confessing his love to Rachel and them getting back together. These two toxic characters were given a "sweet" sendoff, and I am sure many of the 52.5 million (!) viewers were happy about it. There, in a nutshell, is my problem with *Friends*. Also ... maybe my problem with people? That's something for me to unpack elsewhere. *Friends* can have its spot on '90s sitcom Mount Rushmore. It will be Rachel with her iconic haircut. But, as a tradeoff, can I have Frasier Crane's head up there? That'll work for me.

Buffy the Vampire Slayer: "Angel"

Before he was a superhero movie star, and then Hollywood persona non grata, Joss Whedon was "the *Buffy* guy." He was the dude who had crafted the cult TV show, who would do stuff like puppet episodes and musical episodes, and then eventually do *Dr. Horrible's Sing-Along Blog*. Whedon had a cult following of his own, in fact you would have been hard pressed to figure out where his cult ended and *Buffy*'s began. Maybe they were one of the same. Part of the narrative of the success, cultish though it is, of *Buffy the Vampire Slayer* is a story of creative redemption. Whedon had saved his baby. Me? I'm not so sure about that.

Buffy the Vampire Slayer ran for seven seasons and 144 episodes, though split over The WB and UPN, which is to say outside the realm of "big time" network television. Like I said, it is a cult show, though an adored one. Buffy Summers, played indelibly by Sarah Michelle Gellar (there is a very specific joke from *The Venture Bros.* I am not hearing in my head), is a teenager in Sunnydale who finds out that she is a "Slayer," and, with the help of her "Watcher," Giles, and her high school friends, she battles assorted monsters. Many of them, for the record, are not vampires. In the seventh episode of the show, however, we are introduced to the titular Angel, a vampire with a soul played by David Boreanaz. Angel was a love interest for Buffy, and then later the star of a spinoff show called *Angel*. *Angel* was a supernatural private eye show that debuted in 1999, and it too proved popular, running for five seasons and 110 episodes. Then Boreanaz went on to play "Not Bones" on *Bones* and I presume became generationally wealthy.

Originally, though, *Buffy the Vampire Slayer* was a film, one that came out in 1992. Whedon has screenplay credit, and it was his idea, but the movie was directed by Fran Rubel Kuzui. The film has effectively nothing to do with the TV show, and Whedon is not a fan of the film. Kuzui crafted

Buffy the Vampire Slayer into a "pop culture comedy" about vampires. Whedon loathed this, speaking of writing a scary film about an "empowered woman" and getting his "dude in a 'This is what a feminist looks like' t-shirt" on. Here's the thing, though. *Buffy the Vampire Slayer*, the movie, absolutely rips. Kuzui was onto something. The show, on the other hand, is a real shrug.

It wasn't until I saw the film that the title *Buffy the Vampire Slayer* really clicked with me. In the tone of the movie, that title is a joke, and it makes sense. Gellar's "Buffy Summers" isn't a thing. She's just a person. She fights monsters. That's cool. Good for her. In the movie, though, Buffy Summers is a shallow, stuck-up, disinterested Valley Girl type in Los Angeles. She's a cheerleader. Her friends are equally vapid. She is a *Buffy*, and that Buffy becomes a *vampire slayer*. That's fun! I love the film version of Buffy. I know Kristy Swanson's politics are absolutely trash, but she's great as Buffy. She embodies the concept of "Buffy the Vampire Slayer," which is not really a concept in the show.

Also, literally all she does is slay vampires. Merrick, akin to a Watcher, shows up, and is able to help Buffy realize she is a Slayer, and thus needs to get to slaying vampires. We watch Buffy get serious about it, which means something for this character, but she remains Buffy through it all. Oh, and Merrick is played by *Donald Sutherland*. The movie also has Paul Reubens, Hilary Swank, David Arquette, and a delightful turn by Luke Perry as a sort of LA slacker type. There's actually a voice to the conceit in the movie, which is a ton of fun. Yeah, it's a little low budget. Some of it is cheesy, but the film has so much intentional cheese that is part of the ride. *Buffy the Vampire Slayer*, as perceived and directed by Kuzui, blows Whedon's precious show out of the water.

People can have their Gellar as Buffy and enjoy all their seasons of TV. They can enjoy *Angel*. Maybe they can even enjoy *Bones*. I'm sticking with the movie *Buffy the Vampire Slayer*, though. I'll take Swanson's problematic ass, Perry's slacker goofiness, and Reubens's iconic death scene any day of the week. Is *Buffy* a defining '90s film? Maybe not, but it should be a true cult classic. If society at large wants to kick Whedon to the curb, society should also look past his protestation of how Kuzui "ruined" his screenplay. What she did is churn out a dope, funny, "pop culture comedy" that has more fun with vampires than anybody ever has, Whedon included.

King of the Hill: "Keeping Up with Our Joneses"

FOX has spent much of its history trying to find comedies to pair with *The Simpsons*, with little success. This was especially true after *The Simpsons* became the cornerstone of the network's Sunday lineup. Off the top of my head, I can't think of a live-action comedy that aired on Sunday nights and took off for FOX. Eventually, FOX would find something in *Family Guy*, though it was a circuitous route. Originally, FOX canceled the show, only to bring it back and let it become effectively the driving force behind its comedy lineup. Before *Family Guy*, though, there was *King of the Hill*, which is a show that, at its time, was somewhat overlooked and underappreciated, but has become a favorite in hindsight.

In a way, it makes sense that *King of the Hill* would be overlooked, as it is an animated show that doesn't need to be animated. You could make a live-action version of *King of the Hill* and lose nothing but artistic style, and even the animation of *King of the Hill* felt like it was replicating reality. That, to children of the '90s, may have been a detriment. *The Simpsons* was populated with *cartoons*, and so was *Family Guy*. *King of the Hill* was like the real world was being animated, and that's unusual. It was then, and it is now. This is perhaps why it took retrospection brought on by time for *King of the Hill* to get talked about as a true gem of the '90s animated fare. *Family Guy* announces itself, for better or worse. It will not be ignored. That's not *King of the Hill*'s style. To that end, *Family Guy* seems to exist primarily to polarize, but I don't find *King of the Hill* to create much polarization.

I loved *Family Guy* when it debuted, but I was also in junior high. Before I even graduated from high school I had given up on it, and I don't consider it a good show. *King of the Hill* aired right before *The Simpsons* on Sunday nights much of the time, and as football made its way into cartoons on a Sunday during the school year, I watched what was given to me. I thought *King of the Hill* was fine, but I was never over the moon for it. It wasn't quotable like *The Simpsons*. It didn't hit the jokes as hard. There was subtlety to *King of the Hill*, which was not to be expected from a show co-created by Mike Judge, forever best known as the man behind *Beavis and Butt-Head*. The other co-creator of the show, however, was Greg Daniels, a *Simpsons* veteran who would go on to adapt *The Office* to American television. Perhaps they brought balance to Arlen, Texas.

Ostensibly, *King of the Hill* centers on Hank Hill, a seller of propane and propane accessories. I say this because the show's characters consist primarily of Hank's family, friends, and neighbors. The defining image of the show, after all, is Hank, Dale, Bill, and Boomhauer standing on the side of the road drinking beer. First-season episode "Keeping Up with Our Joneses," though, focuses on the Hill family, including Hank's relationship with his son Bobby.

Hank's attempts to be a good father to Bobby drive a lot of stories, and a lot of comedy. Often, it is built around Hank's worries that the boy "ain't right," as Bobby isn't interested in sports and instead has interest in things like cooking or prop comedy. This time around, though, *King of the Hill* tackles a classic trope of pop culture, as Hank catches Bobby smoking a cigarette. As so many parents in movies and TV do, Hank's punishment is to make Bobby smoke an entire carton, trying to drive him off of smoking for good. Instead, Bobby becomes addicted, as do Hank and Peggy. It's a clever, dark twist on a classic story beat. Hank does the "traditional" thing, and it backfires for everybody. Also, imagine a storyline like this on network TV nowadays. It feels like you'd be more likely to see full-frontal male nudity than somebody puffing on a cigarette, especially without it being a symbol of evil or moral decay.

"Keeping Up with Our Joneses" captures the sensibilities, style of humor, and family dynamic of *King of the Hill* well. Of course, it doesn't feature either of my two favorite characters, Dale and Boomhauer, all that integrally. Dale is probably the closest to a great, iconic character *King of the Hill* crafted. I gave up watching the show sometime during its run, but it kept going … and going. In the end *King of the Hill* ran for 13 seasons and 259 episodes before being abruptly canceled to make way for *The Cleveland Show*. Although, much like with *The Simpsons*, there is a contingent of fans who speak of a "zombie *King of the Hill*" starting with season 7, at which point Judge and Daniels were not really involved anymore and the producers stopped aging the character and started retconning a bunch of stuff.

In high school and college, I would occasionally catch a rerun of *King of the Hill* and think to myself, "Hey, this is a lot better than I remembered." I wasn't sure, though, how much of that might be the loopiness of watching TV in the middle of the night. Watching it in a solidified frame of mind, it remains a pretty good, unremarkable show to me. Others, though, speak of a love for *King of the Hill* in a way I never anticipated. Hank Hill gets memed. Dale Gribble gets memed. Sure, *Family Guy* has surpassed *King of the Hill* for the silver medal in terms of successful FOX cartoons. But there's nothing wrong with the bronze, especially for a humble propane salesman from Texas.

Ellen:
"The Puppy Episode"

There had been gay characters on American television before. Jodie Dallas from *Soap* is often cited as an early example, and being played by Billy Crystal certainly helped keep Jodie in this conversation. Sure, Crystal isn't gay, but he's also not Sammy Davis Jr., and that's never stopped him. Seriously, never stopped him. There had also been gay people on television who were not "in the closet" or hiding their sexuality. As a fan of the '70s version of *Match Game*, I assure you there were many jokes about Charles Nelson Reilly's sexuality, including from Reilly himself. In a later-in-life interview, Reilly noted that he never considered himself in the closet or hid the fact he was gay from anybody. All that being said, there is no denying the cultural weight of "The Puppy Episode."

Originally called *These Friends of Mine* for its first season, *Ellen* starred Ellen DeGeneres as Ellen Morgan (no relation), a bookstore owner in Los Angeles. So, in essence, *Ellen* combined the '90s affinity for handing successful standups their own sitcom with the '90s affinity for hangout sitcoms about friends, like, oh, *Friends*. This made *Ellen* unremarkable. It was *a* show on TV. *Ellen* got decent ratings, even if DeGeneres settles in around the Jerry Seinfeld level of acting acumen. Then, in the fourth season, "The Puppy Episode" happened, and DeGeneres's career—and life—changed.

DeGeneres, herself a lesbian and not out, was looking to pull a double whammy and have her character come out as well. Ellen Morgan had effectively not done any dating during the run of *Ellen*, and one of the main reasons for a show to have a main character who is single is so that they can be out there dating, and purportedly Michael Eisner, head of ABC's parent company Disney, suggested that Ellen could get a puppy if her character wasn't going to date. Thus "The Puppy Episode." DeGeneres and her writers wanted Ellen, the character, to come out, and after much negotiation and handwringing, a script was approved and "The Puppy Episode" dropped as an hour-long affair at the end of the fourth season.

It is not overly terse to say that the plot of "The Puppy Episode" is "Ellen Morgan comes out as gay." That's it, more or less. Prior to the episode airing, DeGeneres had come out, even appearing on *Oprah* with her then-paramour Anne Heche, which is a very '90s memory. Heche was, as they say, totally cuckoo bananas. Undeniably, DeGeneres and Heche appearing on Oprah Winfrey's show was a huge cultural moment. It also featured three deeply unlikeable people. I haven't mentioned it yet, because it is not part of the linear timeline at this point, but after Ellen became a titan of daytime television a litany of people who worked for her said that she was a nightmare. Now, I don't know what's legitimate, what's an overreaction, what's an ax to grind, but there is probably some validity in there. She also said she's friends with George W. Bush, so there's that. Anyway, DeGeneres is likely not a chill person.

Prior to "The Puppy Episode" there were groups protesting Ellen Morgan coming out. Some companies pulled advertisements. The cultural moment was significant, however, and 42 million people watched "The Puppy Episode." It was the highest-rated episode of *Ellen*. It probably got a fifth season greenlit. Weirdly, there was a parental advisory on fifth season episodes, which does suck. The fifth season would be the last. Naturally, some presume that it was because Ellen Morgan was now gay, and that the show was "too gay." This was the '90s, before every show seemed obligated to have a gay character for the street cred. What if, though, the show just still wasn't good?

Ellen Morgan being gay didn't make *Ellen* an interesting show. It didn't make DeGeneres a better actor. The show was mediocre before "The Puppy Episode," it was mediocre after, hell, it was mediocre *during* the episode. There is a reason Ellen DeGeneres never had a successful acting career. Neither did Jerry Seinfeld, I'll grant you, but he happened to have a show teeming with great writers and other people who were great actors. Also, Seinfeld was funny. Ellen has never been funny. Good for her that she fought to have her character be gay, and to in turn come out herself, but that doesn't make her talented or interesting.

Sometimes I say that I have a misanthropic sense of equality. Men, women, non-binary people, cis people, trans people, straight people, queer people, and people of all races and ethnicities are, by and large, not very interesting. A lot of people suck. A lot of people aren't likeable. In 1997, treating Ellen DeGeneres with equality meant allowing her to be open about her sexuality, and to have her TV character be able to be gay as well, but also to assess the quality of her show and her work as you would any straight person. Ellen is gay. That's totally fine. Ellen is not talented. That is my opinion. "The Puppy Episode" is probably the biggest "queer moment" in '90s television, and it's also not very good TV. Hey, most TV isn't good. Perhaps that makes it a true moment of equality. Behold, a lesbian mediocrity.

Todd McFarlane's Spawn: "Burning Visions"

The "Xtreme," Surge soda version of the '90s has not been prominently featured in this book. I'm a little surprised by that. Sure, the X Games didn't have any "episodes," so I couldn't go down that route, and Zima ads don't count as episodes of TV either, but there is a certain strain of '90s culture so encapsulated by all this. It's Poochie, but even more in your face. "Xtreme" came to comics in the 1990s in full force, best exemplified by two characters: Venom and Spawn. One man, Todd McFarlane, played a key role in both of them.

I was not a comic book reader at all in the '90s, and as I have mentioned previously, if it doesn't involve Archie and the gang, comics-wise, I'm not interested. Although, if it's a *Little Archie* comic, I'm firing it into the Sun. I was still well aware of Venom, though, because if you were into comics and, say, under the age of 14, Venom was the coolest thing on the planet, and I knew such kids. He's an alien with a giant mouth full of fangs, and he's all weirdly muscular and veiny. Oh, and mostly jet black. Venom debuted in the late 1980s, but he was maybe the biggest thing in comics in the '90s, or at least that was my impression. David Michelinie was the writer at the forefront of the conception of Venom, but McFarlane was the Marvel artist who first brought him to life.

By 1992, though, McFarlane was busy with Image Comics, which he cofounded. The character of Spawn, and this is completely unsurprising, is based off of a character McFarlane had created in high school. He spruced him up, and McFarlane's creation was brought to life, with McFarlane writing and doing the drawing. *Spawn* was, legitimately, a medium-changing hit. This creator-owned interloper of a comics company became a major player immediately. *Spawn*'s first issue sold 1.7 million copies, a record for an indie comic book. Naturally, in time this would lead to other *Spawn* projects, including in 1997 both a live-action movie

Todd McFarlane's Spawn: "Burning Visions"

and an animated HBO show. While Spawn was a known property at the time, it speaks to the power of the man behind him that the show was titled *Todd McFarlane's Spawn*.

"Burning Visions" is the first episode of the HBO show, and it is an animated program that aired on HBO because, of course, this isn't kid stuff. Presaging the rise of Zack Snyder and his coterie of overly dedicated fans, McFarlane kept things dirty, gritty, and twisted. *Spawn* is not my thing in any way, shape, or form. It has "high school art portfolio" written all over it, but even in high school I found stuff like *Spawn* to be ridiculous, overwrought, and that performative kind of edgy that is just so tedious. "Burning Visions" is laying groundwork, and it gives us an abbreviated version of the *Spawn* backstory. Al Simmons is a black ops assassin who is killed (via flamethrower) and goes to Christian Hell. There he makes a pact with a devil, who sends him back to Earth as a member of his hellspawn army. Does Simmons have a rotten corpse body? Of course he does! It's Xtreme! Spawn just kills dudes ... because? But he doesn't do it right, so another demon, Violator, is sent to Earth to try to get Spawn to kill for Hell. Violator is, of course, a grotesque clown. Eventually, there is a war between Heaven and Hell. I hate this.

Let's say, in theory, somebody was explaining *Spawn* to me. The second this person says, "There's a character named Violator who is a demon who looks like a creepy clown," I am telling them "hard pass" and maybe even telling them to go to (Christian) Hell, so annoyed that I am inclined to shoot the messenger. Keith David, who rules, is the voice of Spawn, and even that does nothing for me. In a piece in the *Tampa Bay Times* promoting the show's debut, McFarlane called *Spawn* "*The Silence of the Lambs*, *The Godfather*, and *Seven* all in one cartoon." Everything about *Spawn*, and McFarlane, feels orchestrated for me to roll my eyes. Even the animation is lame.

Todd McFarlane's Spawn may be my least favorite show covered in this book. McFarlane is, however, a critical figure in discussing pop culture in the '90s. *Spawn* is as defining a 1990s comic book creation as anything. McFarlane took an indie comic he created and was able to turn it into a TV show. Sure, *Teenage Mutant Ninja Turtles* did that, but the show completely reimagined the characters. McFarlane's vision was fully on the screen, for better or for worse. Oh, and it was for worse. Because, you know, this show sucks. At least it sucks in a totally "Xtreme" way.

Roseanne:
"Into That Good Night"

Valerie Harper had broken through as Rhoda Morgenstern, the sardonic best friend of Mary Richards on *The Mary Tyler Moore Show*. She even got a spinoff! Then, in the 1980s, she got another sitcom called *Valerie*. After the second season, Harper wanted a major increase in salary, and when the producers and executives declined, she walked off the show. It had apparently worked for her on *Rhoda*, but this time it didn't work. Valerie Hogan was killed off, and in the third season it became *Valerie's Family: The Hogans*. Then, for three seasons, it was *The Hogan Family*. A show lost the main character, the titular character, but persevered. Which brings me to *Roseanne*, and *The Conners*.

Roseanne encompasses so much of what this book covers. A standup given their own TV show. A belated reboot. Also—spoiler—the "It was all a dream!" twist. I'm starting with the reboot, from the 2010s, because of the strangeness of it all. The show ended its original run in 1997 with "Into That Good Night" but returned for a 10th season in 2017, 20 years later. Much of the original cast returned as well. There was supposed to be an 11th season, but then Barr tweeted stuff that ABC's president called "abhorrent, repugnant, and inconsistent with our values." She claimed she wasn't being racist; others disagreed. She also has supported Donald Trump and said some wild things about George Soros and other QAnon type stuff. Barr was fired, but the show was effectively rebooted as *The Conners*. It has thrived. As of this writing, *The Conners* has run for five seasons and 93 episodes, with a sixth having been ordered. I can only imagine how much better that set and production feels now with consummate professionals like John Goodman and Laurie Metcalf leading the cast, as opposed to Barr. I also imagine it's nice for Goodman, a man who has been open about his battles with alcoholism, to have stability in *The Conners*.

Even in the heyday of Barr's career, and when *Roseanne* was a huge success, she was an out-and-out maniac and seems like a total nightmare to work with. Read any reflection of the production of *Roseanne*, especially when she was with Tom Arnold. Hell, read anything about Arnold and Barr's relationship. She has a "controversies" section on her Wikipedia, and also a section titled "family conflicts." In spite of all that, *Roseanne* thrived for many years, and became a '90s favorite. Like many shows, though, it also seemed to run out of ideas but kept going anyway, leading to the fairly disastrous ninth season.

I didn't watch *Roseanne* much back in the day, but I met somebody whose taste I generally agreed with who said *Roseanne* was their favorite show. Thus, I decided to give it a shot. Watching a sitcom from the beginning can be a bit of an effort, and I made it about eight episodes in. Eight perfectly fine episodes, but not more than that. I could see quality elements, and not just Jackie's many dope fits. It just didn't grab me. Although I was not a *Roseanne* watcher, I still heard tell of the ninth season, and what a fiasco it was. For the book, I jumped over a lot of stuff and dipped into the ninth season a bit, including the series finale "Into That Good Night."

What made *Roseanne* stand out to many was that it was a family sitcom about a blue-collar, working-class family. Both Dan and Roseanne Conner work. Work isn't always easy to come by. The family struggles for money. Their financial concerns feel legitimate. This wasn't *Friends*, where Rachel and Monica could have a New York apartment like that. It was in the show's bones, and then at the start of the ninth season, the Conners (and Jackie) won the Illinois lottery, taking in $108 million (in 1997 money). Suddenly, the Conners were rich. Also, meeting princes, characters from *Absolutely Fabulous*, and getting in wrestling matches. People didn't like it. This was not what they wanted from *Roseanne*, and also it just felt silly. Thus, the one-hour series finale of *Roseanne* became a full-on "loljkjk" situation.

Really, all that matters are the final moments of the final episode. In a voiceover, Roseanne reveals she has been telling the story in a book of her life, and that she has changed a lot of the details. The Conners did not win the lottery. Dan had a heart attack at the end of the eighth season, and it is revealed to have been fatal. Also Roseanne's sister Jackie, not her mom Bev, is revealed to be gay. Now, there are a lot of people online who seem to believe the entire series is a dream, but what I surmise is that just the ninth season, i.e., the stuff people didn't like, was a dream.

"Into That Good Night" didn't appease people. The "It was all a dream" retconning of the ninth season of *Roseanne* was as controversial as the season as a whole was. In fact, when *Roseanne* returned for the 10th season, much of the stuff from the end of "Into That Good Night" is retconned out as well, with Dan being alive and Jackie being heterosexual. Barr, in the end, couldn't get out of her own way. That led to the ninth season of her show being a disaster, the finale being a frustration, and her getting booted from her own titular show, which has succeeded without her. Breathe easy, Valerie Harper (even though you're dead). In the popular memory, *The Conners* will replace *The Hogan Family* as a reference point.

Emeril Live: "Dueling Woks"

Food had been showcased on television before. Cooking shows had existed. Julia Child had developed a devoted following. There was a market for food television, but an entire food network? That's what, well, the Food Network banked on when it launched in 1993. Given everything that has happened since then, the gambit has proved quite successful. The Food Network has minted stars and notable names, such as Bobby Flay, Alton Brown, and the network's patron saint, Guy Fieri. First, though, came the original face of the Food Network, Emeril Lagasse, who proved so popular that he had a successful cooking show with, somehow, a live audience.

Yes, like David Letterman or Jay Leno or Oprah Winfrey, Emeril did his thing in front of a live studio audience. Also, like Oprah, he was effectively known by one name. He was, and is, Emeril. In addition to being the network's first star, Emeril was one of the first people involved at all. He was the host of *Essence of Emeril* beginning in 1994, but this was much more in the vein of the staged-kitchen, here's-how-to-cook-this-recipe show that was the staple of food TV for decades. What *Emeril Live* did was, well, kick it up a notch.

Sure, it was still a guy cooking, but Emeril had an audience to play off of who was into what he was doing. He had an in-house band, which is utterly bonkers for a cooking show. Emeril got to build his personality, because he had engagement. The chef crafted catchphrases, with talk of kicking things up a notch, seasoning- and spice-wise, and his signature "Bam!" which he exclaimed when upping intensity. His audience would "Bam!" right along with him. All he was doing was cooking, for an hour, but *Emeril Live* proved able to grab an audience. Emeril was building a cult of personality. He was getting people to watch Food Network.

I know the first Food Network show I ever saw was *Emeril Live*. He was all I know of food television, of cooking shows. The tics of Emeril permeated culture. People knew "Bam!" Emeril would be parodied, including by *Futurama*, a show I will get to later in this book. In "Dueling Woks," Lagasse was joined by another TV chef, Martin Yan. Yan had been in the food TV space for years already. His cooking show—*Yan Can Cook*, focused on Chinese dishes—began airing on PBS in 1982. Of course, *Yan Can Cook* came from that old-school style of presentation. Before Food Network, the conception of what cooking shows were largely came from PBS shows like *Yan Can Cook*. It was not about kicking things up a notch, or in-house bands. Emeril was more Tim Taylor, less Bob Vila. In "Dueling Woks," both worlds come together. Also, Yan once appeared on *Space Ghost Coast to Coast*, which of course I must mention.

Emeril Live ran from 1997 through 2007 on Food Network, before being moved to the Fine Living channel, now the Cooking Channel, from 2008 to 2010. Well before *Emeril Live* ended, though, food television had passed him by. Lagasse's show, in truth, was not an evolution of food television. It was taking what existed to its furthest reaches but was a tweak on a formula. Then, food television, and the Food Network, became less about cooking and more about competition. Television personalities had to be "television personalities" more and more. It's not unlike how on almost every game show, save for *Jeopardy!*, contestants are all people who act like lunatics who have never been so happy or pumped in their whole lives. Years ago, I got a job with a game show because I had auditioned for it and did the best of anybody on the testing but did not have a "game show personality," so they (also taking the fact I worked as a writer into account) gave me a behind-the-scenes gig. Emeril was not kicked up enough notches any longer. The age of *Chopped* and (on another network) *Top Chef* had arrived.

And yet, I have to admit I never really watched *Emeril Live* after a few times in the 1990s. I watched *Iron Chef America* for years. I watched *Chopped* until it got too gimmicky and asked me to have any interest in Martha Stewart, a tedious person who eats everything with chopsticks. Then again, does Food Network exist long enough to take its current form without *Emeril Live* holding the network up? Does Guy Fieri have a career if Emeril wasn't able to capture an audience and build a following? How many people first absorbed the existence of Food Network into their brains thanks to Emeril Lagasse? He was the network, and then the network left him behind. Time comes for us all. Bam!

Walker, Texas Ranger: "Lucas"

You may have never watched a full episode of *Walker, Texas Ranger*. Perhaps, unlike me, you did not find yourself sitting on the floor of your great-grandparents' home in some suburb around Tampa Bay, watching a *Walker* or two in lieu of continuing to "play" the *Jurassic Park* theme on the electric organ or riding an exercise bike in the covered patio room not protected from the summer humidity. But if you are reading this book, there is a good chance you are to some degree of a sensibility similar to mine. If so, you have probably intuited the episode of *Walker, Texas Ranger* I have chosen, even if you don't know the episode by name. It all comes down to one iconic, infamous line: "Walker told me I have AIDS."

Pedro Zamora, wherever you are (I mean you're dead and have zero consciousness, but I am being existential here), your death was a tragedy and your work was admirable, but "Walker told me I have AIDS" is maybe the funniest damn line of '90s TV that wasn't meant to be funny. *Walker, Texas Ranger* and Chuck Norris exist more as memes than anything else at this point. Chuck Norris facts took over the internet for a minute in the 2000s, but they were built off the absurdity of Norris, an actor lacking in talent, a person with trash politics whom I utterly loathe on a human level. Norris is a joke, and thus turning him into a source for jokes was cool with me, though Chuck Norris facts got old fast.

Norris was in some bad action movies in the '80s, but by the '90s water found its level with *Walker, Texas Ranger*, a show that ran on CBS from 1993 through 2001. It is a quintessential CBS procedural. Norris stars as Walker, who is, well, a Texas Ranger. Mostly it's a chance for Norris to play a moralistic (Norris is Christian to a disconcerting level) crime fighter who uses martial arts. Hey, he may believe in intelligent design. He may have supported Roy Moore for the Senate. However, Norris's martial arts bona fides are legit, so there's that.

Look, nothing that happens in "Lucas" matters other than one moment. The titular Lucas, by the way, is a kid played by Haley Joel Osment, a quintessential child actor who grew into an adult who can do solid character work and is a fan of *Comedy Bang! Bang!*, which is cool. At one point, effectively out of nowhere even if it is an ongoing plot point, Lucas, a seven-year-old child, declares, "Walker told me I have AIDS." The thing is, it's true! Lucas has AIDS, and Walker is the one who told him.

How did this line come to my awareness? Thanks to my favorite late-night host, Conan O'Brien. In the 2000s, O'Brien started doing a sketch called "*Walker, Texas Ranger* lever" on *Late Night*. The premise was that he would pull a lever, and it would show a clip of the show. It was always something that, out of context, was absurd and funny. You see, *Walker* was made by incompetent people, hacks lacking skill, awareness, and talent. There was comedy in the specificity of it being solely a *Walker* bit, but the show also provided a lot of fodder. After the sketch was effectively done, it was brought back one more time, with Conan promising a real doozy. He wasn't lying. We got the definitive *Walker* clip, which culminates with Osment delivering those infamous six words. The audience erupted. I laughed my brains out at home. It was a glorious moment. Also, a 2000s moment, so that's the end of that!

Funnily enough, both *Walker, Texas Ranger* and *Late Night with Conan O'Brien* debuted in 1993. They have, um, very different cultural legacies. In fact, *Walker*'s legacy now is essentially only the lever bit from Conan's show. Many people only have one memory of *Walker, Texas Ranger* and it's "Walker told me I have AIDS." O'Brien has the legacy of brilliance in the '90s and beyond. Norris is a joke. As it should be. Any show that would give us an episode like "Lucas," which is two parts, by the way, and a moment like the one Conan made infamous deserves to be remembered for its absurdity. All the dumb martial arts fight scenes and all the cringeworthy lines of dialogue are only fodder for laughs now. *Late Night with Conan O'Brien* trafficked in brilliant absurdity, but the writers of that show never crafted a moment as absurd as "Walker told me I have AIDS."

Jerry Springer:
"I Refuse to Wear Clothes"

Jerry Springer was born in London to Jewish parents who escaped Nazi Germany. He grew up in New York and then got a law degree from Northwestern. Springer worked on Robert Kennedy's campaign until RFK's assassination. He was the mayor of Cincinnati at one point! Springer married Micki Velton in 1973 and, while there is conflicting information, never divorced. He died on April 27, 2023, at the age of 79. Springer died an icon. He died a pop culture legend. Oh, and he did it as the face of "trash TV," the lowest form of entertainment imaginable. Jerry Springer's talk show was socially irresponsible, definitely problematic, and changed the face of television. The hustle is respected. Nobody has had a life quite like Springer's.

Maybe it's the *Seinfeld* lover in me, the guy who admires the willingness to have contempt for your characters, to not try to have your cake and eat it too. Oprah Winfrey would not shy away from "trashy" topics, from what is sometimes called "tabloid talk show" content. Jerry Springer hid nothing. Well, he got there eventually. In truth, when *Jerry Springer* debuted in 1991, it was a low-key political talk show. Ratings were bad. Cancellation loomed. Thus, Springer and his producers did not take the high road. They created the most salacious, lurid show they could get away with on daytime television. The audience ate it up, and *Jerry Springer* became a phenomenon. It wasn't some "Is this what you want?" cynical offering laced with content. No, it was more, "This is what you want!" Viewers said, "You're right!" Springer and his audience went all *Thelma and Louise*, holding hands and driving off the cliff of taste.

How to describe an episode of peak *Jerry Springer*. Well, maybe in a collection of imagery. There is a topic at hand, sure, but the episodes are about more than that. Guests yelling at each other. A live audience whipped into a raucous, frothing chaos. Fights breaking out, with security on hand to break it up. One security member, Steve Wilkos, became so notable he got his own show. Bleeped profanity. Pixelated nudity. Women in the crowd would occasionally flash for "Jerry Beads" like it was Mardi Gras. Oh, and a crowd chanting, "Jerry! Jerry! Jerry!" over and over. Episode topics, and therefore episode titles, are designed to be salacious and enticing. I chose "I Refuse to Wear Clothes" because it is indeed representative of the lowbrow, prurient nature of the show, but also it's a topic that is not gross or, um, problematic by modern standards. *Jerry Springer* was full of sexual deviancy, some of it theoretically illegal. It also featured a litany of transgendered folks in a way that would flip a lot of wigs these days. "I Refuse to Wear Clothes" is maybe not as fight-inducing as some topics, but it was a great opportunity for pixelated nudity and performative horniness from the crowd. The show would produce videotapes, DVDs, and pay-per-view specials called *Too Hot for TV* that was basically uncensored *Jerry Springer*.

"I Refuse to Wear Clothes," from the tail end of 1997, is part of the peak era of *Jerry Springer*. In the 1997–98 corridor, *Jerry Springer* was beating Oprah in the ratings some days in some markets. Springer's fame peaked in 1998. That year, he appeared in *Austin Powers: The Spy Who Shagged Me* in a parody of his show, and he even starred as a fictionalized version of himself in a movie called *The Ringmaster*. Controversy permeated, and hands were wrung. Famed pearl clutcher and doofus Joe Lieberman called for the show to be pulled from the airwaves. When Lieberman was speaking out against you, you knew you had made it. In the 2000s, *Jerry Springer* started to wane in popularity, controversy started to turn the tide on the show, and *TV Guide* called it the worst show ever. And yet, it would still run all the way to 2018, because it remained cheap to produce, and pixelated nudity and bleeped swearing remained in style to some.

The title of his film, *The Ringmaster*, was indicative of how Springer saw himself. He was the emcee of his sordid circus. Springer would note that he never jumped into the action. He was still a host in a suit, not swearing, not fighting, not partaking in any nudity that needed to be pixelated. Springer was a conductor, but a conductor of a train that everybody wanted to see derailed, making his job even easier. What role did Springer really play in the success of *Jerry Springer*? Was his greatest role his willingness to be a part of something so crass, so tawdry? If you or I had been willing to wield a microphone and stand there getting "I Refuse to Wear Clothes" from point A to point B to point C and on and on, would it have been as popular? I think it is a legitimate question. I also don't have the answer.

Jerry Springer was a bad show, by and large. It was at times offensive. It was always stupid. The salaciousness always felt sweaty and desperate.

If you are smart enough to see the sausage being made, it is hard not to roll your eyes. I don't think it "hurt society." I am not bothered by bleeped swearing or pixelated nudity (or unbleeped swearing and unpixelated nudity, for that matter), but *Jerry Springer* is just so dull. There's also the fact that the legitimacy of people and events on the show has often been called into question. Some claim that events, specifically fights, were staged. I heard somebody on a podcast who said he was on *Jerry Springer* a few times and the way he presented himself was a put-on in every instance. Which, I mean, sure, I could see that being true. Nobody is holding out hope for the sanctity of *Jerry Springer*, right? *Jerry Springer* was "trash TV," but it is the most successful show of that ilk ever. Springer himself is the icon of that genre. Like Sinead O'Connor, Springer died after this chapter was originally written. He was 79. Springer's legacy is no less complicated than O'Connor's. How he will be remembered going forward remains to be seen, but back in 1997, he was one of the biggest things on TV. He was the ringmaster. Take care of yourselves, and each other.

Ally McBeal: "Cro-Magnon"

If you weren't around in the '90s (and if you weren't, thanks for reading), you might see some dodgy special effects or computer-generated graphics and presume we all thought it looked good at the time, that we were wowed by what we were seeing. While it is true that some CGI graphics have not aged well and time is not kind to technology in many ways, often, the special effects clearly sucked, even then. That is to say, I feel that basically everybody was floored when *Ally McBeal* dropped that damn dancing baby on us, in part because it looked so weird, so creepy, and so fake.

I was aware of *Ally McBeal* as a ratings ploy–heavy legal show on FOX. Starring Calista Flockhart as the titular lawyer, it seemed to craft plots based on being able to cut together sensationalistic promo ads. This was, after all, a time when promo ads would be seen during other shows, and when you might be willing to check into a program you hadn't really watched. Maybe it was that a pre–MCU, post-legal troubles (and also pre-other legal troubles) Robert Downey Jr. was joining the cast. Maybe it would just be a bunch of good-looking TV people passionately kissing. *Ally McBeal* was the opposite of subtle. I picked that up just from the ads in the late '90s and early 2000s. This was a David E. Kelley show, after all. I talked about him in the *Picket Fences* chapter, but this was perhaps his greatest achievement in "more is more" entertainment. I almost said "more is more storytelling," but, well, the stories didn't really matter, near as I can tell, other than as vessels for sex and soap operatic plot twists.

I haven't gotten to the *Futurama* chapter yet—as of the date of "Cro-Magnon" airing it hasn't even debuted—but they once did a parody of *Ally McBeal* called "Single Female Lawyer." It was all short skirts and judges sexually propositioning lawyers in unisex bathrooms. Turns out, "Single Female Lawyer" was maybe not all that much of a stretch in terms of the reality of *Ally McBeal*. I knew I was going to be writing about the first appearance of the dancing baby for this book. It's the piece of *Ally McBeal* that permeated culture and became defining. In the process, though, I read a lot of plot synopses of *Ally McBeal* and, wow, this show was ABSOLUTELY BONKERS. Every episode seems maximalist. I can't imagine bingeing this show. It would be exhausting.

"Cro-Magnon" is a perfect example of this. Ally's plot is that she is horny for her 19-year-old client. Additionally, Ally and a couple of her female compatriots are taking an art class (as TV characters often do) with a nude model (another TV staple). This happens to be a nude male model with a large penis. So, in one storyline, Ally has the hots for a teen young adult, and in the other, she's doing art of a well-endowed model. Sex! Now that I have your attention, *Ally McBeal* might as well have been *Sex and the City* without the access to actually showing nudity. Oh, and then there is the dancing baby.

Now, the dancing baby was not created for *Ally McBeal*. They just took an existing animation from the '90s that was worked on and tweaked, over time, by individuals including Michael Girard, Susan Amkraut, Robert Lurye, and Ron Lussier. What *Ally McBeal* did was take this rudimentary animation of a baby doing the cha-cha (which Girard had tossed for being too "disturbing") and put it on network television. Also, soundtracking it with Blue Swede's cover of "Hooked on a Feeling." Plus, the baby no longer existed in a vacuum. It was in Ally's apartment, with real human Calista Flockhart sharing the scene. Dancing to the "oogachaka" strains of "Hooked on a Feeling," this nightmarish looking, desperately fake baby took center stage. Flockhart did her best to act opposite nothing. This was before that was how, let's say, 99 percent of movies were made. You see, Ally had a ticking biological clock, and the dancing baby was there to represent that. Yes, this was also about sex, at least sort of. I mean, there are other ways one can get pregnant, thanks to modern science, but in *Ally McBeal*, everything is about sex.

"Cro-Magnon" was the 12th episode of *Ally McBeal*. It aired on January 5, 1998, and it immediately got people buzzing about the show. By this point, some people were on the internet. "Water cooler talk" was still a thing. Those promo ads I mentioned? They were perfect to showcase this insane bit of early computer animation. "Cro-Magnon" was the highest-rated episode of *Ally McBeal* at the time, even higher than the pilot. The next two episodes were both even higher rated. Kelley and company kept on tossing the baby out there. It was a phenomenon, but because it was so weird. People didn't think it was good animation. I don't think Kelley even thought that. My guess is Kelley thought, "This will get people talking," and he was right. I was a kid when I saw the dancing baby in ads for *Ally McBeal*, and my thought was, "That is so weird and creepy, what are they doing?" Well, they were doing the same thing they were doing with the barely legal romances and the well-endowed nude models: whatever it took to get people talking. Mission accomplished, you weirdos.

3rd Rock from the Sun: "36! 24! 36! Dick"

As a kid, I watched *3rd Rock from the Sun* on occasion, and I remember it as being fairly funny. Of course, this was the '90s, which meant I caught it when it was on, if I wasn't watching something else, because otherwise I'd have had to catch a rerun. My first real experience watching *3rd Rock from the Sun* actually came in 2020, when it was a pandemic binge of mine. Hey, remember the novel coronavirus? I really enjoyed it, more than I expected. Yes, it is a silly, broad sitcom, an old-school multi-cam affair, but one of the better examples of that from the '90s. The cast is stellar, which helps. French Stewart's Harry Solomon is now a style icon in my mind. Given my recently discovered affinity for *3rd Rock*, I wanted to include it in the book, and figuring out how to do so was fairly easy. You see, "36! 24! 36! Dick" is a post–Super Bowl offering.

First, *3rd Rock*, then the Super Bowl (and then also some more *3rd Rock*, probably). The high-concept premise is simple enough. Four aliens have come to Earth to observe it, and they pose as a family of humans in Rutherford, Ohio. Dick Solomon, played by John Lithgow, is the leader of the mission. Sally is played by Kristen Johnston, and is the security officer. The game with her character is the alien figuring out the female body, and being a woman on Earth, as the alien is not "female" in any human conception. Tommy, played by a young Joseph Gordon-Levitt, is the oldest of the aliens, but is in the body of a teenager. Harry, whom I already mentioned, is kind of a robot? He has a transmitter in his head? Basically he's the weirdo. They interact with humans, fall in love, fail to understand basic societal norms—you know the drill.

It's very broad, with everybody mugging, even the human characters played by the likes of Jane Curtin and Wayne Knight. Subtlety doesn't have much of a place on *3rd Rock from the Sun*. Sometimes, that makes for cheesy comedy, but a lot of the time it's quite funny. Few shows are more reliant on the cast to sell the jokes, though. You put a different ensemble together, and it probably doesn't work as well. Lithgow, in particular, is a gem. I'm not the only one who thinks this, as he won three Emmys for the show (Johnston won two). If you want clever, nuanced comedy, you don't watch *3rd Rock*. If you want to watch Lithgow at his hammiest, Johnston's physical comedy, and Stewart being a weirdo, then go nuts! I like this show quite a bit.

"36! 24! 36! Dick" is a two-part episode that aired in the middle of the third season, on January 25, 1998. My first reaction upon seeing that was, "Wow, the Super Bowl was still played in January that recently, huh?" As you presumably know, the Super Bowl is the NFL title game, and the biggest sporting event in the United States. It's also a ratings bonanza. Most of the highest-rated TV events in American history are Super Bowls. Once the Super Bowl became a sensation, and a massive ratings boon for whatever network was airing it, the idea of the Super Bowl "lead out" show became a bigger thing, and something for a network to mull over. If you aren't interested in sports, you might still be interested in the Super Bowl ads, and in what show is going to air after the Super Bowl is over.

Sure, it wasn't always this way, and after three of the first four Super Bowls an episode of *Lassie* aired. Everybody expected, though, that it would become a thing. Often, the Super Bowl is used as a launching pad for a new show. Some programs to debut after a Super Bowl include *The Wonder Years*, *Homicide: Life on the Street*, and *Family Guy*. A couple times, CBS used the opportunity to premiere a new season of *Survivor*. Occasionally, networks have turned to popular shows to try and create a supercell of ratings. NBC has done this with *Friends* and *The Office*, and the *Friends* episode was watched by almost 53 million people, so that worked. Then, there are the times where it feels like a network is trying to goose the ratings of a show that could use a pick-me-up. This seems to be the case with "36! 24! 36! Dick."

The episode is actually centered around Super Bowl XXXII in San Diego, which finished just before "36! 24! 36! Dick" aired. ABC got lucky, as that particular Super Bowl saw the Denver Broncos eke out a 31–24 win over the Green Bay Packers, giving John Elway his first title. That meant a lot of people were still tuned in when the game ended, ready to watch Elway lift the Lombardi trophy and then stick around for some *3rd Rock from the Sun*. Oh, and *3rd Rock* didn't just have the Super Bowl to promote itself. It also had supermodels.

A bunch of beautiful women suddenly appear in the small town of Rutherford, Ohio, and they are all over the men of the town. Some of these women are played by the likes of Angie Everhart, Beverly Johnson, and Cindy Crawford. It turns out they are Venusians, who are seducing these men for their nefarious purposes. After taking over Rutherford, the plan then is to go to San Diego, for the Super Bowl, to bring their plan to the world at large. The plan fails, naturally, and the Venusians are never seen again.

In *3rd Rock from the Sun*, ABC was fortunate in that they had a show on their hands that could do such an overt "Super Bowl" episode and have it make sense. Everybody going down to San Diego? A bunch of supermodel cameos? Viewers of *3rd Rock* weren't going to blink at any of that. There were no square pegs when it came to *3rd Rock*. Anything, in theory, could work. "36! 24! 36! Dick" is fun, if overstuffed. It's far from my favorite episode, but I am glad *3rd Rock* got to be a Super Bowl lead-out show. Unfortunately, if ABC wanted to give the show a boost, it didn't really work. Now, a ton of people did stay tuned to watch after the Super Bowl, as "36! 24! 36! Dick" was watched by more than 33 million people. The next episode, a few days later, had slightly higher ratings than normal, but then things drifted back to normal. *3rd Rock from the Sun* aired three more seasons, but the series finale had lower ratings than any episode from the second season, for example.

Likely thanks to a great Super Bowl, and a lot of pretty ladies to promote, "36! 24! 36! Dick" is, as of this writing, one of the 10 highest-rated Super Bowl lead-out shows ever. This, from a show that was never a major hit and that isn't often thought about when discussing '90s sitcoms these days. Maybe people think of *3rd Rock* as "that show Joseph Gordon-Levitt was on as a kid." Well, for one night, the show got to be, if not the center of the television universe, at least close to it.

Veronica's Closet: "Veronica's $600,000 Pop"

Not every show succeeds. Even with a litany of things going for it, a show might fail to take off. In the '90s, even in 1998, you may have had fewer options of what to watch, but you still had options. Also, you increasingly had options away from network TV, or from TV in general. *Veronica's Closet* is a sterling example of such a circumstance, and makes sense to stand in for other shows of this ilk for this book. It was an unremarkable show with an unremarkable run, even with so many things theoretically going for it.

For starters, *Veronica's Closet* was created by David Crane and Marta Kauffman, who had also created *Friends*. They effectively had a blank check from NBC, and they used it to get *Veronica's Closet* on the air, hoping to find another cash cow (while *Friends* was still going strong, by the way). The show starred Kirstie Alley, still a popular sitcom star in the years after *Cheers*. Behind the scenes, and in front of the camera, *Veronica's Closet* had cachet. That wasn't all! To try to ensure success, *Veronica's Closet* debuted as one of the quintessential "hammock" shows. Hammocking a show is when you stick it between two popular, highly rated programs hoping that people will stick around and watch it in between the two shows they really enjoy. Obviously, this was more viable in the '90s, when people watched TV as it aired. *Veronica's Closet* debuted hammocked between *Seinfeld* and *ER*.

Alley plays Veronica "Ronnie" Chase, the owner of a thinly veiled Victoria's Secret analog that lends its name to the series itself. In the pilot, Veronica chooses to leave her philandering husband, even if it hurts her image, and the series goes from there. "Veronica's $600,000 Pop" brings to the table another classic ratings ploy. In this 14th episode of the first season, airing right before Valentine's Day 1998, Veronica's ongoing divorce proceedings get in the way of her rekindling a relationship with an old flame. That previous paramour is played by none other than Ted Danson. Danson and Alley, of course, had spent years sparring on *Cheers*, one of the most popular sitcoms of all time. By casting Danson in "Veronica's $600,000 Pop," the show was riding on the coattails of *Cheers*, while also riding the coattails of *Seinfeld* and *ER*. That's a lot of coattails!

The thing is, the hammocking worked. *Veronica's Closet* was the third highest rated show on television its first season, and fifth its second season. However, NBC either did or didn't know exactly what it had on its hands, which I recognize is a substance-free statement on the surface. One possibility is that NBC realized it had a low-quality show on its hands—*Veronica's Closet* is not good—and recognized it was wasting a prime timeslot on it. The other possibility is that NBC saw the ratings for *Veronica's Closet*, assumed it had fans who would follow it to another night, and hoped to bolster a different day's lineup, with Thursday a juggernaut for the network. Moved to Monday night for season 3, the first episode of that season had nearly a double-digit drop in terms of millions of viewers from the last episode of the second season. *Veronica's Closet* would end up getting moved to Tuesdays, and even moved around on the Tuesday lineup. None of it worked. The ratings tanked, nobody cared, and *Veronica's Closet* was canceled.

Maybe you have one of the stars of *Cheers*. You might have the creators of *Friends*. Hell, you can even bring a TV icon on for a quasi-reunion that you can promote into the ground. Sometimes, none of that matters. *Veronica's Closet* ended up a full-on shrug of a sitcom, finishing off after a three-season run earned not by its own quality, but by the quality of the shows that aired around it. It turns out that hammocks need to be held up by something. Otherwise it's just a weird net on the ground.

South Park: "Mecha-Streisand"

In the realm of post–*Simpsons* animation, there are two shows that can make the argument for the next biggest show: *Family Guy* and *South Park*. Both debuted late in the 1990s, with *South Park* arriving first. Notably, *South Park* also took a shot at *Family Guy*, lampooning it for its lack of quality and its reliance on "random" humor and pop culture references. I'm no fan of *Family Guy*, but here's the twist: *South Park* is also not a good show, and "Mecha-Streisand" is in many ways representative of the kind of humor Trey Parker and Matt Stone took *Family Guy* to task for.

Now, *South Park* is better than *Family Guy*. There are episodes that are good, especially earlier in the show's run, but overall I don't like it. Parker and Stone heavily rely on shock value and gross-out humor. So much of the comedy comes down to, "Isn't this messed up?" Which, I mean, sure, but that doesn't make for a good joke, or even a joke really. Even in high school, I had a friend who loved to make "dead baby jokes," but I would just think to myself, "He's just saying the grossest thing possible, and indeed he is being gross, but what am I supposed to find funny? What's the joke?" Anyway, hope you're doing well Gianpaolo. Sorry I forgot how to stylize, or even spell, your name. He was the kind of kid who loved *South Park*, though, and a lot of those kids were out there.

"Mecha-Streisand" is the 12th episode of South *Park*, airing on February 18, 1998. By this point, it was already a buzzed-about show, and a staple of the "parental disapproval genre." *South Park* was definitely a no-go from my parents as a kid, as it was declared inappropriate for young children. Accurately, I should say. While I snuck the show from time to time, there was also an instance where my dad, while noting my mom would be displeased, put on *South Park* for like 10 seconds for me and my siblings. What I recognize now is that, in that brief period of time, the cop character was performing cunnilingus on the mayor lady. A tough beat for my dad on that one, but as the appointed disciplinarian parent he earned the ability to try and balance that out by being the "cool, lenient" parent as well. This moment was not atypical for *South Park*, though. It was filled with scatological humor, swearing, sexually explicit content, animated nudity, sexual deviancy, and generalized crassness.

Of course, this element of the show was enticing to kids, and like Bart Simpson before him, Eric Cartman became a staple of shirts worn by kids, and probably led to some shirts being banned from schools across the country. A lot of the comedy of *South Park* is unpalatably gross, and sometimes morally dubious. Now, it is animated, so I'm not rallying against *South Park* being on TV, but I find some of the grosser stuff unpleasant. More pointedly, my issue with Parker and Stone, especially early on, comes from their whole snide, snotty smart alecks vibe. They were grown men who had never matured out of the "dead baby joke" phase. Initially, they also oozed a lot of libertarian, smarter-than-everybody-else social commentary. Infamously, self-defined libertarian Stone gave a quote in 2001 saying that he hated conservatives, but really hated liberals. Parker once called himself a registered libertarian, but also "not overly political." Basically, early *South Park* has a lot of, "Isn't it stupid that people care about stuff?" vibes. Memorably, the show dedicated an entire episode to making fun of Al Gore and his quest to inform people about climate change, calling it a hoax. Later, Parker and Stone would do a "my bad" episode where they acknowledged that, yeah, they were wrong about climate change. Over the run of *South Park*, Parker and Stone have ground a lot of axes against celebrities, often mean-spiritedly making fun of anybody who they disagree with or who dares to criticize the show.

Specifically to "Mecha-Streisand" and its relation to Parker and Stone's criticism of *Family Guy*, in this episode Barbra Streisand becomes a robot kaiju version of herself in the vein of Mecha-Godzilla. Film critic Leonard Maltin also becomes a giant kaiju robot to fight her, followed by Sidney Poitier as a Gamera-style turtle, with Robert Smith, frontman of The Cure, turning into a Mothra-esque monster, defeating Mecha-Streisand in this process. What is this plot if not an assortment of pop culture references apropos of nothing? Parker and Stone are clearly fans of The Cure, so I get them wanting to shout out Smith. Streisand complained about her portrayal on *South Park*, which I imagine Parker and Stone were counting on. She is famously somebody who can't help but take the bait. There's even a phenomenon known as the "Streisand effect" speaking to the idea of trying to suppress something or fight it but only adding fuel to the fire in the process.

There are a couple funny moments in "Mecha-Streisand," sure. It's not one of the bad episodes of *South Park*. At the time, this was the highest-rated *South Park* episode, though again it was only 12 episodes in. That's more indicative of the rise of *South Park* en route to being a true cultural phenomenon and the most successful show in Comedy Central history. I know I am fighting against the tide in saying *South Park* is not a good show (it's less of a fight against the idea of Parker and Stone being smarmy, self-satisfied libertarians), but *South Park* isn't personally in my top 20 animated shows, or even the top, say, 10 Comedy Central shows. Its strengths exist, but its flaws are many. As a child, I couldn't resist the siren song of *South Park*, forbidden fruit of the televisual variety. In my teenaged years, even into early adulthood, I admittedly regularly watched it. Ultimately, though, the flaws became more apparent. Also, I grew up. Parker and Stone never did. There will always be teenagers with bad taste in comedy. Shock-value humor will always be beloved by high school kids. And, yes, there will also always be adults who never grow out of it. They've had *South Park* for decades. Mecha-Parker and Mecha-Stone can't be defeated.

Boy Meets World: "If You Can't Be with the One You Love…"

ABC's TGIF lineup was built around family-friendly shows, but it also served a target audience of tweens and teens not quite old enough to be out on the town on a Friday, specifically kids not yet old enough to drive. Otherwise, in the '90s, you might just randomly cruise around your town in a 1989 Dodge Shadow, because that was a thing that happened. Given that, there were the family sitcoms like *Full House* and *Step by Step*, but there were also *Sabrina the Teenage Witch*, the previously covered *Clueless* adaptation, and *Boy Meets World*. What *Boy Meets World* had was staying power. It is, perhaps, the '90s show that the most kids of the era "grew up with," going through the same experiences as the characters at roughly the same time.

In the first season of *Boy Meets World*, which debuted in 1993, Cory Matthews and his friends were 11-year-old middle schoolers. By the time the seventh season came to a close in 2000, we had seen the crew graduate from high school and go to college. Cory and Topanga get married in the seventh season, which, now that I'm an adult, makes my teeth sweat. I hope that is one way in which the kids who grew up on *Boy Meets World* didn't reflect the experience of the characters on the show. And if, like Cory and Topanga, you did get married in college around the turn of the millennium, I hope your second marriage is going well. Cory, Shawn, and Topanga may not have meant anything to adults of the '90s, but they meant a ton to kids at home on Friday nights. There's a reason why three members of the *Boy Meets World* crew got into the bizarrely lucrative world of "rewatching your old show and podcasting about it." Rider Strong (Shawn), Danielle Fishel (Topanga), and Will Friedle (Cory's older brother Eric) are successful enough that *Pod Meets World* can tour.

"If You Can't Be with the One You Love..." aired during the fifth season, which culminates with the massive event (for teenagers) of high school graduation. That wasn't the only drama of that season, though. This episode is two episodes after Cory and Topanga break up, which likely sent shockwaves through teenagers of 1998. "If You Can't Be with the One You Love..." is also one I would classify as a "very special episode." You see, it involves teenage drinking, and rarely do teens get to drink on television without it becoming as disastrous as possible.

Cory, tired of being a "downer," drinks at a party and has a good time, so he convinces Shawn to drink as well. By the end of the episode, Cory and Shawn have gotten in trouble with the police for underage drinking, and Shawn has immediately started drinking every day—including at school—and becomes a full-blown alcoholic. No, seriously. In the span of less than a week and a half, Shawn fights his half-brother, pushes a girl, and then tells said half-brother that he is going to get his alcoholism in check and never drink again. Did Ben Savage do a PSA about alcohol abuse after this episode aired? You bet!

A "very special episode" is defined by serious subject matter and a tonal shift, which is why in truth all "very special episodes" come from sitcoms, because dramas are, well, dramatic. When something grim happens on *Law & Order*, nobody is surprised. It's literally the thrust of the show. But they also tend to be moralizing. And, of course, they also tend to be bad. Actors and writers lacking the skill set to craft serious television are left flailing, and on occasion, admittedly, behind-the-scenes creatives are hindered by having a moral imposed upon them by the network. "Very special episodes" have a fandom, but one built out of an ironic affinity for the awkwardness, for the fiasco feel of it all.

I will say that "If You Can't Be with the One You Love..." is better than many, probably most "very special episodes," but it still suffers from some of the trappings. It's not laughable, which clears a bar many don't. This isn't Johnny Dakota smoking a jay in the Bayside bathroom. Still, the drama lands more as melodrama. In order to hammer home the "teen drinking: don't do it" message, everything had to happen in the course of 22 minutes of television. Shawn had to immediately start abusing alcohol, immediately become a violent drunk, and then swiftly bring an end to his drinking, because otherwise the show would have to keep dealing with it in future episodes, and *Boy Meets World* wasn't about to do that. Why, that would make a fool out of Ben Savage and his PSA! If you were a teenager, you shouldn't drink. If you did, you needed to stop immediately, which is easy. Just look at Shawn: he did it.

There is, obviously, no subtlety here, no nuance. It's both too messy and too tidy. I will even grant *Boy Meets World* the fact that a teenager who drinks for the first time and enjoys it could lack an effective governor and decide to do it often, even every day. The way it happens, though, strains credulity, specifically in the way Shawn is treated not as a kid who doesn't know how to reasonably consume alcohol, but as a full-blown alcoholic. This, in turn, makes the swift ending to his drinking more implausible. At least *Boy Meets World* had better actors than *Saved by the Bell*. To its credit, there is no "I'm so excited! I'm so scared!" moment in "If You Can't Be with the One You Love…." Maybe it even scared some kids off of drinking in 1998. I don't know. I never watched *Boy Meets World* growing up. Not an episode. These characters mean nothing to me other than Topanga being a funny name.

Notably, "If You Can't Be with the One You Love…" was not included in reruns on Disney Channel, where *Boy Meets World* had a successful secondhand run, which probably led to *Girl Meets World*, which proved less successful. Undeniably, *Boy Meets World* was a big show to kids of the '90s, even if it wasn't for me. It defined many a childhood of the decade. Also, it probably behooves me to include a not-terrible "very special episode," given how prominent those were in the '90s. They weren't all "Jessie's Song." That is some heavy-duty faint-praise damnation, to be fair. Oh, also, this episode aired the week after a slasher movie parody episode. They wedged that in between Cory and Topanga breaking up, and Shawn being a weeklong alcoholic. TV is weird sometimes.

The Larry Sanders Show: "Another List"

There are the big, iconic HBO shows. They largely aren't found in the 1990s, though. The rise of HBO as a powerhouse started in 1999, and I will get to that, but the '90s weren't devoid of quality TV on HBO, or rather "not TV" on HBO. To me, the best '90s show from HBO is *The Larry Sanders Show*, which actually debuted in 1992. In 1998, it would speed through a sixth and final season that was quite effective. That started with "Another List," the season premiere. It features, in a key role, another figure of culture that, like HBO, would be a force in the 2000s.

The Larry Sanders Show is a sharp, pointed, occasionally cynical comedy. It chronicles a late-night talk show hosted by Larry Sanders, played by Garry Shandling in his defining role. There is a creative conceit to *The Larry Sanders Show* in which the behind-the-scenes stuff is shot single camera, in a quasi-documentary style at times. When we see the show-within-a-show *Larry Sanders Show*, though, it is lit and filmed like an actual talk show. Sometimes, the show even bounces between the two. Many celebrities appeared on *The Larry Sanders Show* as themselves, though Shandling and the creatives on the show did not let them get away with building up their brand or gently skewing their personas. When you were a celeb on *The Larry Sanders Show*, you still had to act, and it wasn't just some easy PR stunt.

Sanders is a solid talk show host, which is another part of the sensibilities of the show that I appreciate. They don't make Sanders the best host in late night, but he's also not bad. He's decent at his job, fairly popular, but not as big as David Letterman or Jay Leno. Of course, this only helps to fuel Sanders's anxieties. Larry is vain, egotistical—you name it. Shandling is great as Sanders, but there are two other characters from *The Larry Sanders Show* who are among the best characters of the '90s. They would be Artie, Larry's ruthless producer, and Larry's sidekick on the show, the iconic Hank "Hey Now!" Kingsley. As many personality issues as Larry may have, he has nothing on Hank, a man as narcissistic as he is talentless. These characters are great, and the actors who played them were fantastic in the roles.

Now, Artie was played by Rip Torn and Hank by Jeffrey Tambor, two guys who, by all accounts, are/were nightmares to work with. Well, as far as Torn goes, it seems like he was a nightmare to work with, to be friends with, or to see walking down the street. Although, and this is the slightest of caveats, I once heard Ed Harris described as a difficult personality who is hard to work with but an "equal opportunity yeller." That is to say, he's not using his status to bully crew members or only yelling at those who can't really stand up to him. He'll yell at directors, at bigger stars, at dudes who could probably take him in a fight. It's not so much that he's abusive or a bully. He's just a jerk with anger issues. Torn and Tambor seem to be of that school of overarchingly problematic people. All of that said, they were both great on *The Larry Sanders Show*. Torn won an Emmy, deservingly, and Tambor should have won one as well.

"Another List" is the opening salvo to the story of the final season of *Larry Sanders*, which culminates in Larry, fed up with the network, deciding to leave the show. Starting in season 5, the network clearly has an affinity for a guy who has become a recurring guest host for Larry's show, so much so that Larry begins to worry about being usurped. After another successful guest hosting spot, the network is turning the screws on Larry, seeing a potential replacement host in the mix. This guy is younger and hipper. He's a Gen X comedian, perhaps what the network wants, or needs, in 1998. Oh, and he's a real person as well. See, this guest host is played by Jon Stewart.

Nowadays, Stewart needs no introduction. He's one of the faces of political comedy of the new millennium. He's also one of the key figures in a whole generation turning to other avenues for their news. Mostly, Stewart rose to fame and admiration as the host of *The Daily Show*, which he oversaw the transformation of in the 2000s. When *The Daily Show* debuted in 1996, with Craig Kilborn as the host, it was more of a spoof of newsmagazine shows. When Stewart took over in 1999, it started to transform into political satire. This shift really started with "Indecision 2000," their coverage of the 2000 presidential election. As the name indicates, the premise was that people really didn't know whom to pick between Al Gore and George W. Bush. In hindsight, that feels wild. Thus, this version of Stewart is a new-millennium creation. No, what we're dealing with here is '90s Stewart.

Before becoming an icon of political satire, Stewart was mostly associated with MTV. There, he hosted *You Wrote It, You Watch It* and *The Jon*

Stewart Show, a half-hour version of the late-night talk show. This is the Stewart who plays himself on *The Larry Sanders Show*. He's the cool MTV guy, which Larry very much is not. Though I watched almost the entire run of Stewart's time as host of *The Daily Show* (I watched off and on even in 1999 and 2000, before becoming an every-episode viewer) and am a fan, the guy isn't the best actor. Getting to play himself, though, helped. I also want to point out the other main plotline of "Another List" before I bring this chapter to a close. Hank meets a huge fan who is a Hank Kingsley lookalike and, oh man, the contempt that Hank has for this guy, and the way Hank ends up laying into him. Tambor is great in this episode. I love *Arrested Development*, but Hank Kingsley is Tambor's crowning achievement. Hey now! And while I'm at it, "Another List" is co-written by Shandling and Adam Resnick, the latter the writer and director of the infamous '90s film *Cabin Boy*.

With how much I espoused the virtues of the ethos of *Seinfeld*, it is perhaps no surprise I have a real affinity for *The Larry Sanders Show*, which is deeply ensconced in contempt and loathing for its characters. It's also really funny, though. "Another List" is a great example of the quality of the show, but also the entertainment landscape of the era. It is, after all, an episode of a six-season show dedicated to the production of a late-night talk show, and in "Another List" the hot, young comedian is played by Jon Stewart, now a veteran figure of pop culture. These kinds of shows simply don't have the same place in our culture anymore. I used to be a regular viewer of late night, be it Conan, Craig Ferguson, or Stephen Colbert. I don't even watch clips these days, although that's partially because clips of Colbert's show became increasingly bleak to me. I want to remember him as a comedic genius not as a *looks side to side and lowers his voice to a whisper* quasi-hack. The idea of crafting narrative entertainment around a fictional late-night show would feel out of step with the modern landscape. Off the top of my head, I can't think of anything of this ilk in the last 15 years or so other than the movie *Late Night*, which sits in the "wait, is Mindy Kaling not talented?" genre. That's all right, though. Even I have moved beyond the late-night talk show. Conan is a podcast host. Letterman has a beard. Shandling has passed on. *The Larry Sanders Show* is a cultural artifact, but it's a wonderful one. You may now flip.

The Drew Carey Show: "What's Wrong with This Episode?"

Of the significant, successful '90s sitcoms, the one most in danger of fading into the background of culture is *The Drew Carey Show*. Make no mistake, *The Drew Carey Show* was a hit, running for nine seasons and 233 episodes, and finished in the top 20 in the ratings three times (and once finished 22nd). There's a reason Carey had the cachet to replace Bob Barker on *The Price Is Right*. But I rarely hear anybody talk about *The Drew Carey Show*, priming it for a spot in the memory hole. It just doesn't have any of the things necessary for a show to really have that stickiness a sitcom needs.

Part of that is there aren't a lot of people espousing the qualities of *The Drew Carey Show*. It wasn't critically beloved, and doesn't get included in "best of" lists. The Emmys didn't much care for it. It was successful enough to, again, air 233 episodes and be a top-25 show for almost half its run, but it wasn't adored. Then, there's the fact that *The Drew Carey Show* has been exceedingly difficult to see for over a decade. It has never been streaming anywhere, which is a death knell in terms of finding a new audience and rekindling an old audience. There are many who refuse to watch any show they can't stream and binge, especially the ludicrous out there who talk about waiting for something to be on a streaming service so they can watch it "for free," showing a lack of understanding of the "subscription" part of "subscription streaming service." It goes beyond that, though. During the pandemic, I bought the complete series of *Newhart* on DVD because at the time it wasn't streaming anywhere. You can't even do that with *The Drew Carey Show*, as only the first season ever came out on DVD.

I used to watch the show in syndication, back when it aired on network TV in that fashion. There was also some time when it aired reruns on

TBS, but the "syndication era" of *The Drew Carey Show* effectively ended in 2008. Rarely do people watch reruns as they air these days as is, and I feel like the crest of the networks like Buzzr and MeTV has already come and gone, but *The Drew Carey Show* never even landed on one of the major over-the-air nostalgia channels. From 2015 through 2019 it aired on Laff, the sitcom network, and as of this writing since 2021 it has been on something called RewindTV, which I admittedly had never heard of. Even then, if you have RewindTV, you are at most catching two episodes a night Monday through Friday. Beyond watching the first season, though, this is currently not just your best, but your only option.

Then again, does every good sitcom need to have a long shelf life? I will join in with the general consensus that *The Drew Carey Show* is a solid sitcom but nothing more. That also comes with the caveat that the last couple of seasons aren't good, and I gave up watching before the show ended its original run as a result. There's a reason the ninth and final season was burnt off over the summer of 2004. I wish I had seen the series finale at least, but, well, obviously that's not looking like it will ever happen. I'm sure there are good not great sitcoms from before my time that have been lost to the ages. I just don't know about them, so I have no feelings about that. *The Drew Carey Show* is one I watched, many episodes multiple times thanks to reruns. It was part of the course of my life, but does it need to be for those who missed it? Maybe not.

Yet another example of "standup gets sitcom," Drew Carey didn't even bother changing his character's name at all, and the show is also set in his hometown of Cleveland, Ohio. For the most part, the show focuses on Drew, his friends, and his workplace, which is the fictional department store Winfred-Lauder. He hangs out with Kate, Oswald, and Lewis; he quibbles at work with Mimi and his boss, Mr. Wick. The usual stuff from a sitcom of the '90s. To the extent *The Drew Carey Show* stands out, it's in the fact that it was willing to get absurd and out there, not always with the best outcome. Sometimes, it was fully fourth-wall breaking, and "What's Wrong with This Episode?" was the first in what became a series of episodes that were, frankly, not about the plot at all.

There were two types of recurring gimmick episodes on *The Drew Carey Show*. One was when the show would do live episodes, which would entirely break the fourth wall and were built upon the success of *Whose Line Is It Anyway?*, the only(?) successful improv comedy show ever on television. Carey served as the host of that show, and *Drew Carey Show* cast member Ryan Stiles became a beloved comedy figure thanks to it, so these live episodes of Carey's sitcom would often stop cold to basically play a short-form improv game. Even as somebody who has done a lot of improv, the exasperation point on watching a sitcom pause the action for

The Drew Carey Show: "What's Wrong with This Episode?" 227

some short-form improv is hit fairly quickly. The "What's Wrong with This Episode?" conceit holds up much better, though even there, they probably went to the well one time too often.

The four episodes of this ilk were done as close to April Fool's Day every year as possible, with the first one landing right on the day. Honestly, the plots of these episodes truly don't matter. They are built around a different premise. Namely the production has included a bunch of intentional errors—from the glaringly obvious like the wrong actor in a role to subtler stuff—and your job is to try to find as many of them as possible. I feel like there was maybe a contest aspect to this, but if that was the case, like so much associated with *The Drew Carey Show*, that has been lost to time. The lily-gilding became heavier once the premise had already been done, and proven successful, but "What's Wrong with This Episode?" doesn't suffer from being overstuffed. Also, I probably don't need to say this, but I didn't rewatch this episode for this book. Because, you know, it isn't legally available anywhere other than RewindTV, which I do not have access to even with my over-the-air antenna.

The real joy in these episodes, though, was when they aired in reruns. See, at this point, the show would point out every single error they included. How did *The Drew Carey Show* go about doing that? By mimicking *Pop-Up Video* and having informational bubbles appear on the screen. Now that I have broached the subject, I was also a big *Pop-Up Video* watcher in the '90s. The VH1 show would air music videos and have facts pop up during them. I will fully admit, when the show was rebooted in 2011, I tried to get a job writing for it. No dice. Watching "What's Wrong with This Episode?" and its sequels with the *Pop-Up Video* formatting is baked into my brain. There are so many people who will never have that experience. It has been left to the '90s. Also, any errors in this chapter are in homage to this episode. In fact, this whole book is a spiritual sequel to "What's Wrong with This Episode?" Totally my plan this whole time.

Monday Night RAW: "April 27, 1998"

There have been culture wars throughout the years. The cola wars were so bad that Billy Joel could no longer take it. Leno battled Letterman. Then, there was the Monday Night Wars. In the '90s, we suddenly had two professional wrestling companies going head-to-head on Mondays, each trying to take the other down. On April 27, 1998, one of those companies literalized that to some degree … and looked like doofuses in the process.

It feels like both lampooning and defending professional wrestling are well-worn positions at this point, so doing either would feel unnecessary and over explanatory. Maybe you don't like professional wrestling as a medium, but the idea of wrestling fans being slack-jawed yokels who think it's real is an antiquated cultural take. Some people probably think most wrestling fans are like that, but some people also think the Earth is flat. By that token, if you are aggressively defending wrestling as a form of entertainment, well, who are you fighting? Professional wrestling blends reality and fiction into one another in a way that has become the defining form of reality television. Also, like, in the '90s there was a wrestler who was ostensibly also a garbage man. Wrestling can be very silly.

I watched wrestling as a child and was a big fan, but I actually stopped watching in the mid-'90s, before I picked it up again in the late '90s. Then, I didn't watch it for years, before starting to watch it with a bit of irony in college, as I was able to appreciate the silliness but also enjoyed some of it with sincerity. This lasted a couple years, before I stopped watching again, and then watched for a couple months in my late twenties for work, which got me watching for maybe a year or so. These days, I am tangentially aware of wrestling, mostly because something wrestling related seems to be trending on social media every 20 minutes. I find it to be a good medium for consuming in brief highlights. Why was it that, every time I got back into watching wrestling for a bit, I would burn out within a year or two? Well, professional wrestling isn't that good. In total, at least. It can be quite good at its best. When two (or more) talented wrestlers are killing it in a match, it's as good as any fight scene in a movie but with the added dimension of it being done live before an audience. On occasion—and I stress *on occasion*—something funny will happen too, because every now and again somebody with a strong sense of humor enters the picture in pro wrestling. The highs are what would get me interested. What would kill that interest is everything that happens between those highs. The last time I was trying to follow wrestling I realized that, over the course of a two- or three-hour show, I'd actually be watching, like, a half-hour tops. The rest of the time, I'd be flipped to another channel, apathetic about whatever wrestlers or storyline was happening at the moment.

Wrestling these days seems to be in the vein of a lot of entertainment, in terms of violence and content, that MCU-style soft PG-13 level. Admittedly, when the '90s began, pro wrestling was goofy as hell. In WWF, now WWE, gimmicks were quite cartoonish, and the staged violence lacking in substance much of the time. The WWF was delivering entertainment in the parameters of "professional wrestling," but then you had WCW, which was viewed as a "rasslin'" product. That was all well and good, but Ted Turner's WCW wanted to challenge WWF. On my birthday in 1995, WCW debuted *Monday Night Nitro*, which went up directly against WWF's *Monday Night RAW*. Soon, WCW started to pull ahead, relying on big stars and the popularity of the group known as the New World Order, or nWo. How would WWF counter? By developing an attitude. Specifically, the attitude of the unchecked id of a 13-year-old boy.

In 1998, the WWF was in the midst of what has become known as the "Attitude Era." This was a time of envelope pushing, "grittiness," and offering the kind of "mature" product that WCW was not. I'm a liberal dude with politics far to the left, but often I find myself exasperated with complaints about the inappropriateness of content and the wrongness of previous generations of work. There are occasions I wish somebody would pump the brakes on their self-aggrandizing crusade against anything not within a bubble of politically perfect content. I imagine these individuals would be happier if they just spent their downtime reenacting the final scene of *Boogie Nights* but with them saying, "I call them sex workers" over and over into the mirror. That being said, Attitude Era WWF was about as racist, misogynistic, and homophobic as I can recall television ever being. Sometimes, they even managed to squeeze a bit of transphobia into the mix for good measure! It's some revolting stuff. It also helped make WWF "cool" again, at least to kids in junior high. When the April 27, 1998, episode of *Monday Night RAW* aired, I was finishing out sixth grade, and not really watching wrestling. By the time I started seventh grade that fall, I was watching WWF, because it was the thing to do. And seemingly every boy at my school had a D-Generation X shirt.

There are several key figures from the Attitude Era of WWF. "Stone Cold" Steve Austin, a beer-swilling, bird-flipping redneck, is somehow maybe the least problematic in hindsight. The Rock, now movie star Dwayne Johnson, emerged during this time. Vince McMahon turned himself into a character and then used his on-screen persona to jack up his ego and seemingly act out his deranged fetishes on national TV. Then, there's DX, best known as the grouping of Triple H, Shawn Michaels, Chyna, the tag team New Age Outlaws, and hanger-on X-Pac (sorry, Sean Waltman). It takes a second to square the circle but, indeed, in 1998, the face of edgy counterculture was still found in Gen Xers.

Basically, everything objectionable about this era of WWF can be found in DX's antics. Also, a lot of what isn't objectionable but is just lame. When WWF content wasn't being problematic, the attempts at lewdness and shock value often just felt cheesy. Most people aren't funny, but it feels like the percentage of unfunny people is even higher in wrestling. DX was adored by teens, though, mostly teen boys, who loved the sexual innuendos and general fratty attitude towards women. They also popularized the phrase, and gesture, which I can't really relay without just saying it: "suck it." This was the rallying cry heard in the halls of many a middle school and junior high in 1998. The phrase was also paired, or sometimes replaced, with a "crotch chop."

DX was "at war" with the establishment of WWF, but they were also "at war" with WCW. On April 27, 1998, that was literalized. The matches on *RAW* that evening aren't relevant, to be honest, a collection of squashes and non-finishes. What mattered was that *RAW* was emanating from Hampton, Virginia, while WCW's *Nitro* was taking place in Norfolk, Virginia. Hey, those cities are pretty close! So, DX dressed up like they were going as "army" for Halloween, crammed into a Jeep they called a "tank," and went down to where *Nitro* was happening to "invade." After goofing around with some fans outside and wasting the time of security guards, DX just stood around outside the arena's shut metal gates pretending to talk to wrestlers on the other side.

It was not an effective stunt, utterly lackluster in payoff, and also it was just packed with lame jokes, because of course it was. The DX "invasion" didn't move the needle on the Monday Night Wars, but it still stands as emblematic of said wars. DX were the faces of the Attitude Era. The comedy involved was juvenile. The battle between the companies was literalized by WWF on a random April night, simply because the two shows were happening in the same general vicinity. Ultimately, WWF won the Monday Night Wars, though by that time they were WWE. You might say the raunchy, offensive content won out and, sure, there was something to that. Mostly, though, WCW's programming just got bad and boring, with a roster overstuffed with uninteresting wrestlers and self-aggrandizing egos. WWE bought out WCW in the early 2000s and, soon after that, I'm pretty sure I stopped watching wrestling again. It feels like wrestling is bigger now than it was in 1998, and though I don't watch it I assume it has to be more entertaining. Even if that is true, modern wrestling can't be synthesized into a situation as neatly comprised as the Monday Night Wars. Also, I miss when there was a wrestling hockey player called The Goon. That is the America I dream of returning to.

Cousin Skeeter: "Mo' Skeeter Blues"

Puppets interacting with people and not being treated like puppets has been happening on television for decades. It's a staple of the Muppets. The robots on *Mystery Science Theater 3000* are puppets, and only the occasional fourth-wall-breaking joke would reference that. While puppets often have popped up in family-friendly entertainment and kids' shows, rarely were they seen on Nickelodeon. Now, Nick Jr.? Those dudes were drowning in puppets. On Nickelodeon proper, though, this phenomenon is mostly limited to *Cousin Skeeter*, a marginal success commercially, at best, and a failure critically as far as this critic goes.

The premise, devoid of one key detail, could be a million sitcoms. A family is turned upside down when a relative comes to stay with them. The focus is on Bobby, in terms of the Walker family, but obviously the titular character is Cousin Skeeter, who moves from Georgia to New York to stay with his cousin and the rest of the kin. Skeeter just happens to be a puppet. Now, he's never referenced as a puppet. His height is commented upon, but Skeeter is not, in the world of *Cousin Skeeter*, a puppet. It's just … the barest of premises to justify the show existing?

Skeeter is more Poochie than Poochie. He's loud and brash, but he's cool and everybody loves him. For some reason he's friends with Dennis Rodman and MC Lyte. The dial on Skeeter was turned to 11, and then broken off. Because he's a puppet, maybe they thought it would work, but for me it very much does not. It didn't when I was a kid, and it definitely doesn't now. Skeeter is one of the more irritating characters I can recall. The puppet is voiced, though not puppeteered, by Bill Bellamy, a figure so ensconced in the '90s that I feel like he has not been mentioned since Dick Clark rang in the new millennium. He has fallen so far from his peak of popularity that, if not for the convenience of Wikipedia, I would have feared he was some Mandela effect figure. Where

Cousin Skeeter: "Mo' Skeeter Blues" 233

some believe Sinbad played a genie in a movie, I believe Bill Bellamy existed.

"Mo' Skeeter Blues" has a plot very much in the vein of your usual *Cousin Skeeter* fare. In his typical chaotic, perpetual-sugar-rush style, Skeeter accidentally destroys the cassette tape of a new single. Don't worry, everything works out in the end, because Skeeter walked so Vinnie Chase could run. Of course, he walked in that shambling puppet way. A plot hinging on the destruction of a cassette tape is very '90s, to be sure, but that's not why I chose this episode. No, it's two people credited with working behind the scenes that intrigued me, and made this a real statement of 1990s culture.

One, the episode is credited as having been written by Nick Cannon. Yes, that Nick Cannon. *The Masked Singer* guy. Mariah Carey's ex. A man with a negligent approach to birth control that borders on the morally indefensible. In 1998, though, he had joined the cast of *All That*, his first taste of fame and success, and he also got credit for writing "Mo' Skeeter Blues." I keep using the word "credit" with intent. When it comes to television writing, in general, the person credited as the writer of an episode has usually seen their work tweaked by others, often extensively. You got the assignment, you started it, you got notes, there were drafts done, the room worked it over, and depending on how hands-on (or egotistical) the head writer/showrunner is, they may have worked it over a lot. John Swartzwelder, the icon among icons of *Simpsons* writers, still only contributed, like, 75 percent of the material in his scripts at peak performance. The credit writer on a TV screen rarely, if ever, is solely responsible.

That being said, I emphasized credit because, well, I'm skeptical just how much what Cannon wrote made the cut. When "Mo' Skeeter Blues" aired, Cannon was 17. Look, I don't care how talented a writer somebody becomes, no 17-year-old is delivering a viable television script, even for a show that isn't good. And as to Cannon specifically, it's not like he had a long, illustrious career as a writer. I'm not saying he turned in a script written in crayon, or filled with drawings, or containing several threatening references to the UN, but if I have to speculate, his name is on a script that the producers and other writers had a heavy hand on. Brian Robbins, longtime Nickelodeon bigwig and current head of Paramount, was one of the creators of *Cousin Skeeter*. You think he isn't getting his hands on this script? Having Cannon's name on it was a selling point, a novelty. "Teenager writes TV script!" is a headline—"Seasoned TV vet with alimony payments writes TV script!" is not.

In addition to Cannon's writing credit, this episode was directed by Shaquille O'Neal. I feel like that deserved more emphasis, because *Shaq* directed an episode of *Cousin Skeeter*. With all due respect to Michael

Jordan, Shaq was the biggest celebrity athlete of the '90s, partially because he gladly did everything he could with his fame. There were the commercials, sure, and Shaq still seems to do any commercial for any company that will throw him 20 bucks and a turkey sandwich, but also the rap albums, the video games, the bad movies. He actually played a genie! That isn't the Mandela effect!

In 1998, Shaq was in the middle of his run with the Los Angeles Lakers, in the thick of Hollywood. He tried his hand at directing, and it is much easier to do that with television. Yo, in 1998 if I had a TV show and Shaq asked if he could direct an episode, I'm letting him. I'm not worried about competence. The marketing opportunity is massive. Now, it seems that directing didn't take for ol' Shaq. He has all of two directing credits. One, "Mo' Skeeter Blues." Two, his own music video from 1998. Too much work, perhaps, for a man who now has the reputation as the laziest analyst in all of sports television.

I did not expect to write this much about a not good episode of a not good show, but that's the power of celebrity. Shaquille O'Neal and Nick Cannon are bigger than *Cousin Skeeter*. They are the kind of famous people Skeeter would have inexplicably been friends with. This was one of Nickelodeon's bigger misfires, though. Plus, you can't have famous people write and direct every episode. That was not a viable plan. Wacky schemes may have worked out for Skeeter, but reality is a harsher beast than the world of *Cousin Skeeter*.

Will & Grace: "A New Lease on Life"

With *Ellen,* hands were wrung about the main character coming out as gay, alongside the actress that played her. Advertisers pulled out from the show. It would not have much of a shelf life after "The Puppy Episode." Though, as I noted, *Ellen* just wasn't that good of a show to begin with, and the lead actress wasn't all that talented at, you know, acting. Not much later into the '90s, *Will & Grace* featured gay characters—and gay actors—out of the gate, and it became one of the most successful NBC sitcoms. The times, they were a-changing.

"A New Lease on Life" is the second episode of *Will & Grace*, and effectively the first episode of the show going forward. More than even most sitcom pilots, the pilot of *Will & Grace* is doing a ton of table setting. It's basically getting the characters from point A to point B, with point B being the jumping-off point for the show. For some reason, a lot of pilots like to start with the characters in a completely different place in life and then jump so many hurdles to set up the premise. *Will & Grace* fell into that, but it survived.

Will, a lawyer, is best friends with Grace, an interior designer. These are sitcom characters who live in New York, after all. Will is gay, so he is sort of the "gay best friend" of a straight lady, but as the lead characters of the show, there is a bit more nuance to that. In the pilot, Grace is proposed to, Will advises her not to marry the guy, the marriage doesn't happen, and, in "A New Lease on Life," Grace moves into Will's apartment. That's one key thing that happens in this episode to really set the show up going forward. The other is that Jack and Karen meet, thus bringing the four main characters of *Will & Grace* into one another's lives.

As the two lead characters, Will and Grace have sitcom-y personalities, but within reason. Grace has a lot of romantic comedy lead in her. In addition to her job as a New York City interior designer, and also in

Will & Grace wasn't just modern because it had gay characters on it. Look at that prop newspaper! It has the word "downloaded" on the back page! Eric McCormack and Debra Messing are up front, Megan Mullally and Sean Hayes are in the back (NBC).

addition to her gay best friend, she is obsessed with food. If you can't make a woman in a comedy clumsy, you make her preoccupied with food. This is the case, even if Debra Messing is one of television history's thinnest actresses. Will is more of an everyman, calm to balance out Grace being written as high-strung and neurotic. He's the closest thing to a sensible character in the show. I note that, because Jack and Karen are both absolutely bananas characters untethered to reality.

Now, Sean Hayes and Megan Mullally both rode *Will & Grace* into fame and success. Jack and Karen will forever be their defining roles. Notably, all four main actors (I haven't mentioned Eric McCormack by name yet, so I will now) won Emmys, with Mullally winning two. As characters, though, Jack and Karen are like two Kramers, but with the amp turned up to 10 and the knob broken off. They are craven, hedonistic, selfish, scheming, deranged id machines. They are not nuanced. They are not subtle. Jack and Karen could suck the oxygen out of the rainforest, let alone a room.

Jack and Karen are also the reasons why I never got into *Will & Grace*. They are annoying characters, especially Karen. I like both Hayes and Mullally as performers, and, from what I have seen, as people. Their characters are written in such a way that they were likely doomed to be unbearable, but the performances don't help. Truly, I can't stand Mullally as Karen. She's a cat on cocaine's nails on a chalkboard. Clearly, I am in the minority, because the show only ramped it up with Jack and Karen. Neither was ever reeled in.

Culturally, though, the show is certainly significant. Here, in the '90s, we had a sitcom where two of the main characters, and one of the lead characters, were gay. While McCormack is heterosexual in real life, Hayes is gay, meaning a gay man was playing a gay character. Sure, he was the most flamboyant gay man this side of a Mel Brooks comedy, but sitcoms aren't always subtle, and *Will & Grace* never was. Maybe part of progress is a gay man getting to play an annoying gay character. It shouldn't be only straight characters annoying the hell out of us! Change comes in many forms.

Will & Grace ran for eight seasons in its original run, and then after a one-off character reunion to try to encourage voting in the 2016 US elections (oops), the show was rebooted. I would call it one of the more successful reboots, owing to the fact that they added three more seasons and another 40-some episodes into the mix. By the time of the reboot, gay characters on TV weren't a novelty. They were a status symbol. To the credit of *Will & Grace*, even back in 1998, Will and Jack were more than "gay." One of them was characterized much more by being very annoying. In that way, it was like many sitcoms, and that's the way it should be.

Hang Time: "High Hoops"

Medical marijuana was legalized in California in 1996, but marijuana was still viewed with a jaundiced eye by many people. While Ronald Reagan was long out of power, and his crony (and former head of the CIA, which is wild to think about) George H.W. Bush had failed to successfully ride Reagan's coattails beyond one term, Bill Clinton was very much a War on Drugs president himself, as he was effectively a conservative-leaning moderate who just happened to represent the Democratic Party. In television, even into the late 1990s, marijuana was still often treated as akin to hard drugs. When it came to TV aimed at teenagers, in the '90s an anti-marijuana episode was almost an obligation, and *Hang Time* did not shirk this responsibility.

Hang Time is essentially, "What if *Saved by the Bell*, but basketball?" It's even set in Indiana, like *Good Morning, Miss Bliss*, the predecessor to *Saved by the Bell*. Additionally, *Hang Time* was paired with *Saved by the Bell: The New Class* on TNBC, NBC's teen-centric programming block on Saturday mornings. If that wasn't enough of a connection, starting with the second season of *Hang Time*, Peter Engel was the showrunner, the role he had performed on *Saved by the Bell*. This was a bad, poorly produced show about high schoolers, but in this instance the focus was on the Deering High Tornadoes, the basketball team. If anything defines *Hang Time*, it's the perpetual cast changes. Only two characters, Chicago transplant turned hooper Julie and rich-girl cheerleader Mary Beth, lasted the entire run of the show. In fact, beginning with the fourth season of *Hang Time*, former NBA player Reggie Theus was out as Coach Fuller, replaced by Coach Katowinski, played by ... NFL great Dick Butkus?

Speaking of a cast in chaos, the primary driver of the action of "High Hoops," Rico, is only in the fourth season. He starts to smoke weed, and it immediately begins to ruin everything for everybody. There's also a "B" story about some of the kids taking auto shop to get an easy A, which somehow leads to one of the kids being trapped in the trunk of the teacher's car? Well, that doesn't really have anything to do with '90s culture. There was never a wave of teens getting locked in trunks accidentally.

The lesson imparted by many a show of *Hang Time*'s ilk to the ostensible teenage audience is "never drink alcohol and never smoke weed." Well, the message is more anti–underage drinking, but marijuana is viewed as an everlasting evil. It is never okay to smoke weed, even as an adult. At the time of "High Hoops" in 1998, it was not really legal much of anywhere, which probably played into this. To a certain mindset, "illegal" means "wrong." The Republicans may have hated Clinton, but the GOP and Slick Willie shared a love of "law and order" politics. Do what you are told, because you are told to do it.

At least *Hang Time* took efforts to show marijuana impacting Rico's life, though in a way that was melodramatic. Things culminate with him forgetting to fix the brakes of Nick Hammer's motorcycle, leading Hammer to have an accident. Rico also starts to be bad at basketball, which, well, if he was puffing enough herb probably would be the case, although many an NBA player of the '90s might argue otherwise. This is in juxtaposition to *Saved by the Bell*, though. In "No Hope with Dope" it is essentially taken as read that marijuana is evil, and anybody who smokes it is a bad person. Take that, Johnny Dakota!

That's not to say I support teenagers drinking alcohol or blazing up. I just think both can be done without it yielding utter disaster. It would be a bit unreasonable, I admit, to ask *Hang Time* to show Rico smoking pot and having a good time, but just once in the '90s couldn't a teenager have smoked a little pot and had a perfectly fine time? Plus, I mean, this was a high school kid in some random Indiana town in 1998. The dude is smoking swag and is probably as high as if he had drunk a bunch of hot sauce. Rico wasn't getting his hands on modern dispensary marijuana. Where's the verisimilitude? We should have seen Rico roll a C-plus joint filled with stems.

"High Hoops" did win something called a Prism Award for "accurate" depiction of drug use, but I did a smidge of research and the Prism Awards seemed like a weird group with some sensationalistic anti-drug vibes. *Hang Time* was a show that couldn't sufficiently portray teenagers playing basketball or sitting around a table at a diner, much less smoking weed. Also, what was Peter Engel's obsession with kids hanging out at diners? And if they are hanging out at diners, why aren't they smoking cigarettes and all sharing one plate of French fries for five hours?

Peter Engel didn't want teenagers to smoke weed. He was afraid of it, it would seem. "High Hoops" is a mild entry into the anti-weed archives of the War on Drugs era. It's not terribly didactic, but it is silly. Did these producers realize they could just, you know, not mention marijuana at all? That might have worked out better for all parties involved.

Sports Night: "Intellectual Property"

All due respect to *Sports Night*. Aaron Sorkin's show, his first TV program, was a critical success. It gets bandied about from time to time in "canceled too soon" articles. The show lasted two seasons and 45 episodes, which is a solid run for a network comedy. "Intellectual Property" features a storyline that is built upon a semi-common '90s trope. It was written by Sorkin himself, who will get more attention in a later chapter. However, *Sports Night* is a half-hour comedy-drama about a fictional sports news program called "Sports Night." It is heavily based on ESPN's *SportsCenter*, which is the true '90s titan to discuss. Picking an "episode" of *SportsCenter* to cover would have been, if not impossible, fruitless. Writing about *Sports Night*, though, is a backdoor way for me to tackle the behemoth that was *SportsCenter* in the 1990s.

I watched so much *SportsCenter* in the '90s. There was a stretch when I probably watched it every day. I was far from the only one. People of all ages, provided they were sports fans, tuned into *SportsCenter* on ESPN, or occasionally ESPN2. It aired multiple times a day. There was a morning version they would repeat throughout the morning (which was annoying when I'd be home sick from school and, on occasion, would find myself watching the same *SportsCenter* twice). We'd usually get an early-evening episode at 6 p.m. ET. Then, there was the jewel of ESPN's schedule in the '90s, the 11 p.m. ET *SportsCenter*. This version's peak was when it was hosted by Dan Patrick and Keith Olbermann. *Sports Night* is based on the Patrick and Olbermann 11 p.m. *SportsCenter*, with Josh Charles playing the Olbermann analog and Peter Krause the Patrick figure.

As a kid, the 11 p.m. *SportsCenter* was not always a watch for me, but I caught it on occasion. Although, by 1997 Olbermann was out, and Kenny Mayne had replaced him. I was more of a Kenny Mayne guy. He is my all-time favorite *SportsCenter* anchor. *SportsCenter* was built around showing the highlights of sporting events. The 11 p.m. show was dedicated to that day's events, often leading with whatever big games were going on (and over by the time the show began). Occasionally there would be interviews or reports from the field as well. Mostly, though, it served as a sports highlight show, with the personalities of the anchors becoming vital. They were the faces of ESPN. Yes, if you loved sports, you might tune into *SportsCenter*, but some people were tuning in for Keith and Dan (or Kenny or Stuart Scott or whoever).

What I have just written is probably one of the most far-afield descriptions of anything in this book to anybody under a certain age. These days, I watch condensed versions of sporting events I missed on YouTube. Highlights abound on social media. I listen to sports podcasts, read up-to-date box scores in the evening online, and am generally never lacking in current information, and content, related to sports. As somebody who is an avid sports fan, this is great. If you came of age in an era of YouTube, much less an era of Twitter and Instagram, being fully informed on the world of sports at any given moment has always been easy. In the '90s, this was not true.

I would read the sports section of the *Detroit Free Press* every morning as a child, and sometimes they would not have box scores for, say, a hockey game that happened in Vancouver because it ended too late to make the cut. I remember mornings getting on the school bus hoping to hear what happened in a Red Wings game because the paper did not have that information. At some point in the '90s, ESPN debuted the "Bottom Line." This was a ticker on the bottom of the screen that would inform you about the sporting events of that day. It even would tell you what was happening in *ongoing sporting events*! That was a game changer. Prior to that, I might not have a clue what was going on in a game. I didn't have the internet to look it up. If it wasn't on TV, my options would be the *Free Press* ... or *SportsCenter*.

To me, *SportsCenter* was entertaining, but also valuable. Kenny Mayne was funny, yes, but I was seeing highlights. I was finding out who won games I cared about and how they did it. *SportsCenter* allowed me to be an informed sports fan. There were mornings I watched it before school, and nights I fell asleep with it on. The show was vital. It was the conduit for sports highlights and game info. *SportsCenter* was at the center of life for sports fans until the internet became substantive enough to push it to the wayside. It still exists, but I can't tell you the last time I watched it.

Thus, it makes all the sense in the world that, in 1998, Sorkin created a show about a fictionalized version of *SportsCenter*. Also, it would make sense to focus it on pseudo versions of Olbermann and Patrick, whose run had just ended. They were the titans of the genre. Side note: at one point

Sports Night: "Intellectual Property"

Kenny Mayne had a web series on ESPN called *Mayne Street* featuring a fictionalized version of himself, and the show featured pre-fame Aubrey Plaza and Ben Schwartz (plus fellow future *Parks and Recreation* actor Alison Becker). Kudos to the casting staff on that one! Anyway, "Intellectual Property" features Dan getting in trouble for singing "Happy Birthday" on the air, leading the network to have to pay the copyright holders. This was such a thing for so long. Patty and Mildred Hill, those miserly old crones (I'm stealing a Paul F. Tompkins joke to coast on the esoteric value of referencing it), had songwriting credit for "Happy Birthday," but it was Warner Chappell Music who got the copyright in 1988 and demanded royalty payment for *every public performance* of "Happy Birthday." That's why restaurants would have their own birthday songs, and why it wouldn't appear in TV or movies. In 2015, the copyright claim was invalidated, "Happy Birthday" entered the public domain, and Warner Chappell paid back $14 million in licensing fees.

Sports Night was canceled in 2000. *SportsCenter* is no longer a cultural force. "Happy Birthday" is in the public domain. Mildred Hill apparently died in 1916? Scott Van Pelt could sing "Happy Birthday" for an hour straight on *SportsCenter* these days and not have to pay a dime. Alas, how many people would be watching?

Celebrity Deathmatch: "Masters of Martial Arts"

Claymation, a variation on stop-motion animation built around characters made of clay materials, has been around for a while. Usually, claymation is family friendly. *Gumby*, for example. Those awful Nick Park movies that bore me to tears if I accidentally see two seconds of a trailer. And, of course, Green Jelly's music video for "Three Little Pigs." Wait, maybe not that last one. In 1998, MTV got into the claymation game, a little surprising for a network synonymous with cheap, fast production. *The State* used to get, if I recall correctly, seven bucks per episode. It paid off, though, because for a minute there, *Celebrity Deathmatch* was a big hit. To me, the reason why is clear. Namely, people love celebrities, and they love animated violence.

Even people who are squeamish about gore in live-action movies and TV shows sometimes enjoy the artificiality of cartoon violence. *Celebrity Deathmatch* was not exactly realistic, even by the standards of animation, either. MTV believed its audience of teenagers would find it funny if animated versions of Hanson were violently squished to death, and they were right … for a while. Returns diminished steeply when it came to *Celebrity Deathmatch*.

The premise is simple. Celebrities fight to the death. The end. *Celebrity Deathmatch* was a lowbrow show, built on scatological humor and violence. They made fun of the images of celebrities and went after a lot of low-hanging fruit. This is the kind of show that would champion the "Stone Cold" Steve Austins and Marilyn Mansons of the world but take great glee in violently killing, say, Rosie O'Donnell. In the first episode after two pilots, the first fight saw Hillary Clinton taking on Monica Lewinsky. It was 1998, after all.

"Masters of Martial Arts" was the finale of the first season. Though it aired just before Halloween in 1998, there is nothing particularly

"Halloween" about it. Of course, this is a show where celebrities violently murder one another. Maybe it didn't need to be goosed up for the occasion. Roseanne fought Kelsey Grammer. She sits on him for two rounds (why yes, those are crickets you're hearing) until Grammer slips out of his skin, Roseanne sees his skinless body, and she has a heart attack. Courtney Love loses to Brandy when, um, she is mauled to death by bears. In the main event, Jackie Chan squares off with Jean-Claude Van Damme. Van Damme kicks special guest referee Chuck Norris in half, and then Chan rips Norris's arms off and uses them to decapitate JCVD.

Yeah, "Masters of Martial Arts" is a fine summation of *Celebrity Deathmatch* in a nutshell, and also a real depiction of the celebrity landscape of 1998. Roseanne and Courtney Love get made fun of. Jackie Chan and Jean-Claude Van Damme get to be badasses, while Chuck Norris's violent death is supposed to be gleefully received. Sure, maybe you didn't want to see Norris kicked in half in real life, but a clay version of him? Why not?

More effort went into creative deaths than celebrity matchups or comedy. Eventually, even the deaths started to flag as well. I was a watcher of *Celebrity Deathmatch* for a couple seasons, but eventually the premise lost steam. Reflecting on the show now, you can get a wide swath of the celebrity landscape. Hey, "Masters of Martial Arts" did have sitcom stars, action stars, and musicians. Kelsey Grammer and Brandy came together. Or, rather, clay versions of them did. Making clay models and doing stop-motion animation are both time consuming, so *Celebrity Deathmatch* deserves credit for the effort. Of course, this was MTV, so I worry sufficient compensation was lacking. Then again, the *Celebrity Deathmatch* crew could have always crafted claymation versions of MTV's executives and, say, run them through with the MTV flag on a pole or dropped them in a pool of acid. Creative violence was the name of the game. That, and easy jokes about celebrities. Hey, those are two popular things. Always have been, always will be.

That '70s Show: "That Disco Episode"

Let's say you were a teenager in the 1970s. For the sake of ease, let's say you were born in 1960. You turned 13 in 1973. By 1993, you would be in your early thirties. By 1998, you would be 38, likely established in your career, possibly flush with disposable income. Maybe you have a kid or two, and on a weeknight you're likely home and watching TV. It's 1998, so you aren't streaming anything. You aren't running to Blockbuster on a weeknight, more than likely. There's a show, and it is about being a teenager in the 1970s. Why wouldn't you check it out? That logic train, plus generalized nostalgia, is the crux behind the creation of *That '70s Show*.

Fascination with bygone decades arrives in time over and over. In the 1970s, we got *Happy Days*. In the 1990s, we got *That '70s Show*. Granted, the bulk of *That '70s Show* aired in the 2000s, but the beginning of a nostalgia for/curiosity about the 1970s began in the 1990s and hit the airwaves in 1998. It was created by Bonnie and Terry Turner, the husband-and-wife team that also created *3rd Rock from the Sun*, as well as Mark Brazill, who had been a writer on *3rd Rock*. I don't know for sure, but I speculate that the Turners brought Brazill along because he was born in 1962, and was thus a teenager in the 1970s. The Turners were both born in the 1940s.

The seventh episode of the show's run, written by the Turners, is "That Disco Episode," which aired on November 8, 1998. In making a show about 1970s nostalgia, and poking fun at the trappings of the 1970s that fell by the wayside, invariably there would have to be an episode centered on disco. Frankly, the only surprise is that six episodes preceded "That Disco Episode."

Disco is a style of music long associated with the 1970s. It became a punching bag, and even a rallying cry. Fans of rock music would loudly proclaim that "disco sucks," and the antipathy to disco would culminate in Disco Demolition Night at Comiskey Park in Chicago in 1979. There would eventually be an overcorrection to the facile and easy jokes about disco that would posit that the driving force behind most people's disdain for disco was that it was a musical subgenre populated by, and popular with, minorities and gay men. This strengthened disco as a weird touchstone of identity politics. It is very much possible not to like disco because you don't enjoy the way it sounds. It is also entirely possible to declare that "disco sucks" solely because you find that to be a signifier of the kind of "serious" music fan you consider yourself to be.

In "That Disco Episode," the gang all decide to go to a discotheque in Kenosha, Wisconsin, and since this is a book steeped in '90s pop culture, I must now reference the "Buddy Holly" video by Weezer, which is itself riffing on *Happy Days*. Hyde, very much characterized as the kind of guy who would define himself as being against disco, only goes to try and get with Donna (who is not paired off with Eric fully at this point). First he has to learn to dance, which he does by taking lessons from Kitty, Eric's mom. This leads to some traditional sitcom miscommunications, which lead to a rumor that Hyde and Kitty are having an affair, which is then naturally smoothed over, as these things often are.

So we have a triangle formed between Eric, Hyde, and Donna, but also Jackie, Kelso, and Fez. You see, Kelso can't dance, but Fez turns out to be a marvelous dancer. This, in turn, leads Kelso to tell Fez to stay away from Jackie. Meanwhile, Hyde dances with Donna when Eric doesn't want to, but when Hyde makes a move on her, she quickly declines. I will say this for *That '70s Show*: it wasted no time mining the overwrought interpersonal dynamics of teenagers for intrigue and stakes. Nothing about these two love triangles feels forced or false. If you were a teenager watching this in the 1990s, the emotions on display in these teenagers from the 1970s would feel entirely relatable, by and large.

Are there easy jokes about disco? Of course! This is a multicam sitcom from the 1990s! On the other hand, I would frankly have been disappointed in a show in the vein of *That '70s Show* if it had not delivered on that front. We needed a disco episode as much as we needed an episode about trying to get alcohol when you are underage or going to see *Star Wars*. Ultimately, *That '70s Show* would go on for too long, key actors would leave the show, Josh Meyers would show up, and apathy set in. I will admit I have never seen the eighth and final season of the show. There is no Topher Grace as Eric, so why bother?

While I was cognizant of disco when I watched "That Disco Episode," I had no firsthand knowledge of the 1970s, or disco of the era, and I cannot view the episode through that prism. I will have to wait until a sitcom of the future weaponizes emo shows at Legion halls for humor to understand that perspective personally. In an era where pop culture rarely stays buried, Netflix brought us a sequel series in 2023, *That '90s Show*. I have not seen it, and frankly I don't know if I want to indulge. Not that I am begrudging any of the parties involved. This is my third book on 1990s television. I know when to bite my tongue.

Total Request Live: "November 9, 1998"

In the long run, the internet effectively killed MTV, or at least the music video element of it. First, though, the internet helped give MTV's music video cache a second wind. *Total Request Live* became a favorite of music fans, especially teenagers. Specifically, the kind of teenager who might dream of someday screaming indiscriminately into a microphone held by Carson Daly. *TRL* became a must-see because it changed the landscape of the music videos MTV showed in a key way. Namely, it gave the viewers control.

TRL, as it was known for the sake of brevity, was a fusion of *MTV Live* and *Total Request*, two shows already in existence. Daly was even ported over from *Total Request*, a show already dedicated to showing videos being clamored for by MTV's audience, for this new live version. *TRL* debuted in September 1998, and it swiftly became the face of MTV, a position I'd say it held until, oh, probably 2002 or so. Airing four days a week, Monday through Thursday, there was a lot of *TRL* in the mix. Naturally, it would air in the hours after middle school and high school kids got home from school. We, as children of the '90s, graduated from watching Nickelodeon after school to MTV.

People could vote online or over the phone for the music videos they wanted to see, and then *TRL* would count down the top-10 most-requested videos. Did this lead to a ton of repetition? Of course! The show was on four days a week! Sometimes, you'd be happy about this, sometimes, not so much. Videos would be retired after a certain length of time. Daly was the primary host, and he rose to fame as the face of *TRL*, and thus the face of MTV. Other VJs would join the fray in the 2000s, but there were a couple other individuals of note from the '90s. I was surprised to find out that MTV first did their "Wanna Be a VJ" contest in 1998, the same year the show debuted. The winner was to be given a one-year contract to be a host on *TRL*. In the end, the victor was … incompetent weirdo Jesse Camp. This is what happens when an audience primarily consisting of teenagers gets to vote in a contest. Runner up Dave Holmes was much more in the "consummate professional" vein of Daly, and it isn't surprising he had a much longer, more successful run on MTV. I was, and am, a Holmes fan. It's a bummer he had to spend so much time on *Say What? Karaoke* alongside Teck from *Real World: Hawaii*, a notable homophobe even by the standards of *Real World* castmates.

I was able to find the songs that made the countdown on November 9, 1998, and it is a typical collection in terms of *TRL*'s usual voting results. Specifically, the top two songs come from Backstreet Boys and NSYNC, respectively, with 98 Degrees popping up at eighth as well. This was the era of the boy band. In third and fourth we have the "alternative" to boy bands, with Korn and Marilyn Manson showing up. If you hated boy bands and pop music, but still wanted to tune into MTV for some reason, you could cast your vote for a band like Korn. The Offspring's "Pretty Fly (for a White Guy)" also made the cut. When I was a *TRL* watcher, it was the pop punk bands that I supported. Also, Tom Green, but I was in junior high so cut me some slack.

TRL debuted right after I started seventh grade, pretty much perfect timing for me, but if I made it into the 2000s watching it, it was probably only just barely. Like I said, I was behind the pop punk outfits showing up on *TRL*, but eventually even Green Day or blink-182 was too mainstream for me, "sellouts" as it were, so I stopped watching *TRL* and mostly listened to … pop punk bands that didn't get MTV airplay. Remember when people cared about bands selling out? I'll admit, as an elder millennial with some traditional Gen X sensibilities, I still don't love it when a musician I like becomes popular.

Nowadays, the idea of tuning into a TV show hoping to see the music video you want to see is archaic. You go on YouTube, you call up any video you want. Watch NSYNC's "Tearin' Up My Heart." Check out "Father of Mine" by Everclear, which came out at five on November 9, 1998. Carson Daly had his own late-night show for 17 years (no really!). He has hosted New Year's Eve events. Daly has been the host of *The Voice* and on *Today* for over a decade. And yet, if you were between, say, 11 and 16 years of age around the turn of the millennium, he will forever be the host of *TRL*. There are fewer screeching teenagers for him to deal with these days, at least.

NYPD Blue: "Hearts and Souls"

Amongst '90s cop shows, for many *NYPD Blue* rises to the top of the charts against all that competition. It did run for 12 seasons and 261 episodes and was the longest-running one-hour drama in ABC history until the immortal *Grey's Anatomy* passed it. It began as a vehicle for David Caruso, who left after two seasons to try to find movie stardom. This didn't take, which led to *CSI: Miami*, which did take, but in the "I know nobody who has ever seen an episode of this show, but it has been on forever" way. When Rick Schroder (Ricky to a certain generation) needed a role in adulthood, he stopped by *NYPD Blue*. Mark-Paul Gosselaar basically kindled his adult acting career by stepping into the last four seasons of the police procedural. When Caruso left, Dennis Franz's Andy Sipowicz became the de facto lead. Among Sipowicz's many partners on the force, Jimmy Smits's Bobby Simone is the most famous and most beloved. With "Hearts and Souls," the show said goodbye to Bobby.

Smits was nominated for five Emmys during his time on *NYPD Blue*, and him leaving the show was a cultural moment. The news had already leaked out, and executive producer Steven Bochco had commented on it. People tuned into "Hearts and Souls" knowing this would be the end of Bobby Simone. How would he be written out? Would Simone die? Speculation ran wild, including on the nascent internet. Airing on November 24, 1998, "Hearts and Souls" was a 90-minute special episode, and it began with *five minutes* of "previously on" footage chronicling the entire run of Smits as Bobby Simone to that point. Clearly, this was an "event" episode.

It was already known that Simone needed a heart transplant, and when "Hearts and Souls" begins, he's had the transplant and is dealing with the aftermath. Simone never gets out of the hospital. There are ups and downs, infections and improvements. Ultimately, Simone gets last

David Caruso left *NYPD Blue* in search of movie stardom. Dennis Franz stayed. Things worked out for one of them. From left, the first season cast of *NYPD Blue*: Sherry Stringfield, James McDaniel, Dennis Franz, David Caruso, Nicholas Turturro, and a young Amy Brenneman, who also didn't last long (ABC).

rites, a parade of coworkers (and Smits's costars) say their goodbyes, Simone has a waking dream of his mentor, and he goes into the light. So yes, *NYPD Blue* killed Bobby Simone off, but not in a sensationalistic way. It was all about emotion, about interpersonal connections. Bobby Simone did not die in the line of duty. He died surrounded by his friends and family. It was a "proper" sendoff, as they say.

Much of the attention *NYPD Blue* got was from pushing the limits of network television. The show would use language not used by other shows, and once got an indecency fine for, essentially, too much naked lady. It was not "edgy," per se, but unafraid of working to tell the gritty stories Bochco and David Milch desired. Milch would go on to create and craft *Deadwood*, which is 95 percent a paean to swearing and full-frontal nudity. "Hearts and Souls" isn't on that trajectory. It's all about the human element, about character investment. Simone got a compassionate sendoff, which probably felt good to Smits. Sometimes, creatives and producers will get petty when somebody decides to leave a show. Not Bochco and Milch, at least when it came to Smits.

"Hearts and Souls" got huge ratings, cashing in on the news of Smits leaving leaking. It was watched by 22.1 million viewers, second most of that week, and the biggest ratings for *NYPD Blue* in three years. Beyond that, many call it the best episode of the show, and one of the best TV episodes ever. Of course, the show didn't stop down. "Hearts and Souls" aired during the sixth season and, as I noted, *NYPD Blue* ran for 12. Police work continues when cops die. Television shows continue when characters in an ensemble leave. An appeals court overturned the FCC's fine over all that nude lady stuff. It was a big show in the '90s, but also in the 2000s. As I head toward the end of this book, that feels fitting. This is the last episode of 1998. All that's left is 1999. Y2K is nigh.

The PJs:
"Rich Man, Porn Man"

Fun fact: Animation used to primarily employ professional voiceover actors. It's true! During the early days of Disney, characters were voiced by people hired because of the quality of their voice work. The most famous member of the *Simpsons'* voiceover cast when it began was ... Julie Kavner? Harry Shearer? A sea change happened in the '90s, starting with *Aladdin*. Robin Williams was cast to play Genie, and he became the central figure of the advertising and promotion (much to Williams's chagrin). Nowadays, Chris Pratt is the voice of Mario. It has come to television as well to a lesser degree. The point of no return, when the boats were burnt on the shore, probably came with *Shrek*. Dreamworks, looking to keep pace with Disney and Pixar, threw a ton of cash at a big name cast and were rewarded with such a success that others followed suit. Eddie Murphy, of course, voices Donkey in the *Shrek* films, which is a nice transition as he also was the name brand, and voice, that got *The PJs* on the air.

FOX threw a lot of weight behind *The PJs*, and why not? They had Eddie Murphy! When the show debuted in 1999, Murphy was still a movie star, though on the wane. He was a couple years removed from *The Nutty Professor*, and one year removed from *Dr. Dolittle*. Animation takes some time, so Murphy was carrying cachet when he was made the face and voice of *The PJs*. Oh yeah, *The PJs* was animated. Specifically, stop-motion animation of the clay variety. Every episode reportedly took two months to craft. That's a lot of effort, so FOX probably needed a name like Murphy's to try to get people watching.

The PJs is set at the Hilton-Jacobs public housing project, where Thurgood Stubbs, as voiced by Murphy, is the superintendent. I watched the show on FOX, and I recall that my mom asked me, in what felt like an accusatory fashion, if I knew what "the projects" were. I had never been to summer camp, but I was not asked if I understood *Salute Your Shorts*. My mom never said a word to me about my lack of knowledge of Minneapolis news departments in the 1970s. I don't know why *The PJs* drew a line of skeptical questioning. Well, I was 13 when the show debuted, so perhaps my mom figured further questions were worth asking. Also, no, I had not heard the term "the projects," but I understood the low-income, dilapidated nature of the building that they were all living in.

The PJs is packed with broad characters, and would be classified as a "Black Sitcom," though animated. It is a show where Thurgood would say things like, "Whitney Houston, we have a problem." Most of the characters were Black, and many of them were stereotypes. Cultural sensitivity was not the name of the game on *The PJs*. There is "Haiti Lady" and a character was referred to through the first three episodes as "Mr. Crackhead." There is also a Korean man who "considers" himself Black.

"Rich Man, Porn Man" is the fifth episode of the show, airing on Groundhog Day of 1999. Thurgood fixes up a broken down movie theater, which he then inadvertently turns into a porno theater. Basically, the premise was, "What if we made a bunch of jokes about porn?" *The PJs* was not the most intellectually rigorous show. It was broad and raunchy. What's odd about the lowbrow humor is that the show was co-created by Steve Tompkins, a former *Simpsons* writer and Harvard graduate, and Larry Wilmore, a familiar face to *Daily Show* fans. He had that show after *The Daily Show* that replaced *The Colbert Report* for a bit. I watched like two episodes. It wasn't that good.

I liked *The PJs* as a kid, but as I already noted I was 13 when it debuted. The raunchy humor was, in and of itself, worthwhile to me. While the stop-motion animation is interesting, it doesn't look that good. I dislike the character design on *The PJs*. Now, I'd credit the voice cast, led by Murphy, but here's the thing about that. Reportedly, according to the actor Phil Morris, he provided the voice for Thurgood in some episodes. Basically, Murphy would record his dialogue when he felt like it. When he didn't, Morris did. So, it turns out Murphy was really just the name brand FOX and *The PJs* was banking on.

That didn't work out. *The PJs* lasted for two seasons on FOX before it moved to The WB, where they hoped a "Black Sitcom" could find footing. No dice! Only 10 episodes aired, leaving three unaired. By that point, Murphy was voicing Donkey. Then, his live-action movie career tanked. That's the story of Murphy in the 2000s, though. In the '90s, he was a star, so much so he became the focal point of a FOX sitcom on voice alone … even when he wasn't actually doing the voice work.

The Sopranos: "College"

The Sopranos is the defining HBO show. It's arguably the defining show of the 2000s. This, of course, is a book about '90s television, and '90s culture. Even so, "College" belongs in this book of defining episodes of '90s TV. Not just because it is considered by many one of the best, maybe the best, episode of *The Sopranos*, which is saying a lot. It also was a defining '90s moment, because "College" was a sign in February of 1999 that "the '90s" were coming to a close, and fast.

The rise of the antihero on television, the focus on the criminal family man that is central to so many shows of the new millennium, can be traced back to the significant success of *The Sopranos*. In fact, all those HBO shows you have tuned into in recent years owe a debt of gratitude to David Chase's mob show as well. The viability of the network as a force in original programming began with *The Sopranos*. While the first few episodes have fans, lovers of *The Sopranos*, and there are many, point to "College" as the episode where it really took off as a show. It showed that there was something special here.

James Gandolfini became a TV icon thanks to his turn as Tony Soprano. He is a high-level mob boss in New Jersey with a wife and two kids, and he tries to balance his family with his work, which causes tension. This is often seen in Carmela, Tony's wife played by Edie Falco, who has to balance the luxury she lives in with how that luxury is funded. Additionally, at the beginning of *The Sopranos*, Tony starts seeing a psychiatrist, Dr. Melfi, after he has a panic attack. This was part of the "humanizing" of Tony Soprano. Not in an empathetic way. David Chase found Tony loathsome, and didn't want you to root for him or care for him. He also wanted him to be a three-dimensional protagonist.

Chase co-wrote "College," which was a synthesizing of Tony, mob capo, and Tony, girl dad. Tony is taking his daughter Meadow on a tour of

The Sopranos: "College"

James Gandolfini in the role that defined his career, Tony Soprano (HBO).

colleges. In the process, he sees a former member of the DiMeo crime family that flipped on them. The former soldier, Febby Petrulio, notices Tony and tries to kill him. He fails, and the next day Tony takes a side trip away from his daughter's college tour to find Petrulio and strangle him to death. There's also some stuff about Carmela finding out Dr. Melfi is a woman and then hitting on a Catholic priest, which is when I realized that I had actually seen part of this episode.

Yes, while I am a huge television fan, I have only seen a handful of episodes of *The Sopranos*. I was well aware of "College" but did not think I had seen it. In reality, it turns out that I had seen some of the Carmela and the priest stuff when my dad was watching it. Have I seen *The Many Saints of Newark*? Of course I inexplicably have! Fortunately, through cultural osmosis I could come to "College" understanding the gist of it. The acting, of course, is high level. Gandolfini does give a seminal performance on this show, and Falco is no slouch. Granted, it is probably easier to jump into what is only the fifth episode of a show as well.

Retroactively, "College" has become considered a testament to the quality of *The Sopranos*. *Time* named it the best episode of the show. In 2009, *TV Guide* called it the second best TV episode ever. In hindsight, it is also pointed at as being when *The Sopranos* cemented itself. This is, of course, something that can only be recognized with hindsight. I didn't watch "College" when it aired, and I don't know how it was received at the time. Certainly, nobody was saying, "Mark my words, *The Sopranos* will be viewed as an all-time show and this is the episode where it rose to a higher plane of quality!" This is the sort of thing that can only be recognized looking backwards.

The Sopranos wasn't the first original HBO show, but it is the one that started the buzz about the network. *Oz* didn't do that. *The Sopranos* won Emmy after Emmy. HBO had some successful comedies already, such as *The Larry Sanders Show* and *Sex and the City*. As a dramatic force, though, *The Sopranos* is where it all began. The idea of HBO as being the home for acclaimed drama started with Chase's domestic mob program. Network dramas have all but been forgotten by critics and the Emmys. It's all about HBO, Showtime, and streaming platforms. The first step of that change was *The Sopranos*.

Network television was the dramatic force of the '90s. HBO was the dramatic force of the 2000s. The debut of *The Sopranos* in 1999 is the pivot point, and "College" has become the face of that change. People didn't know how different things would become when "College" first aired. Sure, maybe watching Tony strangle Febby while touring colleges with his daughter felt "different," but the changes that would follow proved seismic. The '90s conception of television was falling away. HBO woke up one morning and got itself critical cachet.

Futurama: "Space Pilot 3000"

How fitting, as this book winds down, to cover an episode that is literally about the end of the millennium. Two millennia, in fact. *Futurama* wasn't about Y2K, the pseudo-technological concern many felt as the year 2000 loomed. No, it had sights set further than that. One thousand years further, to be exact.

After all the success Matt Groening's co-creation *The Simpsons* had brought FOX, he finally got himself a second show with the network. Groening, and former *Simpsons* writer David X. Cohen (credited writer on "The Itchy & Scratchy & Poochie Show") brought us *Futurama*, which brought the sensibilities of *The Simpsons* to the world of science fiction. Groening and Cohen had created their show about the sassy robot, and it all began with "Space Pilot 3000."

Though the events of "Space Pilot 3000" are set on New Year's Eve, the episode aired on March 28, 1999. This is one of those classic "setting the stage" pilots. Philip J. Fry is a dumb, lazy slacker who delivers pizzas in New York. Thanks to a prank pizza order he ends up at a cryogenics lab, falls into an open pod, and then wakes up on New Year's Eve in the year 2999. Suddenly, Fry finds himself in New New York dealing with a different world. Over the course of the episode, Fry teams up with Bender, the amoral robot, and Leela; they find Fry's relative Professor Hubert Farnsworth; and the trio takes a job as his delivery crew at Planet Express. There you have it. Also, Richard Nixon's head is there.

From that point on, *Futurama* is built upon all sorts of outer-space adventures and quasi-future Earth events. As to "Space Pilot 3000," it is perhaps the best "laying track" pilot since *Cheers*. It's a really good episode that proves funny, sharp, and illuminating while getting all the pieces in place. I feel like I get Fry and Bender, though less so Professor Farnsworth and Leela. That would take a little longer. Fry and Bender are also two of

Leela and Fry enjoy (?) a trip around New New York in *Futurama* (FOX).

the best TV characters ever, with excellent voiceover work done by Billy West and John DiMaggio.

The Simpsons is my favorite show ever, but *Futurama* comes in at an easy number two. It's a great show. *Futurama* is hilarious, with some of the funniest jokes any show has ever crafted, helped by the excellent voiceover cast. Given the sci-fi nature, it can do stories *The Simpsons* never could. Why, even the idea of a person being frozen in 1999 and waking up in 2999 is not feasible on most shows. I also appreciate the future that *Futurama* depicts. It's the rare sci-fi future that is neither utopian or dystopian. Basically, New New York is like New York, but with more advanced technology. That's more impressive, frankly, and also more realistic, all things considered. Although, in truth, in the year 2999 robots probably won't look like drawing from 1950s sci-fi books. Sorry, Bender. You still rule as a character.

It's great to be able to watch a comedy pilot that doesn't feel like work to get through, waiting for the rest of the show. *Futurama* hits the ground running. Then, we get almost a second pilot with "The Series Has Landed." Here, we meet a few more key characters like Hermes, Amy, and Zoidberg, and the logistics of Fry in the future—and of Planet Express—are laid out. It's also laying a lot of track, but really funny. *Futurama* is so good! While almost as good as *The Simpsons*, the show never found the same audience or got the same support from FOX. I remember *Futurama* airing, in theory, at 7 p.m. ET Sundays on FOX. During football season, though, it would almost always be pushed, if not outright cut from the lineup. Though I enjoy football, I wanted to see *Futurama*! Show the cartoon, chumps and chumpettes!

Futurama originally aired for four seasons on FOX, ending its run in 2003 on that network. The show with the pilot built on the turn of the millennium ended up going well into said millennium. Also, oddly, the whole first season aired in 1999. The first episode to actually air in the 2000s is "Why Must I Be a Crustacean in Love?" which is one of my least favorite episodes. Still funny, though! There are no bad episodes in the initial run.

I say "initial run," because *Futurama* is the face of "no show ever truly dies." There were four direct-to-DVD *Futurama* movies, at least two of them good. This was exciting, but also a sign that perhaps sometimes dead is better. These movies got Comedy Central to bring *Futurama* back. The movies were turned into the fifth season, followed by two more seasons. The Comedy Central episodes are a little spotty. Some of them are outright bad. In the original run, *Futurama* didn't get a proper series finale, though, and this time it did. "Meanwhile" is the best episode of the Comedy Central seasons, or the second best at worst, and a good finale … for a while. *Futurama* came back again. Now, it is on Hulu. Characters in *Futurama* were reincarnated. It's fitting the show has been brought back to life multiple times as well.

Even by March of 1999, the idea that the millennium was ending had come to television. *Futurama* played out events yet to come, though not with perfect accuracy. "Space Pilot 3000" is a highly successful pilot and a highly successful sitcom episode. If you have never seen *Futurama*, I highly recommend it. At least, watch the FOX episodes. If not for me, then for Scruffy.

Star Trek: Deep Space Nine: "What You Leave Behind"

Star Trek, the umbrella entity, is vast and varied. I am not the one to parse it all. My knowledge on the subject is reasonable, as I am a cultural magpie who has pieced much together over the years. Thus, I can tell you the characters and cast members from the original *Star Trek* show from the '60s, even if I have never seen an episode. I have seen both William Shatner and Leonard Nimoy play murderers on *Columbo*, though. When it comes to *Star Trek: The Next Generation*, I know a few of those characters, I know people are into how Jonathan Frakes sits in chairs, and I saw *First Contact* in theaters with *zero* knowledge of the show. I had heard of *Deep Space Nine*, but I will admit when I dove in for this book I had assumed that this was the one with Seven of Nine in it. Turns out, that's *Star Trek: Voyager*. Three different *Star Trek* shows aired episodes in the '90s! *Deep Space Nine*, though, is the most '90s of the *Star Trek* programs, having debuted in 1993 and ended on June 2, 1999, with the two-part series finale "What You Leave Behind."

Dropping into the series finale of a show that you have never seen previously can be difficult. Sure, the first *Seinfeld* I ever saw was the series finale, but there is a lot of reflection and callback in that episode. Also, I didn't fully know what was going on there either. That being said, two hours of science-fiction storytelling designed to bring an entire show into the station is a lot to try to follow. The only character from *Deep Space Nine* I recognize is Worf, who was ported over from *The Next Generation*. Protagonist Benjamin Sisko was entirely new to me. There's talk of a Dominion War and Captain Sisko being "Emissary of the Prophets." It seems like quite a bit of storytelling is culminating, and from reading reviews, it would appear that "What You Leave Behind" was viewed as a mostly satisfying conclusion. I do think it is a good title for a series finale, at least.

I don't know what *Star Trek* lovers think of *Deep Space Nine* among

Star Trek: Deep Space Nine: "What You Leave Behind"

all the branches of this universe. I can't recall anything Comic Book Guy from *The Simpsons* or Noel from *Frasier* had to say about it. The finale did nothing for me, but that likely would have been true even if I knew the show better. *Star Trek* has always felt more like a sphere for lovers of world building. People who get hyped for maps of Middle Earth and things of that ilk. That's never excited me in and of itself. While I thought the three Chris-Pine-as-Kirk movies were solid, mostly I liked the action. *Star Trek* has largely left me cold when I have tried to indulge. On the other hand, obviously it is a beloved entity, and I am sure *Deep Space Nine* has devoted fans.

Then again, while I can name off the top of my head people like Picard, Data, Jordi, Janeway, and Seven of Nine, Benjamin Sisko was not a name that meant anything to me. I want to call him "Jeremy Sisto" at every turn. *Star Trek* had a strong toehold in '90s TV, though, before really disappearing for a while, only to see a robust return in the last few years. *Deep Space Nine* is the most '90s of the bunch. It debuted early in the decade and ended a handful of months before the new millennium began. What did it leave behind, though? Scant name recognition? A bunch of characters left out of the limelight in terms of chronicling and cataloging the universe of *Star Trek*? It was there, though, episode in and episode out, for most of the 1990s. Maybe in the shadow of Patrick Stewart, Jeri Ryan, and William Riker memes, now if not then, but it was there.

The West Wing: "Pilot"

Aaron Sorkin soared in the era of Bill Clinton's America. His particular sensibilities, political and otherwise, tracked in the 1990s, when the country wasn't really in any wars and Clinton's conservative-leaning moderate nature was shrugged off. Of course, Clinton was a de facto lame duck by the time the fall network TV season began in September of 1999. George W. Bush would be elected in 2000, but *The West Wing* would continue, remaining a "Clinton Era" show during the Bush regime, to the joy of some and the frustration of others.

That is, by and large, Sorkin in a nutshell. Any show he does is a mixed bag, but his work never really delivers as a 50-50 split. He's pop culture's most "writer-y" writer. Sorkin has given us the screenplays for *A Few Good Men* and *The Social Network*. He has also given us *Studio 60*, *The Newsroom*, and *Being the Ricardos*, the last of which he also directed. Some people love Sorkin. Some loathe him. Many just wish he could be in *The West Wing* mode more.

With the benefit of decades of more Sorkin content to parse, though, the pilot of *The West Wing* hits differently. The man loves to turn a phrase, harkening back to the era of '40s films when everybody quips and nobody talks like humans tend to do in day-to-day life. In entertainment, that's fine, though mileage can vary. It comes down to execution, because when stylized dialogue doesn't hit, nothing in pop culture is as aggravating. I'm looking at you, Diablo Cody, and your war crime of a script in *Juno*. *The West Wing* is that kind of show from the beginning, and it also became famous for Sorkin and director/visual language creator Thomas Schlamme bringing the "walk and talk" to the forefront. Sorkin and Schlamme created a show that popped visually and in terms of language. Here, it hits more than in later efforts.

In the original conception of *The West Wing*, the president of the

The West Wing: "Pilot" 265

Definitely not a posed photograph of (from left) Martin Sheen, Richard Schiff, and Rob Lowe. Lowe looks so natural pointing here as Sam Seaborn of *The West Wing* (NBC)

United States was largely going to be unseen, or perhaps even be the government's answer to Maris and never actually appear. Instead, Josiah "Jed" Bartlet is a main character, and also played by freakin' Martin Sheen. Bartlet's senior staff remain crucial characters in what is largely an ensemble show. The ensemble is quite impressive, right from the get-go. I'm talking Richard Schiff, Allison Janney, Rob Lowe, Bradley Whitford, and on and on. The first season takes place early in Barlet's administration, when the Democratic president and his staff are having a hard time getting anything implemented. It's a low-stakes version of high-stakes circumstances, or maybe a high-stakes version of low-stakes circumstances. Either way, it exists in a world where American politics isn't in a crisis every moment, which has become more commonplace in political fiction, aside from the cynical *Veep*, a show I love that is dedicated to overarching contempt for anybody who has ever dipped their toe into politics.

The West Wing's pilot sees Bartlet crash his bike, which he later reveals he did because he was distracted because his granddaughter was threatened (via a doll with a knife stuck in it) for declaring herself pro-choice. Meanwhile, Whitford's Josh Lyman creates a stir for saying during a debate, "Lady, the God you pray to is too busy being indicted for tax fraud." That's a line worth quoting directly, because it is Sorkin in a nutshell. There's a lot of religious chatter in the pilot, though Bartlet ends up atop the heap after he corrects somebody attending a debate between

Lyman and a "Christian activist." It comes so close to tipping over into "bad Sorkin" but avoids that by the skin of its teeth, more or less.

The difference between *The West Wing* and, say, *The Newsroom* is that by the time of *The Newsroom*, Sorkin seems to have seen himself as the star of the show, and he mostly seemed interested in scoring points with … somebody. Maybe himself? A common complaint about *The Newsroom*, in addition to characters who don't act like real human beings in any fashion, is that Sorkin seemed to be rewriting history to his benefit. It was like some liberal version of Mark Wahlberg's "I would have stopped 9/11" rhetoric. With *The Newsroom*, Sorkin seemed dedicated to patting himself on the back. With *The West Wing*, the back patting is largely left off screen.

The vibe of *The West Wing* carried the '90s into the 2000s. In the pilot, though, the show had nothing to work with but '90s politics. It debuted at the tail end of the Clinton administration, which followed an utterly forgettable tenure for George H.W. Bush. Of course, it's built upon "Clinton's America" and "Sorkin's America," but that's the deal you make when you watch a Sorkin property. You buy the ticket, you take the ride, and you probably roll your eyes a few times. Then, he drops a funny bon mot, or a wonderful turn of phrase, and he buys more time from you. You want him on that wall. You need him on that wall. In the world of television, *The West Wing* is definitely Sorkin's defining and best work. Also, I forgot he had co-writing credit on *Moneyball* and sole writing credit on *Steve Jobs*. The dude has had quite the career.

The West Wing lacks the acidity that "Dubya" and Trump pumped into political discourse, and political entertainment. For some, that makes it a refreshing rewatch. To others, it feels like an artifact. Watching the pilot from back in 1999 is a throwback, to be sure. We're never getting back to that world. Josiah Barlet isn't walking through that door. Or, rather, walking and talking through that door.

Felicity: "The List"

Pavement tried to warn her, but Felicity Porter wouldn't listen. The defining hairdo of '90s television belonged to Rachel Green, as portrayed by Jennifer Aniston. The defining *haircut* of the '90s is a different story, though. In 1999, for some reason, people flipped out that Felicity cut her hair. Keri Russell's locks became a focal point of conversation, including on the ever-expanding internet landscape.

By the time *Felicity* debuted in 1998, The WB was well on the move from being a "Black television" network to being TV for teens. In fact, in 1998, *Felicity*, *Dawson's Creek*, and *Charmed* all debuted, following in the wake of *Buffy the Vampire Slayer* in 1997. Keri Russell, in the role that helped pave the way for her semi-stardom, plays Felicity. The show begins at her high school graduation, where her crush, Ben Covington, writes a nice message in her yearbook. This message prompts Felicity to eschew studying premed at Stanford to follow him to the fictional University of New York, a thoroughly camouflaged version of New York University.

Now, there are those who hear the premise of *Felicity* and find her actions completely bonkers. They think it is ridiculous for her to abandon Stanford to follow some boy she barely knows. To which I say: Yeah man, she's a teenager. Felicity's decision is ludicrous and shortsighted, but it also makes total sense to me from a teenager facing a life free of the rigidity of localized schooling for the first time. To dislike *Felicity* out of hand because you don't like the decision that Felicity makes is, to me, a dicey rationale. Maybe to you that is indicative of a character you know you won't like, or will make you feel impatient, and that I can wrap my head around. I mean, I am not writing this as a *Felicity* fan. I didn't watch any of those soapy teen shows on The WB. As an adult, though, I have no issue with the pilot conceit of *Felicity*, which also dissipates as the show becomes more about Felicity and her friends "finding themselves" in that generic collegiate way.

There are four seasons of the show, each roughly aligning with one of Felicity's years of college. "The List" is the second episode of the second season, i.e., Felicity's sophomore year. Now an RA, Felicity has a teenaged existential crisis because one of the students in her dorm is finding a lot of success, if you know what I mean, using tips from a women's magazine. Felicity is also dealing with trying to be who Ben wants. In the end, she asserts independence with a haircut. Then, everybody flipped out.

Russell had long, flowing, curly hair when *Felicity* began, and between the first and second seasons reportedly sent a photo of herself in a short wig to producers as a gag. After a brief freakout, the producers got to thinking and figured that a change of hairstyle would make sense for the character, and given Felicity's general disposition and penchant for impulsive decisions, that did make sense. They found a storyline justification, and the hairdo was done. It wasn't some minor move, either. Suddenly, Felicity—and Russell—had short hair. It was a significant change, and a lot of people didn't like it.

Some just hated change in general, of course. Those people are always there to complain. Some didn't think Russell looked as good. Some thought she looked cool with her substantive head of thick, curly hair. Whatever the reason, there was a lot of negative reaction in 1999 to Felicity's haircut. Russell, for her part, stuck to her guns and refused to wear a wig or extensions to expedite the process of returning to her "classic" look. *Felicity*'s ratings were down in the second season, which was used as fodder by the anti-haircut agenda. It's true that the ratings were a smidge lower for the rest of season 2, but the show had also been moved from Tuesdays to Sundays and was not keeping pace with the ratings from the first season as is. The show would also continue for two more seasons, so Felicity's haircut did not kill the show, though obviously it did lead to some furor. *TV Guide* did try to argue that it was one of TV's biggest blunders, and a reason for the drop in ratings, but that feels like ex post facto reasoning to justify a list entry. Hey, I've been writing listicles professionally for like 15 years. I get it.

Russell would win a Golden Globe for *Felicity* before finding critical acclaim in the FX drama *The Americans*. The guys who created the show did fairly well for themselves also. Matt Reeves directed two of those *Planet of the Apes* movies and *The Batman*. J.J. Abrams is one of the most famous behind-the-camera people in the world. Hey, at least the fandom anger about Felicity's haircut probably prepared Abrams for the reception to the end of *Lost* and *The Rise of Skywalker*.

Who Wants to Be a Millionaire? "November 19, 1999"

By deciding to put this book together chronologically, the only viable decision as far as I am concerned, I did admittedly put myself in the hands of programming choices made decades ago when it came to the final TV episode that would make this book. I was oh-so-close to ending on ... Felicity cutting her hair? That would not have been ideal! Fortunately, in November of 1999, a television phenomenon was in its early stages, and history was being made.

Ported over from the United Kingdom, *Who Wants to Be a Millionaire?* was a game show where the main selling point was the prize. Somebody could win a million bucks for answering some multiple-choice trivia questions. When you were in the hot seat, if you answered all 15 questions, you would win a million dollars, but if you got any wrong your game was over. You were allowed to walk away at any time. You had three lifelines. If you got to $1,000, that became your floor for prize money, and the same once you got to $32,000. Of course, you also had to lock in your final answer. *Who Wants to Be a Millionaire?* was built on tension, stakes, and a ton of vamping. So much vamping.

I like game shows, and the two main qualities that make a game show work are the ability to play along and the entertainment value. *Jeopardy!* is the ideal play-along show, because it is propulsive. *Match Game* has the most entertainment value, in my mind, and you get to play along as well. The issue with a game like *Who Wants to Be a Millionaire?* is that if you figure out the answer, you might be sitting there waiting for the contestant, maybe for a while. Tension could quickly lead to tedium. Sometimes, it felt like the producers were asking the contestants to stretch for time. Contestants might not even finish their run on the game during an episode of the show! That's wild by modern game show standards.

That being said, there was some entertainment value to *Millionaire* as well. Part of that was in the host, one Regis Philbin. Regis was a television staple for decades. He was a good, if not great, game show host. Where he excelled was when enthusiasm was called for. He also managed to garner a catchphrase in, "Is that your final answer?," though that was part of the show's production, not his invention. On occasion, a contestant would be sitting there, in the middle of a rather sleek set, across from Regis. Both of them might be silent, or maybe the contestant is figuring things out aloud. A lot of money is on the line. The tension music is blaring. You, as the viewer, recognized the stakes. There is some entertainment in that.

Who Wants to Be a Millionaire? debuted as summer filler on ABC in August 1999. At the time, it was a half-hour show, and the plan was for it to air for two weeks. Game shows tend to be cheap to produce, even with big payouts like a theoretical million bucks, and ABC could promote its fall shows. Then, *Millionaire* became a massive hit. They decided to bring it back that November, now an hour long. Notably, nobody won the million dollars in that original run. People were dying to see that happen. On November 19, 1999, they did.

John Carpenter was not the director of *Escape from L.A.*, but a 31-year-old IRS agent when he got into the hot seat on *Millionaire*. He proceeded to roll through the questions. Famously, he didn't use a lifeline until he used the "Phone-a-Friend" to call his dad. Carpenter didn't need help with the question. He just wanted to tell his dad he was about to win a million dollars, and he was right. Carpenter nailed it, and he became the first person to win the grand prize on *Who Wants to Be a Millionaire?*. In fact, he was the first person ever to win a million bucks as a prize on a game show. Carpenter went into game show history. Now that people had seen somebody win the million, their hunger for the show only grew. *Who Wants to Be a Millionaire?* was the last TV phenomenon of the '90s, and the first of the 2000s.

In January, ABC added *Millionaire* to its regular lineup. It was no longer a special event. That first season, it was airing three days a week, and bringing in huge ratings. ABC was loving it. In fact, they started to run *Millionaire* a staggering five days a week. The network was operating under the Homer Simpson philosophy: "Everything lasts forever." It was wrong. Starting with the second season, ratings began to wane. Viewers were tired of *Millionaire* by the 2001–02 TV season. ABC fell out of the top spot in the ratings, back when network ratings still mattered. *Who Wants to Be a Millionaire?* was canceled and ended its network run in July of 2002. It was reborn in a syndicated version, but nobody cares about that.

At the time, though, *Millionaire* was the thing. It spawned imitators like *Greed*, and the importation of other British game shows like *The Weakest Link*. Then, in 2000, *Survivor* debuted, and it took over *Millionaire*'s place in the culture, and also in the minds of TV producers looking for cheap, popular programs. Game shows weren't the thing, it was competition blended with reality TV. Then, the "reality TV" end of that dynamic started to win out more and more, leading to shows like *The Bachelor* and all of its spinoffs and imitators. The last time we had a game show phenomenon, it was an app. Even Carpenter's time as the most famous game show contestant ever only lasted a few years until Ken Jennings took the throne for good. That being said, Carpenter remains the best known game show contestant, non–*Jeopardy!* edition. The game show that grabs the general public most often is *Family Feud*, and it is always because somebody said something incredibly stupid and/or raunchy, much to the strained bemusement of Steve Harvey.

Trivia fans and game show enthusiasts already had their options in 1999. *Millionaire* was for a mass audience, as much a "show" as a "game." *Jeopardy!* was way better for trivia fans, and also more of a challenge. The thing that is wild to me now about Carpenter's win is that the question for the million dollars seems way too easy for the final question of such a trivia game. Now, I have been an off-and-on avid *Jeopardy!* watcher, a bar trivia player/host, and all that, but I feel like the fact Richard Nixon was on *Laugh-In* is, and was, fairly well known. When you throw in the multiple choice of it all, it feels anticlimactic. I just played through every question Carpenter was asked on November 19, 1999, and I got them all with no struggle, under a timed clock. Of course, for Carpenter, there was the pressure of the moment, but *Millionaire* was a TV show, and the home viewer wasn't under that pressure.

Then again, here I am in the 2020s, writing about a fad game show from the 1990s, where a guy won a million bucks answering a question about an event on a sketch TV show from the 1960s. Regis Philbin, an icon of television, was there throughout the '90s, popping up on Letterman, hosting his own daytime show where he talked to TV stars, and hosting *Millionaire*. He died in 2020, and an era of TV possibly died with him. That same year, a celebrity version of *Millionaire* with Jimmy Kimmel as the host debuted, because celebrities are the currency of pop culture in this decade. It came and went as well. Nothing I have written about lived forever, or will live forever. That is my final answer … except for the conclusion chapter, where I have some stuff to write about still. So turn the page!

Warm Glow:
A Conclusion

When did "The '90s" end? As I asserted earlier in this book, a few times over, the cultural idea of a decade does not inherently stick to the calendar. We all know when the 1990s ended, which was when December 31, 1999, came to a conclusion. What about "The '90s," the spirit of an era this book worked to define through an assortment of television episodes? There are some historical points that stand out as potential options. September 11, 2001, obviously, was a turning point in many ways, so much so that neither America nor the world has ever been the same since. There's also the day that George W. Bush officially was declared president of the United States, killing the Clinton era for good. I think you could make the argument that The '90s ended on New Year's Eve of 1999, but not when the ball dropped. In America, we knew Y2K was not going to happen, empirically, before it was 2000 here, because we had seen the millennium flip over in other countries already. Once, say, Japan didn't succumb to Y2K, there was no iota of that idea left, and Y2K was one of the last notions of The '90s.

This is a book about TV, though, so what about in that world? I noted in the *Cheers* chapter that the series finale of that iconic sitcom could be pointed to as the end of The '80s. I find no conclusion to any TV show that put the nail in the coffin of The '90s in that same way. *Seinfeld* and *Murphy Brown*, two shows steeped in The '90s as an idea, ended in 1998, and there was plenty of The '90s—and the 1990s—left after that. I definitely do not feel like The 2000s started early, which means The '90s must have ended late, if not on time. *Friends* is an iconic, beloved show, but I feel like it straddled the decades quite well. It doesn't feel overly indebted to either The '90s or The 2000s. *Frasier* also dipped into the 2000s, but it started with a character introduced in the 1980s, and as much as I love it, the end of *Frasier* was not a big enough cultural moment, much less the end of The '90s as a conception.

Warm Glow: A Conclusion

There are two TV moments from the year 2000 that I think are in the running. One came on January 22 of the year 2000, when *Double Dare 2000* debuted. *Double Dare*, and all its iterations, was pivotal to the growth of Nickelodeon in the late 1980s and early 1990s. I grew up as a child of the '90s watching *Family Double Dare* and later reruns of *Double Dare*. Nickelodeon brought the idea back but slapped "2000" at the end of the title to indicate that this wasn't the old *Double Dare*. Also, Marc Summers was gone, replaced by Jason Harris. This was the first instance in the new millennium of an old property being stamped with modernity through the application of "2000" to it. While *Double Dare 2000* flopped, it also may have killed The '90s in the process.

The other TV moment I could see being the choice came on April 12, 2000, when the pilot of *Jackass* debuted. To me, *Jackass* is possibly the first "2000s show." It felt so internet-y, even in the days before YouTube. *Jackass* was built around a bunch of weird, amoral men doing gross and/or dangerous stunts and mean-spirited pranks—just generally messing around. They were just a bunch of dudes with a show on MTV. When *Jackass* debuted, I was in junior high, so naturally I loved it. The show was "water cooler" talk for my friends and me. It was not like anything we had seen on television, and it wasn't like anything The '90s had to offer. Johnny Knoxville allowing himself to be pepper sprayed may have birthed the next cultural decade.

That's about the end of The '90s, though. You've read through 99 chapters covering 99 episodes of 99 TV shows. What was '90s television, then? It was the best decade for television ever, for starters. Now, I may be a longtime proponent of '90s pop culture, but maybe the reason for that is because, through a series of circumstances, we ended up with so much great stuff. These days, the television landscape is oversaturated and all over the place. You have to have several streaming services to watch everything that feels worthwhile. There are shows I want to watch I feel I will never get to. It's voluminous, and not in an enriching, enticing way. In the '90s, you needed cable TV and maybe to throw a few extra bucks in for HBO. On the flip side, options were decidedly limited in the '60s and '70s, and even into the '80s. There was some quality in those decades, but the quantity could leave something to be desired when you had, effectively, three channels to watch.

The '90s gave us almost all of the runs of *Seinfeld* and *Mystery Science Theater 3000*. It gave us all the best seasons of *The Simpsons*. Nickelodeon bloomed into a substantive network for children's programming, and kids could also watch Cartoon Network or the Disney Channel (while also still having Saturday morning cartoons). Procedurals like *Law & Order* and *NYPD Blue* were there. Of course it wasn't all good. I chronicled flops like

Cop Rock, and also commercial successes with long lives I don't think are of any real quality, like *Full House*. Television has always given us a mixed bag, but the highs of the 1990s were so very high. It's probably the best decade of sitcoms, although dramas in the '70s may have been a bit better. That's for another day.

Nineties television was also exceedingly white, especially in those aforementioned sitcoms. Dramatic shows, especially cop shows, featured some diversity, but the world of televised comedy was not as diverse. How we got to that point feels like an amalgamation of factors. In terms of diversity in television in the 1990s, it really just came down to Black Sitcoms, and I choose that capitalization with intent, because Black Sitcoms were seen as an entity. These weren't just shows with largely Black casts piloted by Black leads, but these were positioned, including by Black creatives in some instances, as sitcoms for Black people. *Family Matters* was a show about Steve Urkel (oh, and also the Winslows, I suppose), but it was a TGIF show, which means it was marketed as family-friendly fun, not "Black." Over on The WB or UPN, though, *Living Single*, *The Wayans Bros.*, and shows of that ilk were positioned as Black Sitcoms.

Unfortunately, these Black Sitcoms were rarely all that good. Now, that is true of sitcoms in general, and most TV such as it is. None of the Black Sitcoms of the 1990s, or even the sitcoms with predominantly Black casts, have been categorized as classic sitcoms. People will instead go back to shows like *The Jeffersons*, or perhaps *Good Times*, but even John Amos and Esther Rolle, two of the stars of *Good Times*, won't speak fondly of that show, which became a vehicle for catchphrase spouting. There's also the '80s sitcom that shall not be named, which I was never a fan of to begin with. I also never found the titular individual to be funny. He was a hack, his show was hacky, and all things considered he probably should die in prison.

The diversity largely ended there, though. *All-American Girl* was notable for having Asian Americans in it, and it flopped (because it wasn't good, to be fair). But what about Southeast Asians, Pacific Islanders, Middle Eastern folks, pre–Columbian Americans, and the like? Even Latin Americans were largely in supporting roles in ensemble dramas. Which is not to say that every major show needed to have more diversity to it. Diversity, when wrenched in, feels sweaty at best, patronizing at worst. Plus, let's be honest, Jerry on *Seinfeld* was friends with a high school buddy, an ex-girlfriend, and the guy who lived across the hall. Sometimes, a white person has a few friends who are white, and a Black person has a few friends who are Black; it's just through happenstance, and it makes logical sense. I less wish for more Black people on *Seinfeld* and more wonder if we lost out on a "Black *Seinfeld*," such as it is. Even that, though, sounds like I am looking for a Black Sitcom, when really I just wonder if a Black comedian could have captured the zeitgeist if given the opportunity.

Speaking of *Seinfeld*, and the zeitgeist, those days are over. Not just for network television, but the big moments just aren't as big anymore. Sometimes, television impacts the zeitgeist, such as *Stranger Things* getting a new generation into Kate Bush, but things are never operating on the '90s level. We just have a wider scope to scrape data from. Now, I will not say that the internet or social media or whatever has created a polarization or a negativity that wasn't there in the 1990s. I do not recall who said this, because I read it on social media, but during the Civil War there were people who would hang around at the telegraph office to give their hot takes on whatever came over the wire. This is who "people" have been for centuries. The kinds of ratings shows got in the 1990s won't be touched again. Television monoculture did not die with The '90s, but it was probably the last full cultural decade where we had a clear monoculture of this particular medium.

We have never been without The '90s, at least not since it started, and in the course of our natural lives I do not believe we will ever be without it. The rise of cable, plus the increase in over-the-air networks in the 1990s, meant that the hit shows were readily available in syndication right away. I have been watching reruns of '90s shows since it was still the '90s, and well into the 2000s. *The Simpsons* and *Seinfeld* were daily watches for me. In the 1990s, I also watched Nick at Nite, but it effectively died as a viable concept, as did TV Land. Nowadays, there are those channels like Cozi, MeTV, and Laff. What do they show? A lot of old-school stuff, yes, but also a lot of '90s TV. I've watched *Frasier* on Cozi. You can watch *The Drew Carey Show* on Laff, and effectively nowhere else. Then, of course, there is the streaming of it all. *Seinfeld*, *Friends*, *The Fresh Prince of Bel-Air*—finding '90s TV is arguably even easier than during the 1990s. Certainly, it's easier from an on-demand sense of things. I binged *3rd Rock from the Sun* during the 2020 pandemic days on The Roku Channel. Because the '90s was the last hurrah of television monoculture, and because Gen Xers and millennials (myself included) are still in heavy supply in this world of ours, there is incentive for entities to keep these shows at our disposal. There will always be a market for *Seinfeld* or *The X-Files*. People will probably be watching *Friends* after I die. Could I be any more existential?

While no book built around 99 television episodes and the assessments, asides, and memories of one man could define The '90s in full, I do believe that these 99 episodes cover a lot of ground. You can understand The '90s in these episodes, if perhaps you can't fully grasp it. I began with the first episode of *Twin Peaks* and ended with a man named John Carpenter winning one million dollars on a game show. Laura Palmer was wrapped in plastic, and Richard Nixon was on *Laugh-In*. Poochie went back to his home planet. When you watch the series finale of a show you care about, it always feels somewhat bittersweet, at least to me. The last moments spent watching characters you love, the notes of finality, and all that. You know it's happening, though, which is why you feel it. When *Jackass* aired, nobody felt like it was the "series finale" of The '90s at the time. This book, though, has come to an end, and it is more Sam saying Cheers is closed and less Bob Newhart waking up next to Suzanne Pleshette. Or maybe you want to put me on trial for some of my opinions from this book à la the last episode of *Seinfeld*. However you feel, and however I feel, though, eventually the TV gets turned off, and the book gets closed. The '90s came to an end, the '90s will live forever, yada yada yada....

Index

Ace Ventura: Pet Detective 156–157
All That 128–131
All-American Girl 132–134
Ally McBeal 208–210
American Gladiators 95–96
Animaniacs 91–93
The Arsenio Hall Show 42–43
Arthur, Bea 174

Baby Boomers 49, 51, 98
Barney & Friends 39–41
Baywatch 57–58
Beavis and Butt-Head 81–82
The Ben Stiller Show 64–66
Beverly Hills, 90210 78–80
Blossom 32–33
Bochco, Steven 18–19, 251–252
Boy Meets World 219–221
Buffy the Vampire Slayer 188–189
Bush, George H.W. 20, 42, 46, 48, 83, 238, 266

Carrey, Jim 24–25, 151, 156–157
Celebrity Deathmatch 244–245
Cheers 83–85
Christmas 9, 50, 122, 156–157, 159
Clarissa Explains It All 44–45
Clinton, Bill 3, 42–43, 48, 83, 175, 238–239, 264, 266, 272
Clueless 167–169
Columbo 34–36
controversy 20, 22, 24, 47–48, 54, 206
Cop Rock 18–19
Cousin Skeeter 232–234
The Critic 135–136

dancing baby 208–209
Daria 19, 81–82
Darkwing Duck 30–31
Dexter's Laboratory 164–166
Diagnosis: Murder 97–99

Dinosaurs 110–111
The Drew Carey Show 225–227

Ellen 193–195
Emeril Live 201–202
Emmy Awards 13, 46, 65, 69, 103, 107, 115, 119, 143, 160, 163, 180, 212, 223, 225, 237, 251, 258
ER 143–145
ESPN 241–243

Family Matters 10–12
Felicity 267–268
finale 3, 13–14, 26, 46, 68–70, 84–85, 107–108, 110–111, 157, 160–162, 174, 187, 199–200, 213, 226, 244, 261–263, 272, 276
Frasier 107–109
The Fresh Prince of Bel-Air 62–63
Friends 183–187
Full House 26–27
Futurama 259–261

Gen X 23, 51, 64–65, 128, 223, 230, 250, 275
Goosebumps 150–152
Groening, Matt 136, 259

Halloween 148, 151, 230, 244–245
Hang Time 238–240
Holmes, Dave 250
Home Improvement 102–103

In Living Color 23–25
internet 2, 8, 51, 58, 105, 117, 136, 154–155, 181, 203, 209, 242, 249, 251, 267, 273, 275

Jerry Springer 205–207
Jordan, Michael 171, 234
Judge Judy 173–175

277

Index

Kelley, David E. 118–119, 208–209
King of the Hill 190–192

The Larry Sanders Show 222–224
Late Show with David Letterman 86–88
Law & Order 72–73
Living Single 122–124
Lois & Clark: The New Adventures of Superman 100–101
Los Angeles 27, 34, 47, 50, 62, 72, 78, 98, 130, 173, 189, 193, 234
Lucas, George 76–77

Mad About You 160–163
marijuana 238–239
Married...with Children 20–22
Martin 52–53
Melrose Place 89–90
Millennials 70, 75, 250, 275
Monday Night RAW 228–231
Muppets Tonight 158–159
murder 5–6, 18, 34–35, 49, 97–99, 117–118, 139–142, 235, 262
Murphy Brown 46–48
My So-Called Life 114–115
Mystery Science Theater 3000 176–178

Newhart 13–14
nostalgia 27, 155, 226, 246
nudity 8–9, 112, 191, 206–207, 209, 217, 252
NYPD Blue 251–253

O'Brien, Conan 1, 87–88, 204
O'Donnell, Rosie 123–124, 244

The Parent 'Hood 125–127
Perot, Ross 42, 54
Picket Fences 118–119
pilot episode 5–6, 10, 89, 94, 96–97, 105, 120, 128–129, 143, 164, 167–168, 209, 214, 235, 244, 259–261, 264–267, 273
The PJs 254–255
Pop-Up Video 227

Quantum Leap 49–51
Quayle, Dan 46–49

The Real World 112–113
reality television 112–113, 117, 174, 228, 271
The Ren & Stimpy Show 37–38
Rockapella 59
Roseanne 198–200

Saturday Night Live 54–56
Saved by the Bell 15–17
Saved by the Bell: The College Years 94–96

Schwarzenegger, Arnold 9, 60
Seinfeld 67–71
7th Heaven 170–172
Shop 'til You Drop 28–29
Silk Stalkings 116–117
The Simpsons 179–182
Sister, Sister 120–121
The Sopranos 256–258
Sorkin, Aaron 241–242, 264–266
South Park 216–218
Space Ghost Coast to Coast 104–106
Spelling, Aaron 78, 89
spinoff 10, 30, 72, 83, 89, 92, 95, 105, 107, 129, 153, 184, 188, 198, 271
Sports Night 241–243
Star Trek: Deep Space Nine 262–263
Stewart, Jon 43, 223–224
Super Bowl 25, 85, 211–213

Tales from the Crypt 7–9
Tarantino, Quentin 133, 144–145
teenagers 1, 11, 15, 17, 21, 27, 29, 32–33, 40, 44, 78, 81, 114–115, 120, 125, 186, 188, 209, 211, 218–220, 230, 233, 238–239, 244, 246–247, 249–250, 267–268
That '70s Show 246–248
TGIF 10, 99, 120–121, 167, 169, 219, 274
3rd Rock from the Sun 211–213
Todd McFarlane's Spawn 196–197
The Tonight Show with Jay Leno 140–142
Total Request Live 249–250
Twin Peaks 5–6

Urkel, Steve 10–12, 16, 274

Veronica's Closet 214–215
very special episode 17, 114, 220–221

Walker, Texas Ranger 203–204
The Wayan Bros. 146–149
The West Wing 264–266
Where in the World Is Carmen Sandiego? 59–61
Who Wants to Be a Millionaire? 269–271
Will & Grace 235–237
Winfrey, Oprah 21, 62–63, 132–133, 194, 201, 205–206

Xena: Warrior Princess 153–155
The X-Files 137–139
X-Men: The Animated Series 74–75

Y2K 74, 253, 259, 272
The Young Indiana Jones Chronicles 76–77

zeitgeist 2–3, 34, 36, 105, 110, 145, 180, 275

Milton Keynes UK
Ingram Content Group UK Ltd.
UKHW032208260724
446187UK00014B/150